The Architect's Tale

I dedicate this book to young aspiring architects, to my
long-suffering clients and to those of us who
have 'run the race'

and I wrote it for Vicks my darling wife, and
for Snuffie, Fee and Rob

First published in 2009 by Redcliffe Press Ltd.
81g Pembroke Road, Bristol BS8 3EA
T: 0117 973 7207
E: info@redcliffepress.co.uk
www.redcliffepress.co.uk

© William Bertram (text)

© Stephen Morris (design, new photography)
ISBN 978-1-906593-24-7

British Library Cataloguing-in-Publication Data
A catalogue record for this book is available from the British Library

Design, new photography and publicity: Stephen Morris smc@freeuk.com www.stephen-morris.co.uk
Printed by Gutenberg Press, Malta

The Architect's Tale

William Bertram

redcliffe

Contents

Acknowledgements

A FIRST BOOK IS BOTH A DAUNTING AND A STIMULATING ENDEAVOUR, AND there are many people to whom I owe thanks.

I've taken to heart Kelsey van Musschenbroek's simple but invaluable advice that a good story must have a beginning, a middle, and an end. I am indebted to my long-suffering brother-in-law Ben Ingle, who has not only undertaken the task of deciphering my progressively poor handwriting, but who has been through each chapter making umpteen corrections with stoic patience. Mary and Douglas Home have not only proof-read but have taken immense care in encouraging me to write, and have supplied research material, particularly for 'The Battle for Cavendish Lodge'. Judge John Dixon kept me out of trouble when proof-reading the same chapter. Peter Arnould took great interest in that story as did Dr Tim Mowl, the historian; both are accomplished writers and their warm words and criticisms I took to heart. My sister Elizabeth Wallace-Dunlop acted as another of my invaluable proof-readers. Her speedy and accurate observations on my sometimes wayward grammar have taught me a good deal more than I learnt at school. Andrew Farquharson and Tom McCaw of the Duchy of Cornwall helped me to tread the fine line of approvals through the Prince of Wales's office for the chapters 'A Royal Appointment', 'The Battle for Cavendish Lodge' and 'Win Some, Lose Some'. Tony Nevill produced some memorable phrases which I have included in the text, and my son-in-law Neville Hoyland kept my literary feet firmly on the ground. Douglas Hill was the only person, outside my family, who I knew could comment authoritatively on 'The School Run'. Lord Crathorne helped me get the historical facts right in the Cliveden story, 'A Dry Run', as did Pauline Kennedy. Rick Tyrer gave me support and encouragement at every turn. My godson the Reverend David Middleton confirmed my ecclesiastical references in ''Twas Easier Said'. Luke Rittner, one of my oldest friends, put me right in 'A Royal Appointment' and supplied, through his piece in the Sotheby's catalogue (The Charles And Barbara Robertson Collection: The Contents Of Combe Hay, 2002) some background for the Robertson story in 'The Merry-Go-Round'. References to St Paul's Cathedral were confirmed by Terry Lee, who also reminded me of other details of the hearings in 'Never Give Up'. Roger Humphreys, rector of Bladon, helped me with the story of Churchill's grave: 'The End of the Beginning' and Corporal Kerry Laishley tracked down the names of the Queen's Royal Lancers trumpeters. Victoria Spicka gave me an updated report of the situation with the Salm Palace for 'A Sting in the Tale'. To John Conibear for advice on publishng and promotion. Anne Bertram, my sister-in-law, proof-read the proof-readers, but gave up on my use of the comma! Antonia Johnson edited my text and made useful suggestions and made sense of my eccentric punctuation. Josephine Hoyland, my daughter, drew the bee for me. John Middleton, who tells me he never reads anything, devoured my chapters and managed to flush out mistakes that everyone else had missed. And pre-acknowledgements must go to Andrew Macpherson, Willie Gething and Crispin Holborow, who have given me enough ammunition to write another book! Freddy Flew, my Old Shirburnian mucker, came out of retirement to take many of the photographs for 'The End of the Beginning' and for 'Dry Run'. Philip Pierce was responsible for the stunning photograph (with not a trace of scaffolding on any of the buildings) of the Royal Crescent. Thanks to Samantha Weinberg, whose enthusiasm for my book resulted in my meeting a literary agent who might have been prepared to take me on. Stephen Morris pulled everything together, designed the book and photographed my work. My son Robert who encouraged me to publish. And finally, to my wife Vicks, for whom this book has been as demanding as any mistress, my gratitude. Her support and encouragement has been more than any man has a right to expect.

William Bertram, January 2009

At 30 in 1969, the year I put up my plate at 14 Queen Square Bath

First Impressions

WHEN I STARTED MY CAREER I MISTAKENLY THOUGHT THAT BEING AN architect would consist of sitting in my ivory tower, drawing beautiful things and seeing them built. Every day the sun would shine from a clear blue sky and everyone would think my buildings were masterpieces.

I landed in the real world with a resounding thump. I managed to dust myself off and put such fantasies to one side.

This book is about what it was really like to be an architect practising in Bath during the last quarter of the twentieth century, and about the characters and the odd and humourous situations that combined to brighten his day. The story also delves into the background of that small boy who felt, from a very young age, that he was born to be an architect, and follows the triumphs and disasters of his journey to become one. What this book is not is a compendium of the buildings and their description for which I have been responsible over the last half century.

Ever since a boy I have had the uneasy feeling that the one school subject which was missing from the curriculum was psychology. A good grounding in the complexities of human nature seems to me to be a fundamental part of education if one hopes to enjoy a reasonably carefree existence and rub along in amiable companionship with one's fellow man.

Architectural schools, and I had the good fortune to be tutored at the AA, one of the very best, not surprisingly teach you all about the principles of design, the history of architecture and how to fit all this to a client's brief. Unfortunately what they do not teach you is how best to deal with unhelpful planning officers (you'll know who you are!), incompetent builders, and demanding and difficult clients. If the booby traps laid by those who wish you ill were to be taken seriously, then this book would be the work of a manic depressive. As it is, I have survived the professional roller-coaster with my sense of humour largely intact and with a storehouse of anecdotes. These, I hope, will amuse those who are naturally inquisitive or who like a good gossip and are prepared to indulge my rather childish penchant for name-dropping.

I have also included, by way of illustrations, one or two of the thousands of sketches which I have made for my clients as a speedy way to give them an idea of what they might be letting themselves in for. This ability to draw the pictures that I can so clearly see in my mind's eye has been my most precious asset. These drawings are not all of the same standard; they didn't have to be. Some took only a matter of seconds, others, when my elbow was in good working order, were lovingly prepared and detailed enough to build from. But all, without exception, had a galvanising effect upon my clients, not least the Prince of Wales when first we met at Highgrove in 1987.

Each chapter is a short, or in some cases not so short, story in itself. Whether redesigning the grave of Sir Winston Churchill at Bladon, or transforming Cliveden into an hotel, I have come to know intimately all the characters involved. It is stories of these people and places, interwoven with my own reminiscences, that fill the pages of this book.

The School Run

vis, virtutis, veritas

LEAVING PREP SCHOOL AT THE END OF TERM TOOK ON THE EXCITEMENT OF AN adventure if at the age of eight you were the son of a serving army officer stationed in occupied Germany. In front of you stretched the long and sometimes uncomfortable journey from the south coast of England to a faraway town in the middle of Europe. Owing to the ever-changing circumstances out there the War Office kept regiments on the move so that I knew only at the last moment where I was going.

Amid mounting excitement and the welcome relaxation in school discipline, up on the noticeboard went the lists: those boys who would be collected; those travelling up to London on the school train; and those whose suitcases and tuckboxes were to be ready for collection a day earlier by the aptly named firm of Carter Patterson. In the evening before breaking up, there assembled the full complement of the school: pupils, headmaster, masters and matrons (especially Miss Freda Walters with whom every boy was in love whether they knew it or not), the kitchen staff and even the headmaster's golden retriever. We sang lustily the hymn 'God be with you till we meet again', we boys hoping that perhaps we might be excused from ever coming back… although I would have missed geometry, my favourite subject. Old enemies made up their differences and old scores were forgotten in the heady atmosphere of impending freedom.

We didn't need the school bell to wake us on the last day of term. We were dressed and on our way to the high-ceilinged dining-room clutching our holdalls and jostling good-naturedly into line for inspection. Before we were allowed in the headmaster, J E Maxwell-Hyslop, a towering presence both on and off the sports pitch, walked slowly along the corridor inspecting hands and fingernails as we presented palms and backs, just as we had done before every meal for the past twelve weeks. We scoffed our breakfast and waited impatiently to get away. As form numbers were called so we trundled through the hall to the front door wishing the masters well, before clambering up the shiny metal steps into the charabanc. Then it was a free-for-all and up to those who were strongest to secure either a window seat or perhaps the more coveted one next to the driver, where all of life could be seen uninterrupted. I plonked my school cap on the seat next to mine to bag it for my best friend Ashfield.

When we got to Brighton station the platforms were filled with a mass of school children. The girls' school Roedean was just over the Downs from ours, so we shared the train with the girls, none of whom, in my very considerable experience of such matters, came anywhere near the beauty or voluptuousness of our young matron. The porters, in heavy blue tunics, pushed their trucks full of suitcases towards an endless line of open carriage doors followed by a wave of high-spirited children.

We reached the deputy headmaster, Mr Noel Webster, a full-bodied figure standing like a rock, clipboard in hand, ushering us each into our various compartments.

'Bertram, you're in the one behind me with the blue sticker; your dorm' are all together. Have a good holiday and I'll see you in four weeks' time.' He spoke in his usual booming voice. No time then to gainsay that assumption, only the pleasing thought of the weeks I would enjoy away in Germany where everything was so very different from England which was still struggling to survive rationing.

An unintelligible message over the station tannoy system echoed and re-echoed through the cast-iron roof trusses. Apparently one of our number was lost and the train was not about to jeopardise punctuality by delaying its departure. Doors slammed, windows dropped, and we stuck out our heads to try and see the new engine arriving ready to haul us towards the sunlit South Downs and on to London. The stationmaster

The author aged 8 at sports' day, Rottingdean School near Brighton, 1947

blew his whistle and waved his green flag and we all waved and cheered as we left. The locomotive noisily spun its wheels filling the station with a billowing cloud of grey and white smoke.

The journey took about an hour. We thundered past Crawley where according to our headmaster there was a house called 'Creepy'. Then we entered the endless suburbs of inter-war semis. As we got closer to London these were replaced by the squalid backs of sooty yellow-bricked terraces lining the very edges of the tracks. How, I wondered, could anyone living in such places ever be truly happy?

Victoria is a prince among termini. It may not have the lofty elegance of Paddington nor the architectural exuberance of St Pancras but for sheer romance it has no equal. As we clattered and twisted our way slowly across the silver points towards our allotted platform, there leaving the station was the *Brighton Belle*, with smart chocolate and cream carriages decked out with table lamps and curtains. No doubt its passengers were as excited by the prospect of a weekend on the south coast as I was going in the opposite direction. We drew in alongside the boat train to Dover. Smart men in spats and elegant ladies in furs were embarking ready for the long journey by the *Blue Train*, via the channel crossing, to Paris and on to the south of France.

On such journeys my grandfather used to take great delight in leaving my poor grandmother to settle into her seat, and then going off to get a paper just as the train was about to leave. As the last carriage passed him he would open the door and climb aboard. Minutes later he would saunter back and casually pull back the compartment door much to the consternation or relief of all concerned.

No such pranks on this occasion. I saw the auburn-haired, diminutive figure of Pan, that same long-suffering grandmama, patiently waiting for me, and standing beside her as tall as a church steeple her great friend Muriel Kerr.[1] Pan had been a West End actress and was the most demonstrative of people. When at last she saw me leaning out of the window her hands went up and her eyes became as big as fish saucers. A broad grin spread across her pretty face and she called out my name. I fell out of my carriage door and into her welcoming embrace. I felt loved and safe for the first time in weeks.

Muriel was detailed off to go and identify my luggage from a mountain of leather cases and wooden tuck-boxes which had been emptied from the guard's van. We all three stood by the taxi rank waiting for one of those pre-war black cabs. Eventually it took us across London, past Buckingham Palace, where Pan asked the cabbie to stop and drop the hood. We continued our short journey like royalty with the sun on our faces and the wind in our hair. We pulled up outside Nevill Court in St John's Wood, where my sister, who had also just broken up, was waiting for us. At least the first leg of the long journey had been successfully completed.

---

1 Muriel Kerr was secretary to David Webster who ran the Royal Opera House, Covent Garden. She provided the much-needed organisational skills to this inseparable duo!

We settled down happily to a high tea of scrambled eggs followed by red jelly. Pan showed us two new leather kitbags with shiny zips and strong leather handles which my father had commissioned from his local saddler. It reminded me of the present he had given us when I was six years old and my sister eight. To keep us warm on the trip to Germany he had commissioned two fur-covered teddy bear suits with little pointed hoods. We had tried them on, danced around the dining room, and raced up and down the long staircase. Tired and excited we had fallen into bed early. The day after we'd had to be up with the lark.

Now two years later it was much the same. Liverpool Street was the station which linked London to the port of Harwich. From there ferries plied the channel to the Hoek van Holland, known colloquially as 'The Hook'. The terminus was a busy place indeed. The vast majority of the occupation forces in the British sector passed through this station on their way to and from Germany and Austria. So it was that we found the platforms full of greatcoated soldiers with their kit bags hoisted on shoulders, heads cocked sideways, caps askew, rifles slung, fags drooping from lips, all moving in slow columns towards the trains. It was easy to get lost. To prevent this the WVS, dressed in their distinctive greeny-blue tweed suits and red-trimmed felt hats, took over responsibility for us from our grandmother. They immediately threaded identity labels through our lapel buttonholes. I remembered that on the first of these journeys two years before, dressed in our teddy bear suits, we had climbed onto our luggage which was piled on top of a large trolley, waiting to be told what to do and where to go by our new guides. We were the first of such boatloads of children to go to Germany and the station was crawling with journalists. Suddenly, out of nowhere, a couple of young men appeared; one with a camera the other with a notebook. Before we knew it there was a call to look their way, a flash, a quick question, a scribbled answer and a 'thanks'. A picture of me and my sister appeared on the front page of the *Daily Sketch* the following day under the headline 'Judy and Bill Bertram on the way to join their BAOR father'. Somewhere a faded copy of this article lines the bottom of a drawer.

At just six o'clock in the morning a weak sun had only just managed to lift the mist. Frost still clung to the trees and the icy wind blowing along the platforms between the carriages persuaded those civilians lucky enough to have coats to raise their collars and button up. We were shown into an open compartment with rows of seats either side of a narrow walkway. This was in stark contrast to the cosiness of the usual six-person compartment with its sliding door and comfy seats. No doubt the RTO had worked out that you could move more bodies more quickly like this. I didn't like it at all. And I was so tired. Although the WVS were nominally looking after us, once we had been shown to a seat and our heavy baggage stowed in the guard's van and our hand luggage in the netting racks overhead, we were left to fend for ourselves. I nestled down to try to keep warm and get some sleep. The train was full to bursting as it drew out of the platform on its way towards the sodden marshes of the east coast. Sleep was fitful. As soon as I had dozed off someone would open the door beside me filling my small world with the noise of thundering metal wheels and the numbing cold from freezing draughts. I would tense myself waiting for the door to bang closed and thereby muffle the din and restore relative calm. Until, that was, the next time, the next and the next.

Surrounding me on the train was an assortment of travellers. A large man sat opposite dressed in a smart dark blue uniform, his peaked cap perched purposefully on his knee, his black shoes brightly polished. Here was a staff member of the CCG[2] who were responsible for administering the day-to-day lives of a conquered nation. By their forced unconditional surrender in 1945 the Germans had lumbered the Allies with everything from the re-establishment of local government to the issue of lavatory paper. To me he looked very important and I venture to think he thought so too. Beside him sprawled a soldier who was fast asleep, tunic undone and feet tucked untidily under the seat opposite. There an old lady, determinedly wearing her pork pie hat, sat in the corner seat knitting. The wool was crinkled, no doubt an old sweater being recycled into a few pairs of socks. It didn't look as if she was on her way to

2 Control Commission for Germany

Europe, but then you never could tell.

There weren't many children on board the train. Most were travelling on specially chartered school boats. These were rather intimidating. My sister and I had travelled on one two years before: the *Empire Halladale*, sister ship of the *Empire Windrush* that had taken the first Jewish settlers to Palestine in 1948. It was a troopship, and we, at the tender ages of six and eight, had been en route from Tilbury to Cuxhaven on the north German coast; a two-day journey which I thought should have been less like a floating 'Dotheboys Hall' and more like a cruiseship. However the hierarchy of bullying was simply transferred direct from the schools and imposed upon the hapless children. Boys slept in the hold below decks in vast dormitories, girls' cabins were above water level with portholes. Bedtimes were too early and the food awful. Half way through the first night I'd had enough of being squirted with water pistols and chucked out of my bunk. I had made straight for my sister's cabin where I found four girls who were prepared to put up with me for the rest of the voyage; the genesis perhaps of my preference for the fairer sex. Anyway that's why we were now, two years later, travelling 'civilian' and learning to fend for ourselves in a grown-up world. It did us no harm and gave us a confidence well above our modest years.

There were no stops on our way to Harwich. Just straight through the Essex countryside and onto Parkeston Quay. The train began to slow down so I got up and braved the jolting footplates of the concertina tunnel which linked the carriages, dropped a window and looked out. The wind off the North Sea cut into my forehead. Through my streaming eyes I could see the vast bulk of our ship rising like Beachy Head above the dockside. The train came to a juddering halt and for a moment there was stillness. Then with a sigh the engine's valves were opened and a long wisp of white steam drifted away on the sea breeze.

It seemed an awfully long way down onto the platform. I struggled with my kitbag and we were greeted almost immediately by a mother hen of a WVS lady who clearly had others to account for. She ticked off our names but still appeared to be worried. She strained to see over our heads for the other six children whilst muttering and flapping her metaphorical wings.

There was no Customs Control to talk of, only a short jaunt to an evil-smelling lavatory followed by a fresh administrative stamp on our identity tags. Like little parcels going through the post office sorting system, so we were pigeonholed into the ship. We climbed up the long gangplank, its canvas sides offering little protection from the biting wind. Then we passed through a small bulkhead door halfway up the side and into the warm heart of the boat. The ship's crew ushered our small party to an assembly point along one of the corridors. Everything seemed to be painted white except the floors which were leaf green and parts of the overhead pipe system with its important wheel valves which were painted red. The hum of pumps and dynamos was ever present.

'You lot are on the boatdeck, follow me,' said a rating in white serge uniform and plimsolls. Along narrow corridors, up companion ways, across the wooden deck we trudged, past the white clinker-built lifeboats chocked up and roped to their davits. Eventually we were shown into our own tiny two-berth cabin with its very own porthole and twin bunks. We felt terribly grown-up.

As we stowed our bags and disagreed about who would have the top bunk the loudspeaker outside our cabin door crackled into life.

'Attention please! Attention please!' I stood dutifully to attention as requested.

'Will all those in cabins on the port side of 'C' deck please now assemble for boat drill. Life jackets will be found under bunks.' Excitedly I got onto my hands and knees and looked under the bottom bed. There I found what looked like two canvas pillows with strings. I pulled them out, threw one at my poor sister and opened the door into the passageway. A steward was shepherding passengers onto the boat deck but when he saw us he stopped and took our life jackets from us and gave us smaller ones.

There was a sense of lightheartedness out on deck. Everyone seemed to be very jolly and not really taking things too seriously. The Chief Petty Officer told my sister and me to stand in front of everyone so he could help us put on our jackets.

'Now,' he said, addressing the assembled company, 'I want you all to watch very carefully as I take you through what we call boat drill. If, God forbid, we should have to abandon ship, and we've had quite enough of that in the past, then the klaxon will go off like this' and he pressed a button on a bulkhead and the whole ship was drowned in a ferocious clanging. 'If you hear that, then put on your life jackets immediately and come up on deck to this assembly point 'ere.' He looked relaxed and rather pleased with himself. Then we did the jacket bit: head through the hole between the two canvas buoyancy floats, linen straps taken through the loops behind the waist, pulled tightly and tied in a bow around your tummy. The Chief PO then checked my bow by pulling at it so hard that I nearly fell over. What's more he managed to undo what I proudly thought was a rather useful knot.

'Any questions ladies and gentlemen?' he barked. He didn't wait for a reply but turned to unlash the cover of one of the lifeboats. He showed us what the rope slings round the sides were for and how best to get ourselves pulled in over the gunwales to safety. After getting very cold we were happy to return to the warmth of the mess deck where we had tea. Then I and a friend, without anyone seeing us, sneaked back on deck to see what was going on.

We leant over the ship's rail and looked down onto the quay far below. The dockers were making ready to cast off. The access doors in the hull were being closed with watertight clamps, the gangways lifted away from the side. The fat spring ropes securing bow and stern stretched and creaked. We raced towards the pointed end to watch a tugboat manoeuvre itself into position to take the first of the heaving lines. Bigger and heavier lines followed until the tugboat sailor held to his chest the largest manila rope I'd ever seen. He placed the loop over a solid-looking bollard attached to the deck just behind the wheelhouse and then the little boat took up the strain.

A long deep vibrating blast from our horn filled every corner of the late afternoon gloom. I looked down and strangely had the greatest difficulty in not jumping over the side. Then came the cast-off from the fore and aft bollards. The heavy loops were each lifted by two men, chucked into the water and hauled on board to be neatly coiled by the bow and stern parties. For two small boys it was all great fun. The hull shuddered slightly as the engine revolutions picked up. The sea between ship and jetty began to boil as the tug pulled us away from the dockside and slowly out into the channel. As we passed slowly between the harbour navigation lights three whoops from the ship's siren heralded the start of our passage to Holland and a fond farewell to England.

By seven o'clock that evening a strong sou'-westerly had picked up and the ship lifted to the heavy swell. Stabilisers were not generally fitted to troopships and this vessel was no exception. I'd never been seasick, even though I had been in some pretty powerful storms. I adopted the best method I knew of avoiding it – going out on deck and facing the weather head on. I ran to the rail across a sea-soaked deck and grabbed onto it. I buttoned up my mackintosh and turned up the collar. Behind me the ship's lights bobbed and twinkled in the rigging and the silhouette of the bridge was clear against the dark clouds. I would see out what in my excitement I thought was the best part of the night, pretending now to be a whaling captain harpooning his catch, and now a lifeboatman fighting the sea to save a damsel in distress. I was oblivious of others up on deck who came to heave and retch over the side, till the gunwales ran with vomit. Only when I could neither keep my eyes open nor anchor my feet firmly to the deck did I venture back to my cabin. I slept well and easily, until my dreams were rudely interrupted.

All too soon the dreaded intercom broke through into my numbed brain calling reveille to the entire ship. Apparently disembarkation would be at 0500 hours. I rose but didn't shine. My sister was already up and looking like a rag doll, hair all over the place and still clutching 'Little Teddy', her cherished friend, who had been taken to war in the western desert by my father as a keepsake. The ship seemed already crowded with folk to-ing and fro-ing to the heads. I had to stand on tiptoe to use the urinal, a manoeuvre which always ended in little disasters. But soon we were spruced up and on our way, joining the human tide of legs, hands, coats and suitcases out onto the cold deck. A dark, forbidding scene presented itself. White steam from the funnels lit by the mast lights drifted gently across a dark sky. The stars were still twinkling in the cold grey dawn; the moon was full. The foghorn gave a low mournful call echoing back across the black glittering water from the tall sides of the metal sheds lining the quay. With engines cut back to quarter speed we drifted quietly into the Hook of Holland. As we came alongside we reversed screws and the ship shuddered a little as we lost speed. Again the bowman stood four-square at the prow of our great ship, for it had indeed become our home for a few hours, and judging the distance nicely delivered the guide rope into the hands of the Dutch seaman standing fifty feet below. We edged majestically in towards the dock and in splendid synchronisation both ends of the boat were made fast. A crane swung the gangplank into position and half a dozen sailors made it secure.

Surrounded by yawning passengers we trudged down to the disem-barkation deck and waited our turn to get ashore. As we descended the gangway, the sea gurgled and swelled beneath our feet, and we could see a mixture of broken wood, old oranges, a dead cat and brown froth. It looked a very dangerous place. The first wisps of daylight grew from the east and the wind got up. I shivered an early-morning shiver as I took my first steps onto Dutch soil.

In contrast the quayside canteen was warm and lively. The lights burned brightly overhead. Long trestle tables offered us piping hot baked beans on toast for breakfast. The other half-dozen children travelling with us were all safely accounted for by our Dutch woman volunteer. She sat beside us like a kindly godmother and explained which of three trains standing at the nearby platforms was ours. Identity labels were duly stamped and pretty soon my sister and I found ourselves once again on our own climbing the steep steps into a large green carriage. We were now on the last leg of our journey to Münster in northern Germany.

The carriage was much the same as the one we had so recently left in England, but to get from one to the next you had to leave the warmth and go outside onto a little verandah, across a bridge with handrails and onto the opposing verandah. When you got inside the windows wound down only half way and were wide, allowing you to rest your chin on the bar and see what was happening. To my delight coming slowly down the platform was a large rubber-tyred trolley stacked with chocolate, perfume and stockings. I didn't much rate the stockings and perfume although a good many had been handed up to eager hands and exchanged for guilder notes before it arrived at our window. In heavily rationed England we had to rely on our American friends to bring us candy. 'I've bought you enough Hershey bars to sink a battleship,' were the opening words of Jimmy Cullins, a US army colonel, who when on leave used to visit us in Oxfordshire. Even so I had never seen so much chocolate in one place before. The confectioners at Van Houten's factory had clearly been working overtime. I eagerly handed over my money and in return I became the proud owner of a pack of ten chocolate bars packed five by five either side of a piece of stiff cardboard and wrapped in clear cellophane. My sister had chosen a couple of pork pies and some sandwiches and I'd already decided that she wasn't going to have any of my hoard, even if I was to be ill in the process!

A kindly gentleman joined us in the compartment. He asked us if we were all right. We in return told him where we were going. He offered to look after my chocolate while I explored the platform. The train was not due to leave for another half an hour.

I scrambled down the steps by hanging onto the grab rails on the outside of the carriage. The last step down onto the low continental platform stretched my legs to near breaking. Clouds of steam drifted up from the couplings obscuring for a moment the huge black locomotive that stood at the head of the train. No clean lines of the compact and uncluttered British engines here. The wheels were painted bright red; the front was fitted with massive side plates like blinkers, the size of up-ended snooker tables. The boiler was covered with wires and pipes running its entire length, terminating at the driver's cab. This was so high that a six-runged ladder was needed to get up into it. The fireman was busy feeding coal into the firebox, his face lit by the furnace. I stood transfixed beside this powerful monster.

By the time we drew out of the Hook the sun had risen and the clouds melted away. The Dutch countryside drifted past, flat and wet. The train

'I've bought you enough Hershey bars to sink a battleship.'
Judy and I in lederhosen with US Colonel Jimmy Cullins

ran along beside the banks of the wide River Maas and on into the devastation of Rotterdam. The docks there were slowly getting back on their feet. Massive Stothert and Pitt dockyard cranes swung their cargoes of food from the gaping holds of American Liberty ships into waiting trucks. The Marshall Plan, aimed at feeding Europe, was now well underway and this port was one of its principal sinews. We continued our journey past farmyards with their horse-drawn carts. We saw womenfolk in black dresses and headscarves, their sleeves rolled up, beating their washing out on stone slabs. We sped past roads empty save for the flat-capped man on his sit-up-and-beg bicycle with lunch box clipped to his carrier. Sometimes we ran alongside quiet canals with little wooden Van Gogh drawbridges. Old barges were held by rotten ropes to non-existent rings lying half submerged along the banks. I saw only the occasional seaworthy craft; mostly children were playing in floating tea-chests powered by tea-tray oars. The windmills which had avoided the attention of RAF Bomber Command stood defiant, slowly turning their graceful sails. Holland was waking up to a free world.

I spent the first hour glued to the window. The trackside paraphernalia was so different to the English railways. The points had little boxes attached to them which told you which way they were set. The line was under endless repair so we often had to slow down, especially over bridges. German soldiers had been press-ganged into rail work. They wore their distinctive field-grey peaked forage caps. Leaning on their picks and shovels like a sullen guard of honour they stared at us as we crept by. I had been tucking into one of my sister's pork pies which turned out to be very hard so I decided to throw it out of the window (and I never did see where it landed; I have lived with the thought that I might have killed one of those hapless fellows). Every so often a distant clanging could be heard, which got louder and louder until we crossed a road. There were no familiar white level-crossing gates with red warning plates, nor friendly signalman in his box; only a red-and-white-striped steel bar with a metal skirt that swung down across the road. Flashing red lights warned of our passage and, once past, the clanging faded as we continued our journey eastwards.

Soon our papers were scrutinised by a red-faced fellow who I thought looked as if he might ask me to accompany him to see the guard. He handed back my ticket without comment while he looked out of the window into the middle distance. I followed his gaze and saw a large black and white illuminated sign beside the track heralding the approach of Venlo, the border town between Holland and West Germany. We stopped and I pressed my nose to the window. Venlo was a busy station with massed railway lines and acres of marshalling yards. The signals and lighting stands were operational, but rusty. Electric pylons and over-head feeds crisscrossed the rails like a cat's cradle. Alongside us stood a long line of low wagons loaded with umpteen Churchill tanks, jeeps by the handful and a convoy's worth of ten-tonne trucks. Beyond them were other wagons piled high with war repair materials – timber, metal pipes, plywood sheeting, all provided by the allies to mend a shattered country.

I leaned out of the window. I could smell something cooking on a hot-dog stand. Then we were again asked for our passports. A young inspector raised his eyebrows at the number of stamps we had already amassed.

'Yours?' he asked and we both rather proudly nodded our heads. He held both passports open with spread fingers of one hand while he punched his stamp down with a resounding bang, putting his own mark on a fresh page. He handed them back to us without expression.

As we pulled out of the station into occupied Germany you could feel the pattern of life change. Hardly any of the buildings had been left undamaged. Incendiary fires had gutted what was left after the bombers had been. Gable ends, supported only by their chimney stacks, rose high and slender above brick rubble. Roads had been cleared by hand and brushed clean. Along the pavements sat men and women, with small hand picks, systematically knocking lime mortar off each brick. Once cleaned they were handed to a colleague who would place them neatly on an ever-growing pile ready for reuse in the reconstruction. There were makeshift shelters of corrugated sheeting spanning the corners of bombed-out buildings, enclosed with bales of straw. In this 'home' three generations of the same family might live; and out of these came fresh-faced children with clean shoes and polished leather satchels. The fact that their school had been flattened and their classroom was no more than a Dutch barn with canvas sides did not seem to worry them. Before the war the Germans had made very good maps and records of all their buildings. These plans had been carefully stored to save them from damage. Now, under the authority of the CCG, the German mayors were busily dusting them off ready to recreate down to the smallest detail what had been lost. In contrast English planners invariably eschewed the maxim 'As it was, where it was' in favour of wholesale redevelopment. In the light of experience perhaps the Germans got it right, and we got it wrong.

At level crossings too the vehicles we saw were starkly different from those in Holland. Apart from horse and cart, the most common form of transport was fuelled by charcoal gas. Lorries were favoured which allowed the driver and his indispensable mate to make reasonably long journeys by filling up the bed of the lorry with coal which was then shovelled, even as they went along, into a pot-bellied boiler strapped to the back of the cab – an unnerving activity bearing in mind the state of the roads. The gas produced was held in a large mackintosh bag on top of the cab roof. When full it added five feet or so to the height of the lorry. The other type of vehicle on the roads was the Volkswagen Beetle, which was by then being churned out in substantial numbers from reconstructed pre-war factories. They were painted black for the CCG, khaki for the forces, and grey for everyone else. We saw rusty trams clanging their way through broken cobbled streets, with concertina arms crackling and sparking across overhead wires. By such means and with evident good humour were travel and commerce pursued.

Eventually the novelty of devastation dulled, and succumbing to the fatigue of idleness I fell asleep. But not for long.

'Come on we're nearly there,' my sister said urgently, shaking me awake. I looked blearily out of the window. It appeared that Münster had been flattened. The Naafi was about the only thing standing, and even that was a prefab. We clattered across a Bailey bridge put up by the Royal Engineers to carry the train over the river Ems, the original one lying like a beached whale in the still waters below. I wound down the window, and strained to see round the outside corner of the bending train. Could I see my father and mother in the throng which filled every corner of the long platform? No I couldn't. Perhaps they were right at the back. The Hauptbahnhof, still black with soot, slid into view and we crawled to a standstill beneath its gracefully pitched but glass-less roof. The engine ticked and steamed in moist exhaustion.

Helped by our friendly old gentleman we gathered up our belongings and climbed down onto the platform. The guard raised his green baton, blew his whistle and slowly the long train eased itself out of the station. We were left quite alone on the edge of the platform with our luggage.

'I'm sure we should have seven bits,' my sister said after carefully inspecting the pile. 'Where are the other two cases?' Well I didn't know, or care much; I just wanted to find my parents.

Indeed there seemed to be no one to meet us. We waited amongst the crowd of other passengers who were busily hugging and kissing their relatives and generally organising their way home. Not so for us. But it didn't take long before a German porter asked if he could help. He picked up our bags and told us to follow him. Up some stairs we went, to a little office high above the platform on one side of which was a large window overlooking the station. It was rather exciting. There he left us with a blond girl in charge of the loudspeaker system.

'You are English?'

'Yes, and my name is Wilhelm Beartram,' I replied in my best German accent. She roared with laughter.

'With a name like that you should be a little German boy.' Still giggling she switched on her microphone. Booming across the whole station the announcement went out:

'Will Colonel and Mrs Beartram please come to the station office to collect their two children.'

We made our way downstairs and to our great joy our father, looking very smart with his gleaming leather Sam Browne belt and burnished sword-stick, and my mother in calf-length skirt and a little hat perched upon the side of her head, were waiting to greet us. We then got all the hugs and kisses you could ever wish for. They explained that they had been waiting patiently for us to go through the army security barrier at the side of the station. It didn't seem to matter any more. We'd made it, and we were only too happy to be back, at last, in the heart of our family. My brother, Tom, had come along too. He'd been born just after the Second World War in Germany. He only spoke German, but with touches of Estonian thrown in thanks to his Estonian nanny, Leoni Murmann, so talking to him in our mother tongue proved all but impossible. If you wanted to join in you simply had to learn the language. As a happy result of this I've felt very much at home in Germany ever since.

Armstrong, my father's driver, collected such bags as appeared to be ours and our happy little group walked out into the bright sunshine to find the large Humber staff car waiting for us.

We eventually came to a leafy suburb where the houses were less forlorn, where trees still stood upright and an overwhelming sense of calm prevailed. We entered through the top gates and pulled up in front of a three-storey stone and rendered house half covered in ivy. The shutters were painted white and the front door with its ornate metal grille was of solid oak. The steps up to it had just been washed.

As we tumbled happily out of the car I was taken immediately by my mother to be introduced to an old woman. Her face was lined and her grey hair drawn back into a bun. She was nervously pulling at her apron strings.

'Come and meet Frau Gaedertz,'[3] said Mama, 'she is the owner of this lovely house.' The old lady walked down to meet me and held out a slender hand. After a few halting words of welcome she turned and, in slippered feet, started the long climb up the outside metal staircase to the attic. She lived above us in that house for the years that we were stationed in the town. It must have been terrible for her to see us enjoying her beautiful garden and living in her house with all her furniture still in place. She was kindness itself and my parents treated her with great respect. In similar circumstances of requisition many others in the occupation forces sadly showed no such concerns.

We unpacked. My mother dismissed my sister's concern over the number of suitcases. 'You probably only started out with five – five is quite enough,' she said, and that seemed to be the end of the matter.

Our German butler Herbert Luder and his wife Annie laid the table for tea. As I tucked into a plateful of biscuits I sat back in my chair and dreamt about my holiday to come.

There would be the fun of the early morning rides, with horses brought to the door by our German groom and of being carted at high speed and out of control across flat cabbage fields. The fun of sailing

---

3 I like to think that she was related to one Karl Gaedertz, who in 1888 came across a notebook in the archives of the University of Utrecht which held the only known authentic sketch of the interior of a Shakespearian playhouse. (The Swan Theatre, 1596) The set-up of Sam Wanamaker's 1997 replica of the first Globe Theatre at Bankside, London, is based almost entirely on that rough drawing.

lessons which ended up in the reeds; of skating on floodlit frozen tennis courts; of watching the 3rd Hussars parade behind their glittering, thumping regimental band, marching through the town; the fun of climbing down a hole under the railway tracks and watching the little train from Welbeck thunder overhead; of pinching my father's briar pipe and stuffing it full with dried beech leaves and choking on the smoke; the fascination of watching the old man at the end of our lane make brushes by hand, turning out one every ten minutes. His industry kept him and his family in bread, for which they had to queue for hours. The excitement of the village ShutzenFest, a celebration for young and old to mark the beginning of the hunting season.[4]

Even the fun of experiencing my first evening of opera, listening in rapture to Mascagni's *Cavalleria Rusticana* and Leoncavallo's *I Pagliacci*. They were to be beautifully performed in the one building that the city burgers of Münster had, above all others, made a priority for restoration. I would be entranced by the whole experience and hooked on the romance of opera thereafter.

Dreaming on, my eyes slowly glazed over in that peaceful trance-like state in which one is sometimes caught; a happy, contented, carefree moment. Then the reality of my situation hit me. In only 26 days' time my world would be thrown into reverse gear. That whole, exhausting journey would once again stretch ahead of me, a journey which would take me back to where I had started: back to my boarding school on the south coast of England.

And at the end of our holidays just as we were about to leave again for the station, and for England, a small lorry bumped its way down the drive and pulled up in a cloud of dust outside the back door. Across the face of my sister stole a broad smile. 'There you are,' she said excitedly. 'I knew I was right.' And indeed she was. Out came two rather battered-looking suitcases, still sporting their distinctive blue crosses. Even better, they were conveniently still packed for our journey back!

---

4 My father, officially referred to as Herr Oberst, was responsible for the villagers being allowed to borrow his rifles as a token so that they could have a proper Fest. These were forbidden to Germans at that time.

Brief Encounter

THE GOOD LORD KNOWS WHAT HE IS DOING. ALL THOSE SMALL BOYS WHOM he thinks may find difficulty in working out what they want to do in life, to them is given certainty. He brings them into this world knowing instinctively where they fit in. I consider myself lucky to be one of their number. Sometimes, however, that initial clarity is temporarily clouded. All it needs then is a bit of a nudge to put them back on the rails – in some cases literally.

It happened one day that I found myself on a train going to join the frigate HMS *Roebuck* which lay at berth in Devonport dockyard. I was sixteen years old, travelling to my first naval camp as part of my Combined Cadet Force training from Sherborne School. I lugged my white canvas kit bag into the carriage and found a near-empty compartment. I slid back the mahogany glazed door and asked the only occupant if any of the other seats were taken.

'Nay, lad, come on in,' said the burly fellow in a strong north-country accent. He was dressed in corduroys, a grey cardigan and an open-necked shirt. I sat down opposite him by the window. In no time at all we were sweeping majestically through open countryside towards the west country. It was some half an hour before we got into conversation.

'So,' said my friend suddenly, 'where's thee going all dressed up?'

As I was wearing the uniform of a naval rating, bell bottoms and all, I thought it an odd question. 'Going to join my ship for couple of weeks,' I said proudly.

'What for?' he asked. He was leaning well back into his upholstered corner seat, his long legs stretched out in front of him.

'Well, I thought I might join the Navy and that it might be a good idea to find out what I was letting myself in for,' I explained.

He clearly wasn't impressed. 'Well now you have a great time, young man, and enjoy yourself, but don't for one moment get carried away with romance of it all. I can see you're an up-together-sort-of-chap, and with decent education. Perhaps you should be thinkin' a little bit 'arder about what you really want out o' life.'

'Well then, you must know more about the Navy than I do,' I suggested, hoping that perhaps I might learn something useful before I got to my ship.

'Know 'bout the Navy?' he exploded. 'Good Heavens you need t' know nowt more than it gets very tight at top. No good money to talk of. Not many gets to be admirals, and if you don't make it, they chuck you out at the age o' forty. Not a good age to be told you're no longer needed.' He looked across at me. 'Now, 'aven't you got somethin' else you could do?' He folded his paper and put it down on the seat beside him, and waited.

Eventually I replied rather diffidently, 'Well I had thought I might be an architect.' I'd hardly finished the sentence before he leapt in.

'Now y'er talking. I've got friends in that line o' business and they do very nicely for theirselves; go on as long as they like and make their own way. That's a champion idea of yours, is that.' He gazed out of the window to watch the white steam drifting slowly across the fields. There was a lull in the conversation. I thought perhaps he had fallen asleep and that I could relax for a bit. But I was wrong. With his eyes shut I heard him whisper slowly, 'And if you're goin' t' be an architect,' and he emphasised the arch- allowing the rest to follow as an etcetera 'and if you're going to be an architect, what sort of architect d'you think you're goin' t' be?'

'Look,' I said a bit impatiently, 'it was only a moment ago that I was thinking of joining the Navy. I thought being an architect was, well, just being an architect. I'm pretty good at drawing and I really like build- ings, so it seems fairly obvious that I could make a go of it.' What I couldn't admit was that stewed plums was my favourite pudding.

Counting the four stones left on my plate was what I always insisted determined that I would be a sailor!

'Well, if you'll forgive me,' he said, 'it doesn't seem very obvious to me, son.' He leant forward and I thought was about to tap me on the knee to make his point. 'Take it from me, lad, there's all sorts of architect. If I want someone to design my 'ouse he's not the same chap who I'd ask to design my factory, no matter what. And the architects who design churches wouldn't be any good for your 'ouse. Too expensive and probably take too long about it. No,' and he looked me straight in the eye and in his deep Yorkshire brogue went on earnestly, 'now you tell me, what sort of an architect d'you think you're goin' t' be?'

'I really couldn't tell you, sir, until I've got a bit more experience,' I replied non-committally. He pressed the point.

'Well you get that experience, mind, and when you've got it you make up your mind. Remember if you don't know what sort of an architect you are, how the devil do you expect anyone else to know?' My new friend put down his paper and looked at me long and hard.

God, I thought to myself, I mustn't forget this conversation. No one, not my father, my uncle, nor any of my schoolmasters had ever spoken to me about how life worked in quite such a vivid way. I knew instinctively that the advice I was being offered was invaluable.

'And while we're at it, you might like another bit of advice?' and before I could say a thing he went on. 'When you do decide, as I'm sure you will, that you need to get a bit of really grand experience, join an old-fashioned, steady outfit and learn your trade from bottom up. Say five or six years. That should do, and after you'll want to 'ave a go yourself, I'll be bound.' He raised his eyebrows by way of confirmation and warming to his theme continued.

'And when you do, don't think that it's right to take on private work from inside an office. All that'll do is tell outside world you're a cheapskate and they can get you to work for 'alf price. They'll figure out pretty quick that your employer's paying the bulk of your wages so they won't 'ave to! No. You 'ave courage of your conviction. Hand in notice, stick up a plate and charge full fees. Only then will anybody take thee serious. If

Sixteen-years old: setting
off to join HMS *Roebuck*,
and a fateful encounter
on a train

you've got anything about you, you'll make it. The worst that can 'appen, mind, is you might fail and land back at start. So what's to lose?' and he spanked his knee as a breakwater to this tide of advice.

I looked at this kindly old man who appeared, for no good reason, to have my wellbeing very much at heart. 'That's very helpful of you sir, and perhaps I could now ask you a question?'

'Aye lad, fire away. Fire away!' he said enthusiastically.

'What do you do for a living?'

'Oh, me, I retired long ago, a rich man. I used to be a scrap metal merchant in Bradford. Grand life that. 'Anded over to me son who's doing very nicely.' At this inopportune moment the train started to lose speed as we approached Exeter St David's. He got up, put on his mackintosh and flat cap and turned to shake my hand. 'Good luck, son. This is my stop. Now, don't you forget what I've said. I just hope it will do you some good. I'll be off now.'

And with that he pulled up the brown leather strap to drop the window, and as the train drew to a stop he opened the carriage door, waved me goodbye and left me to my thoughts. I never got his name and not surprisingly I never saw him again. And as things turned out I never received better advice. I remembered every word he said and in the coming years I lived by them.

A year later when I was seventeen I passed my driving test, and on that very same red-letter day I received a card telling me that my application to join a school of architecture had been accepted. I got in with just five modest O-Levels to my name. I think the directors of the school needed all the fees they could get and would, I fear, not have turned away anyone who looked as if they might be able to pay! Anyway I was ecstatic. For the next three years I worked at my studies at the Architectural Association School of Architecture (known confusingly as the AA), housed in a fine Georgian terrace on the west side of leafy Bedford Square, just off Tottenham Court Road in central London. When I was 21 I took my 'Inter', or to give it its full title the Intermediate Examination. Because of the international standing of the AA this was dealt with by way of an internal assessment. It took place at the end of the third year of a five-year course and was judged principally by your third-year master. I didn't rate him as a teacher or an architect, and he knew it. As seems inevitable in life he got his own back when it came to my turn to be assessed by him.

I recalled, rather too late, my father's sensible maxim that it was unwise to make enemies; you never knew when you might need someone on your side! One morning a small knot of students were clustered round the notice board in middle hall, most of them were wreathed in smiles and congratulating one another. When they saw me approaching they fell silent and made way for me to see the list. Eagerly I scanned the names of those who had made the grade into the fourth year and who had not. It soon became clear that my name was not amongst them. My heart sank and I felt wretched. I walked slowly out of the front door, down the wide steps and ambled slowly around the square, deep in thought. Then I plucked up courage to pick up the phone. My palms began to sweat. What on earth would be the reaction of my parents?

It was my father who took the call. 'Well, how did you get on Willie?' I took a deep breath. There was nothing for it. No amount of beating around the bush could disguise the unhappy truth.

'Not good news Papa, I'm afraid,' I said quietly. There was a long pause.

'Oh, I am sorry to hear that.' He sounded as down as I felt.

'I've seen my year master and he has given me two bits of advice.' I said. He enquired what those might be. I explained that he'd given me the opportunity to reapply for a place after spending a year out. I'd have to do another complete third-year design scheme to even stand a chance. If I passed, and there was no guarantee that I would, I could then rejoin the school in the fourth year, alongside the students in the year below. A pretty ignominious fate.

'And the other piece of advice?' he asked gently. I didn't really want to explain much more but felt I had to.

'It was his view, Papa, that I would probably be wasting my time reapplying because he really didn't think I had it in me to become an architect anyway.' As I said the words my voice faltered and I closed my eyes.

My father's voice was quiet but authoritative. 'Come home, dear boy, and we will talk this through together. Just you and me. Telephones are no good for this sort of thing. Drive carefully and we'll see you for supper.' Was he being nice to me or would I be given a piece of his mind when I got home? As I drove down through the Oxfordshire countryside I was dreading the moment of arrival. Here I was, a failure. Couldn't even clear the first hurdle when left on my own. I passed through the large gates, and took the drive down to the house. I pulled up outside the comforting golden stone walls of my home. The front door was open and through the shadows my father emerged, arms outstretched. He gave me a big hug. I hugged him back and we remained like that for a moment saying nothing.

'Your mother's got a cup of tea for us. Come and sit down. You alright?' he said sounding genuinely concerned and putting his arm round my shoulders.

'Oh God, Pa, what a bloody waste of time. Three years of graft and then this. I don't know. If I can't be the best architect in the world then I don't really want to be an architect at all. What's the point?'

'The point, dear boy, is that there are very few of us in this life who reach the top of their chosen profession. Although I would never advocate not aspiring to be the best, you mustn't confuse that with the fun that can be had whilst striving to get there. Look at me. I'm not a Lieutenant-General. I'm a Lieutenant-Colonel – not a rank that sets the world on fire. But I've had a marvellous life: as a subaltern in India in the last days of the Raj; as a soldier fighting Rommel in the western desert, as a planner for D Day at the War Office. I had a fascinating time in Germany after the war acting as liaison officer between the British and Belgian High Commands. Loved every minute of it. Met a lot of very interesting people and made a great many friends. If you really do want to be an architect then don't listen to other people's opinion of you. Just go out and prove 'em wrong. I happen to know how good I think you'll be. I know what enthusiasm you have for buildings. No ..., you take it from me Willie, you've got what it takes to be very good indeed.'

I listened intently to what he was saying. I was so relieved to hear these kind and supportive words. 'It won't be easy, Papa, but what you say is what I desperately wanted you to say, and I wasn't at all sure you were going to say it.'

And a little later when the dust had settled my dear Mama joined us and we sat together beside a roaring log fire with our feet up and whiskies cupped in our hands. It was a good moment at the end of a difficult day.

I took my father's advice and forgot all about the opinions of others which had so unnerved me. I travelled down to the west country and for the next year I joined the old-fashioned firm of Nealons in Bristol. During the daytime I enjoyed working for them as member of staff, and in the evenings I worked on my designs as a lowly but determined student. Eventually and to my great relief I was readmitted to the AA and continued my studies until I had the satisfaction of passing my finals.

As the years passed I always held the memory of that brief encounter with the Yorkshireman who had given me such valuable advice on the train to Plymouth. I knew that what he'd said to me was going to be vitally important if I was going to make anything of my life as an architect. And so it proved to be. Eventually I had the chance to test each part of his philosophy and each time it proved its worth. I often wonder who he was, that man on the train. With a few well-chosen words he managed to change the course of my entire life.

'A Sincere form of Flattery'

'MAY I INTRODUCE MYSELF? I'M JOHN WINTER, AND I'M YOUR FIFTH-YEAR tutor. Welcome back to the AA William.'

He was a tall, elegant man who inhabited a very small office overlooking Morwell Street, at the back of the school's premises at numbers 34, 35 and 36 Bedford Square in Bloomsbury, one of London's more arty quarters. Here he not only set projects for the students in his year, and gave us the benefit of his considerable architectural experience, but also ran an avant-garde private practice of his own; something which the Architectural Association encourage in all its teaching staff. For some reason Winter and I got on. He had a particularly gentle, but direct way of putting over criticism. 'I think you are trying to scratch your left ear with your right hand, Bertram,' he would say, and with that he left you to ponder on a simpler solution to a design. I rather liked that.

'Are you still 'digging' with your grandmother in Green Street?' he enquired, knowing full well the answer.

'Not exactly, John,' I replied. 'I am getting married in a couple of months, and I've just bought a small cottage in Somerset.' My thinking was that as there were no lectures to attend at the school and I only had to see my tutor once a week, I might just as well go up to London and back down again making use of a cheap day return rail ticket.[1] It would be much cheaper than living up in town, notwithstanding the generosity of my grandparents.

'Well, if you don't think that you'll be too much distracted by your young bride,' he said knowingly, 'and as long as you can keep up with

1 In those days a standard class cheap day return was £1-10-6 (£1.52½)

everyone else, I can't see why you shouldn't give it a go.'

In one's last year at the AA a student was considered sufficiently mature to write his own programme of work which culminated in a 'masterpiece' or design thesis, as it was known. It was to this that John now referred.

'Rather more importantly, from my point of view, have you given any thought to what you are going to do about your thesis?'

Indeed I had. I told him of my plan to design an hotel; that if I played my hand carefully I could combine my honeymoon with a modest amount of research. I'd already been to Trusthouse Forte, as it was called in 1963, to interview the managing director. Having talked with him for over an hour I had come to the conclusion that he didn't appear to have any clear idea of how to assess both the number of bedrooms and what range of facilities any hotel, given its location, should have. I found this astonishing. I did press him on the matter but I got precisely no further forward. His method was very much 'think of a number' and see if it made sense. I didn't think that particular intellectual approach would wash with my tutor, John Winter. He confirmed my doubts when next we met to review progress.

'John,' I said, feeling a little depressed, 'I really don't think I'm going to get much help in this country. I need to spread my wings further afield if I'm to get an international perspective on all this.' I then let him into my plan to visit Portugal, ending up in Madeira, on a three-week fact-finding mission to research the European luxury hotel scene. I watched his face for a reaction to this unconventional approach. When I saw that all he did was smile I was encouraged to tell him just how far I had got with my arrangements. 'Immediately after the wedding we fly to Lisbon and will be staying at the Hotel Tivoli for a day or two. I think I'll learn quite a bit there.'

I spent the night before the wedding surrounded by my own family at the Francis Hotel in Bath. When I came down to breakfast the following morning the building was surrounded by a huge crowd of young people.

'Darling,' cooed my mother, 'I had no idea you were so popular and well known in the city!'

'My dear Mama, I don't think this lot are here to see me. It may have rather more to do with an up-and-coming pop group who are also staying called The Beatles!'

On that bright November Saturday in '63 Victoria and I were married in the little Normanesque church in the pretty village of Priston just outside Bath. After spending our first night in the Waldorf Hotel in London (not much to learn there!) we took off from an overcast London Airport and landed in the blissful warmth of late-autumn sunshine in Portugal.

The Hotel Tivoli turned out to be an old-fashioned, rather grand place, and offered some useful lessons in the art of creating space. It had been built in 1933 at the tail end of the Art Deco period. The first thing that struck one on arrival was the magnificent double-height entrance hall with a galleried mezzanine running around three of its sides. Overhead a shaft of sunshine streamed through a Tiffany-style skylight, bathing the carpeted marble floor in a blaze of colour. 'Now that's really what making an entrance is all about,' I said to myself. It was my old muse Sir Edwin Lutyens who remarked to a colleague who had just landed a new commission to design a house, 'Ah my friend, but has your client put aside enough money for a generous amount of circulation?' I was beginning to appreciate just how important that statement was. It was true that the creation of what some might term wasted space was perhaps the key to creating delightful and memorable buildings.

Lisbon was then, as it still is, a cosmopolitan city whose affluence was much in evidence in streets of expensive shops and restaurants, fine architecture, and elegantly dressed women strolling in manicured parks. Step off the patterned pavements and turn down the side streets and you were in a very different world. Whereas our hotel overlooked the Avenida de Liberdade, a wide sun-filled boulevard edged by a double line of plane trees, the connecting alleyways were narrow and dark. From fourth-floor windows lines of washing hung like Christmas decorations. Women in black shawls sat on doorsteps talking with their neighbours and scolding their poorly-dressed children. This disparity of lifestyle did not seem to worry anyone, judging by the warm smiles we got.

Two days later we left that enchanting city and flew to the small, sandy mid-Atlantic island of Porto Santo, situated just off the coast of Madeira.[2] From there we boarded a small banana boat of suspect seaworthiness for the final leg of our journey. After a worryingly choppy crossing we eventually glided into the protected waters of Funchal harbour. Lights twinkled through the dusk of the surrounding hills as our little boat tied up against the rocky quay, sandwiched between a huge cruise liner on one side and a white-hulled, Scandinavian, four-masted, square-rigged cutter, a truly magnificent and romantic vessel, on the other.

A chauffeur in white uniform with 'Reid's Palace Hotel' embroidered in blue across his cap stood waiting patiently on the quay to welcome us. He took our few bags and placed them carefully in the back of the shooting-brake. It only took a few minutes to drive up to the famous hotel. The car came to rest in a cobbled court of patterned black pebbles and we tumbled out in front of a large oak door which was partially hidden under a cascade of passion flowers. I have to admit it didn't look very impressive; not the grand entrance that one might have expected of one of the world's grandest hotels.[3] As we walked into reception I was surprised at how small it was. A modest polished porters' desk to our left was matched by a frustratingly blank wall where there might well have been a stunning view over the gardens and out across the blue Atlantic to the Desertas Islands. I was a bit disappointed. I couldn't think why someone hadn't realised its potential and done something about it.

It was also a bit quiet. There was a church-like hush about the place. People walked softly and talked in low voices. It was the off season which gave the staff an opportunity to spruce up the place before the Christmas onslaught of blue-rinsed dowagers and arthritic colonels.

On the way to our room we passed along wide polished mahogany

---

2 Ironically it was only when the hotel building boom had taken off in Madeira that this old-fashioned Edwardian island got round to building its own airport, which was open for business some ten years after we made our first visit in 1963.

 3 William Reid opened his hotel in 1891 to the designs of George Somer, who had just completed Shepheard's in Cairo.

passages thick with ladders and dust sheets. The porter opened the door to our room, and placing our suitcases on the chest of drawers, flung open the window and invited us to look out. Below us a carpet of blue plumbago and red tree poinsettias filled the tropical gardens. Sweet scents, caught on the evening air, drifted into our room. The shimmering lights on the still black water of the harbour to our left and the lavender-coloured hills up to Quinta do Palheiro[4] could be seen between the sturdy grey trunks of palm trees which in turn were under-planted with the exotic orange flowers of the bird-of-paradise. And at the bottom of the garden, below the cliffs we could hear the steady slap and gurgle of the warm Atlantic. The whole prospect was enchanting, made more so by being lit by a thousand fireflies. With the thought of three weeks of such romantic bliss stretching out invitingly before us, we both flopped into bed, exhausted from our travels. We slept like dormice.

The next morning I awoke early sensing that all was not well. 'Are you feeling alright, darling?' I said, leaning over on one arm and looking down at my pretty bride lying somewhat inelegantly beside me.

'Not really,' she croaked, opening one eye. 'I've got the most awful sore throat and my head's banging.' She tried to sit up but fell back onto the pillows holding the back of her hand across her forehead.

'I'll call Reception and get a doctor to you, you poor thing,' and to my relief a Dr de Silva arrived within minutes. He pulled from his Gladstone bag a thermometer and took her temperature.

He inspected the mercury and said slowly, 'I think a period of time in bed for madam.' Shaking down the thermometer he turned to me and continued, 'You must keep her quiet, and make sure that the curtains are pulled. She's caught a bad chill and should, I think, rest a little. Let her sleep.' He wrote out a prescription for me to get in town, pressed shut his bag and left us, closing the door quietly behind him.

I loosened the covers around the bed, and bent down to kiss Vicks's forehead, then tiptoed out of the room. This perhaps was my chance to

---

4 The Blandys, an English family, had been established in Madiera for 100 years and successfully run businesses ranging from wine, hotels, property development, to transport. Quinta do Palheiro was the Blandy's house to which we were invited for dinner. An evening, supported by an army of servants that could have changed little in a century.

start my research. So I went straight to the concierge and asked if I might see Mr Burca, the hotel manager.

The receptionist rang through to him and nodded to me. 'Of course you may,' he said and pointed me in the direction of the stairs. I climbed the four storeys to the top of the Edwardian building where Mr Burca was standing waiting to greet me.

'And what brings you up to see me so soon after your arrival, Mr Bertram? I do hope everything is all right for you.'

'It's got nothing to do with that,' I said reassuringly, 'I think your hotel is wonderful. I just wanted to pick your brain because I think you, of all people, might be able to help me.' I explained that I was a student of architecture and that for my design thesis I needed to find a suitable site for an hotel and be given a realistic brief for my project. I thought Reid's might be a suitable candidate, and asked if he could possibly put me on the right track?

'You are extremely lucky, young man,' he said, pulling at his cuffs. 'My architect, Leonardo Castro-Freire, he is flying over from Lisbon tonight. I've asked him to talk with me about the possibility of expanding Reid's. I want to double the number of rooms here. It's our first meeting and I think, perhaps, you ought to meet him, don't you?'

'If his English is as good as yours, then I certainly would, sir,' I said eagerly.

'Don't you worry about that, he is very cosmopolitan. We'll be in the bar at six thirty this evening; do join us and you will, I'm sure, find him very amusing and very knowledgeable.'

That evening a thickset, good-looking man in his late fifties, who was enjoying a glass of whisky, rose to greet me. 'You want to steal my job, I hear,' he joshed, 'your timing is impeccable, Mr Bertram.' He turned to Edward Burca, 'do we get a drink from our friend before we release to him the crown jewels?' We enjoyed an easy conversation and to my astonishment within the hour I had what I'd come for: the site on which Reid's stood; a comprehensive brief for an hotel of some 350 bedrooms; what had to be provided to obtain five-star rating; the different seating capacities of all three restaurants; staff requirements; recreational facilities; the number of franchised shops; you name it. In fact everything I needed to be able to begin designing my hotel.

I bade my two friends farewell and as I left, Leonardo called out, 'when you have finished your project, William, be sure to let us see the final drawings. Please ask the desk for my address, and have good luck.'

I sneaked back to my bedroom to find that my dear wife was still fast asleep. As I prepared for bed I couldn't resist humming very quietly to myself. I was ecstatic. I tried not to wake her. I climbed gently in beside her, all warm and cosy. I could hardly believe my good fortune. Buoyed by euphoria I soon drifted off into a deep sleep.

The next morning Vicks was still feeling poorly and felt she needed another day to recover. So I used my time to visit Funchal, the leafy capital city of that small island. I was on the hunt for the city's Planning Department where I hoped to find someone who could give me an accurate site plan of the peninsula on which Reid's sits. Bathed in warm sunshine I walked down the long slope of the Avenida Zarco into the town and along the decorated limestone pavements in the shadow of purple jacarandas. I passed gushing black volcanic rocky grottoes and radiant bougainvillea. I entered the Town Hall through a tall grey stone archway beyond which was a cool fountain courtyard with a large tree to one side. In a corner rose a stone staircase leading to a pillared gallery.

I looked up and saw a wrinkled old man casually leaning over the balustrade, cigarette in hand, looking down at me. I shouted to him in my best Portuguese. Surprisingly he seemed to understand where I wanted to go and laconically raised his thumb. I ran up the stairs two at a time, only to find myself faced with a long row of identical wooden doors. An olive-skinned girl with a pile of papers wedged under her chin stopped to ask me if she could help. She tilted her head beckoning me to follow. I walked behind her until she stopped opposite a mahogany door and nodded her head at it.

I knocked and went in. All eyes looked up enquiringly. One of the clerks approached me, 'You are English?' he asked and I nodded. He turned and shouted over his shoulder, 'Enrico!' A swarthy Madeiran got up from his desk and came over. I told him what I had come for. 'Ah, yes, we do have plans,' he said in a thick English accent, 'all in metric. You, I think, will work in feet, no?' He seemed genuinely concerned. 'I hope that won't be difficult for you.'

He bent down and pulled open a flat drawer in a large plan chest. He flicked through the deep pile of sepia prints and pulling out a large plan, placed it on top of the chest and stood back, 'perhaps this is what you want,' he said folding his arms. I looked carefully at the map. There, quite clearly shown, was Reid's Hotel on its eleven-acre site: the entrance driveway, the gardens with its maze of paths and steps, the bathing lift tower and the rocky terraces down by the sea. It outlined the shape of the high cliffs which supported the site, all in the minutest detail. And over-laying all were half-metre contour lines giving me the third dimension.

I turned to my friend with a broad smile and enquired, 'how much, how many escudos?'

'You have it, take it,' he said , shooing me away good-naturedly. 'It isn't often we have a young architect from England to visit us. If you want it, it is yours.' He rolled up the plan, secured it with an elastic band and handed it to me with a flourish. There was an audible murmur of approval from his colleagues. I took it from him with gratitude, and mounting excitement. I became very fond of the Portuguese; true allies, I thought. A sentiment which has, if anything, deepened over the inter-vening years.

When I got back Victoria was sitting up in bed with the curtains pulled back and looking very much perkier. 'Did you have any luck, darling?' she said quietly.

I leaned over and kissed her forehead. Looking deeply into her eyes I winked, 'yes, my sweet!' I said slowly, 'I most certainly did.'

'Oh good,' she said putting down her book, 'I'm so sorry I couldn't be with you.'

The next morning, 22 November, we were both feeling particularly chipper. We bounced down to breakfast 'full of the joys of love's young dream', anticipating a strenuous day of sunbathing and taking the occa-sional dip. We cheerily wished those in the dining room a very good morning and were rather taken aback when one of the elderly guests asked me what I thought was so 'good' about the morning.

'Haven't you heard the news?' he asked, glaring at us both. 'Kennedy's been assassinated.'

'Good Grief!' I said. 'How awful, I'm so sorry. What happened?'

'Shot in his car in Dallas. Dreadful business,' said our friend, flicking up his paper as a sign that, as far as he was concerned, our conversation was at an end.

Thereafter the day took on a mournful air. Wirelesses in the main rooms played sad music interrupted occasionally by announcements giving us grimmer and more depressing news. It took a day or two for Reid's to get back to some of its old ways.

We fell easily into the gentle rhythm of that life of luxury. Things would be very different when we got home. Back in England, I eventually got down to the serious business of my studies and found to my surprise that I was ahead of the game. My fellow students had used the three weeks we'd been away quite admirably: drinking coffee, discussing the meaning of life and, if being really serious, the finer points of architecture. What most of them had not done was to get to grips with their own design theses. How puffed up I was with self-satisfaction.

We lived not far from Bristol in the village of Blagdon, overlooking a large lake. I'd set-up my drawing-board by the window in the drawing room of our little whitewashed cottage with its bright blue windows and bright blue door, and in this charming setting began the process of design. I allowed the scheme for my new hotel to develop, first in my head and then, when it was quite clear in my mind's eye, on the pages of my sketchpad. Every week, as planned, I took my sketches up to London to discuss my ideas with John Winter at the AA.

I realised from the outset that I would never get the qualifications I'd set my cap at by proposing that the old Reid's Hotel, built in glorious Empire style, should be retained and extended in similar vein, even though I thought that that was what I'd do in other circumstances. What the Architectural Association expected was something new, something that would raise the tutor's blood count. Demolition of all the buildings on this prominent site was to be my only option.

I had made the decision early on that every one of the bedrooms in my new hotel would look out to sea, and the access corridors would be wide and generous, with breathtaking views of the mountains. All this was to be contained in a very long sinuous marble-clad structure of five stories supported on slender concrete pillars to look like the trunks of palm trees. This allowed me to design a free-flowing space at garden level to accommodate the reception rooms, restaurants, shops and the odd palm tree. I chose the shape of the hexagon to give some flexibility and discipline to this fluid succession of interconnecting rooms. But most importantly it presented an opportunity to create the most beautifully proportioned hallway which I designed to jut out into the trees, capturing the spectacular views over the harbour and out to the Desertas, lost in purple haze on the horizon. It was the view which I had yearned to see when first we arrived.

For my final presentation I constructed a five-foot by three-foot balsa-wood scale model of the whole scheme with cliffs made of cork-bark and lots of trees made from sprigs of millet. I took it up to London by train, and to make sure it wasn't damaged I sat for the whole journey on a pile of mail bags in the guard's van until I reached Paddington. Much to the amusement of my fellow travellers and the station staff, I wheeled the model on a flatbed porter's trolley round to the taxi rank.

'Blimey guv, I shouldn't let me budgerigars see that lot,' said my cockney driver as he drew up, 'your millet trees wouldn't last five minutes.' He got out of his cab and helped me load my precious cargo onto the back seat. I installed myself on the flip-seat opposite with my foot firmly out in front wedging the model into the back rest. Shouting over his shoulder as he got behind the wheel, my cabbie suggested where he thought I might want to go, 'Lord Snowdon's birdcage at London Zoo, is it, guv'ner?' he asked, laughing loudly at his own joke.

'No mate, it's 36 Bedford Square,' I said laughing, 'I'll get some friends to help me unload it when we get there, and,' I said, 'if it's all the same, I'd like my model to remain in one piece while we're getting there.'

'I'll drive like your gran'muver guv', you'll 'ardly know you're movin',' and with that he let in the clutch with a fearful jerk and off we sped. As we stopped at some traffic lights he looked at me in his mirror and said. 'You done a lot of work there guv'; where's it goin' to be built?'

'On the island of Madeira,' I said, 'but I'm afraid it never will be. Though if I'm lucky it might just get me through my exams.'

'Hotel is it?' he asked as he pulled away, 'wouldn't mind spendin' a week or two wiv' me old Dutch at a fancy place like that, I can tell you.' Eventually he turned the corner into Bedford Square to find that there was no one about. So Alf, my new friend, and I unloaded the model and took it down into the dingy basement of that very fine Georgian terrace.[5]

'How much is that?' I asked him when we'd finished.

''Ave it on me, guv', you looks as if you need a bit o' luck.'

These lower lecture rooms were a hive of activity. The schemes would be seen in alphabetical order so I was to be first on. Rows of chairs were being arranged in an arc around the screens onto which I would pin my drawings. My model was placed centre stage. The 'crit' which would define the rest of my architectural career was but half an hour away. My mouth was dry and my hands began to sweat.

The essence of education at the AA is to prepare the student for the outside world. So right from the start you are faced with having to stand up and explain your thoughts and ideas to your peers in a formal setting. Practising architects, year masters, tutors and fellow students make up the audience. These occasions can be, and are probably intended to be, bruising affairs.

Cedric Price with his characteristic jet-black hair swept away from his forehead was the first of the jurors to arrive. He strolled up to the display boards puffing on a thin cigar. Dressed, as always, in stiff white collar, black tie and grey-striped shirt he drew up a metal chair and straddling it, looked intently down at my model without saying a word.

'You've been busy,' he said suddenly, looking up at me. 'It'll be interesting to hear what you've got to say for yourself.' That gave me heaps of confidence, as you can imagine.

AA tutors Marius Reynolds, Anthony Mauduit and John Dennis and

---

5 It is hard to imagine a worse example for students of how to convert a Listed Building into an institution than the exemplar of 34-36 Bedford Square, the AA School of Architecture. We should be ashamed of ourselves.

others took their places in the front row, followed by John Winter who was surrounded by a clutch of fourth- and fifth-year students. I'd made it my business to attend the previous year's thesis presentations. I had taken notes on what sort of schemes found favour with the jurors and, perhaps more importantly, how best to deal with the inevitable smart-arses who were out to play to the gallery at the student's expense. For the jurors it was a day out, a sort of intellectual hors d'oeuvres; for me on the other hand it was life or death.

As I walked towards the screens the room settled to a hush. A late-comer crashed through the double doors unaware of the proceedings and tactfully tip-toed to the back of the room. I picked up my pointer, a long wooden dowel, smacked it against my trouser leg, and stood looking across at my inquisitors.

I started tentatively but soon got into my stride. I hadn't planned in detail how I would explain my scheme and I was relieved therefore that a pattern formed in my mind just ahead of the words I was speaking. I had nearly got to the end of my presentation when I was interrupted. From one of the jurors I received a torrent of what could only be described as architectural gobbledygook. Was he making a valid point? By the look on the face of my critic I realised that he intended it to be damning criticism of my precious scheme rather than mere observation. With mounting concern I wondered how best to take the sting out of it? I opted for the simple-officer routine.

'I wonder if you could repeat that,' I said looking at him intently, 'because I'm not quite sure of the point you are trying to make.' Clearly he had not only confused me with his outburst but also himself. He looked round for support, but to my relief found none.

'No, really,' I said in mock concern for his predicament, 'I really do want to know if I can help you to understand this scheme.' He again looked for help along the line of his fellow jurors and when again he realised there would be none forthcoming he dismissively turned away from me, waved his hand in my direction, and quietly subsided into his chair. The episode had a galvanising effect on the room. Suddenly a measure of support for my designs materialised. The others on the panel sat up and started to take much more notice. Even the students chipped in with helpful and amusing architectural comments. And by the time I had explained that the wicker basket chair-lift, which ran from the hotel through the canopy of the palm trees in the garden down to the bathing area, was designed to allow guests to enjoy 'scotch-on-the-rocks', the studio was in uproar!

Looking back on the episode, I reckon that I was fairly treated, even though I hadn't been given an easy ride.

'I guess you'll start polishing your brackets now, William,' suggested a close friend as I wearily climbed the stairs out of the lecture room. I looked at him with raised eyebrows.

'Come again?'

'You know,' he said, 'passing out with flying colours, with the word 'hons' between brackets on the AA Diploma Certificate.'

'Oh, I hardly think so,' I said. 'That's reserved for a very privileged few and certainly not for those, like me, who fail their third-year Intermediate exams.'

But to my astonishment he was right. Whilst holidaying in north Cornwall for a few very hot summer days in 1964 I received a call from David Kemp, my great friend, fellow student and best man at our wedding.

'You need to get back up here as fast as you can, Will. The Diploma Certificate presentation is tomorrow, and the lists are up and your name is at the top of them. Congratulations, my friend.' He sounded genuinely happy for me.

Time went by and I forgot all about Leonardo and Madeira, but within the year I did remember to send a comprehensive set of my design drawings to Mr Burca at Reid's Hotel. I also enclosed with it a series of black and white glossy photographs of the model, which I'd had professionally taken (thankfully before the mice got at it and ate all my trees!). A fortnight later I received a kind letter from Edward Burca, the friendly hotel manager, thanking me. To my amusement he mentioned that Leonardo in his proposals to the Blandy board of directors had not had the courage to knock down the existing building and start from scratch, as I had! He complimented me on producing such a very elegant building and said that he was delighted to have been involved.

I thought very little more about my design for Reid's until my wife and I decided we would take a second honeymoon on the island. It was exactly fourteen years later when we arrived at the Savoy Hotel in Funchal, just along the rocky coast from Reid's. Walking out onto our balcony that first afternoon I sniffed the sea air, stretched and looked nostalgically across the open sea towards those familiar islands on the horizon. Then my eyes drifted round to the harbour where the white cruise liners lay moored in line astern along the breakwater, just as I remembered. And above them, to my utter astonishment, and for all the world to see, there in all its glory was my hotel.

Now, I do realise that to the general public one modern building looks very much like another, but the more I looked the more exact a copy this was. Here was the great curving five-tiered structure with a free-flowing arcade of hexagonally shaped shops threading themselves between great supporting columns. Even the lie of the land and how I'd handled it was identical.

'Just you come and have a look at this, my darling,' I said to Vicks, 'now doesn't that remind you of something?' I said, pointing to my left.

She could hardly believe her eyes. 'My God darling it's yours, isn't it? It's the hotel you designed. It really is. How could they?' So off we both went to investigate.

We walked up to the front door, past the shops selling linens and lace, whilst overhead the great mass of the superstructure curved gracefully towards the sea.

'Welcome to the Casino Park Hotel, sir. Would you like some help?' gushed the girl on the reception desk as we walked through into the polished marble hall.

'Yes, I would,' I said sharply. 'Do tell me, how long has this hotel been up? And who, may I ask, designed it?'

'We have a world famous Brazilian architect, Sir. He has only just finished it. Don't you think it is most beautiful?' She conferred with a

RECONSTRUCTION OF REID'S PALACE HOTEL IN MADEIRA · S.E. ELEVATION 1/16 · DWG NO 10 SET OF 22 · C.W. BERTRAM

My 1964 thesis design for our honeymoon hotel, Reid's Palace ...

colleague talking to her very fast in Portuguese. She then turned back to me. 'Yes,' she said, 'our architect, his name is Oscar Niemeyer. You may have heard of him? I think he is very pleased with it.'

Of course I had heard of him, one of the world's great modernists; I was not in the least bit surprised he was very pleased with it!

Now I know that Niemeyer had worked on a slightly different site from mine but nonetheless to think that one of the most revered architects should have come to the very same conclusions that I, a mere student, had come to was astonishing, not just in the abstract but in almost every particular. It was for me (or so it seemed in the heat of the moment) too much of a coincidence. I was overcome in equal measure by the angst of frustration and the charm of flattery. I could not get over the fact that someone else had, not to put too finer point on it, pinched my scheme. It was both unbelievable and, in a strange way, rather wonderful.

I could not resist the temptation to cast my mind back fourteen years to that dear old cockney cab driver. If only I had taken his telephone number I could have rung him and said 'Hey, Alfie, you remember me

... and in 1977 on our second honeymoon, there in all it's glory, *my* hotel as built: the Casino Park – sadly no longer visible from this viewpoint

and that model of the hotel I designed all those many years ago, you know the one your budgies would have liked? I think I told you then that it would never be built. Well I can tell you now that it bloody well has been built, and what's more, it's pretty amazing.

'Perhaps, after all, you and your old Dutch might like to get yourselves out to Madeira and enjoy the holiday of a lifetime and this time, mate ... it'll be on me!'

A Royal Appointment

Only when one looks back on the way life unfolds can you understand why certain things happen to you and the timing of when they do. So too the chance encounters with characters who unbeknown to them change the patterns of your life. One such person has had a profound effect on me.

Luke Rittner has been a continuing and benign presence in my life. It was he who rang me at the very moment that I had decided to leave the firm of architects for whom I was working in Bristol in order to put up my own brass plate. I was 29 years old. Bath was a close-knit city where the professionals all knew one another and where there was a clutch of ageing architects[1] who were coming to the end of their careers. Just the place to start a new practice, I thought. I had the surprising good fortune to enter the Bath establishment by marrying Victoria Ingle, the elder daughter of Reggie Ingle,[2] a well-known solicitor in the city and one time inter-war captain of the Somerset County Cricket team, and a good friend of the Marquis of Bath.

Luke rang me out of the blue. 'Go and see an old friend of mine, Christopher Blathwayt, who owns a whole house in Queen Square. He may be able to fix you up with a place to start your practice.'

I duly met Christopher at 14 Queen Square, one of John Wood's first buildings which heralded the Georgianisation of Bath. It was November 1969, on a day when the trees in the middle of the square showed all the colours of a Turkish carpet. He took me round; first to the car park

1 Hugh Roberts, Hugh Crallen, Ernest Tew, Molly Gerrard and Alan Crozier-Cole.

2 On one famous occasion, and in failing light, RA Ingle hit a ball bowled by Harold Larwood out of the cricket ground at Trent Bridge.

behind the building. 'You can have one place here,' he said, and to my astonishment went on, 'no doubt in time you'll need a secretary of your own, but you might like to use mine for the time being.'

We walked through the basement to the bottom of the main stairs. He pushed open a panelled door on my right which led into a basement room some 20 feet long and 12 feet wide. A window gave on to the fine square, which allowed me to see the tops of the trees. It was all rather charming.

I was not alone in finding this corner of the city a congenial place. In 1801 Jane Austen and her mother took lodgings at 13 Queen Square and writing to a friend she commented '[it is] far more cheerful than the Paragon and the prospect from the drawing-room window at which I now write, is rather picturesque.' She considered that a prestigious address in Bath was crucial to social ambition, and so did I.

We collected Christopher's son Benedict from the hall and as we climbed the elegant staircase, with its generous apsidal half landing and turned banisters, he expanded on his theme. 'We've got some room up in the attic, looks a bit of a mess at the moment, but Ben wants a studio made from one bit of it and I thought you could make your office in the other.' He explained that the room downstairs would only be a stopgap until we'd finished converting the attic. He opened a door to a low-ceilinged dark space, full of old filing boxes and pigeon feathers.

'What do you think?' he said looking at me with a quizzical expression.

'Well, with the removal of the ceiling to give a bit more headroom, a good roof light and a lick of paint it couldn't be better.'

He looked delighted. 'Now the deal is this. You act as the designer for the two offices up here and in consideration I'll pay for the work to be done. And you will have your office and the car parking free of charge for at least eighteen months.'

'Good heavens, Mr Blathwayt,' I protested. 'This really is most generous of you. I really didn't expect anything like this.'

'Think no more of it,' he said putting his hand on my shoulder to steady himself as we negotiated the tight little stair down from the fifth floor. 'My good fortune is to own the building. It gives me the greatest satisfaction to help young people like you get started. Either you'll be fortunate and your enterprise will prosper, at which point I shall ask you to pay rent, or, sadly, you will founder. I would not be happy to have been responsible for that failure by charging you for the rooms when you could least afford them.'

Some people have fairy godmothers. I on the other hand have been blessed with fairy godfathers. Rittner and his friends were to sprinkle their magic dust over my affairs once again. It was some eighteen years later I heard from him again. 'Is that you, William?' The laconic voice on the other end of the phone could only belong to Luke, who went on, 'Now don't laugh, but last night I was talking to the Prince of Wales and I mentioned your name!'

'I take it you're joking,' I said. 'What on earth were you up to?'

'Well,' he went on enthusiastically, 'in my capacity as Secretary General (of the Arts Council) Corinna[3] and I were invited by the Christies to see an opera they were putting on at their place at Glyndebourne. After the performance we joined our hosts for a drink and I found myself talking to the Prince. The conversation turned to his frustration at not being able to find a sympathetic architect with whom he could work on a project at Highgrove. I told him that I knew of only one person who might be able to help him and he was a Bath man, who lived not too far from Highgrove, and his name was William – William Bertram.' I listened intently as he went on. 'That I thought would be the end of it, but damn me, at the end of the evening he found me and took from his pocket a notepad and pencil and asked for your telephone number.'

'Luke,' I said, 'I'm pinching myself.'

'Don't overdo the pinching, Will, but tell your secretary to expect a call from the Palace. It might be helpful if she takes it seriously and avoids the usual reply on such occasions of 'Oh yes and I'm the Prime Minister'. It's all too easy to get it wrong.'

'When do you think he'll ring? Just so I'm prepared,' I said, beginning to feel rather nervous.

3 Luke's wife

'It won't be him, but his equerry, who'll probably be your first contact. God knows when; he may forget all about it, but I thought I should just warn you.' He giggled, wished me goodbye and put down the receiver with a distant click. I sat and looked at the wall opposite not focusing on anything in particular. I tried to rid my mind of all thought and savour the moment.

Just as Luke had predicted, some days later the telephone did ring and my secretary Joan Potter, who took the call, ran to the top of the stairs at 5 Gay Street and shouted down to me, 'It's Buckingham Palace, William. It really is, it's the Prince of Wales's office wanting you.' It was my turn to be dismissive.

'Oh Joan, stop mucking about,' I said, 'Just because I told you that it might happen there is no reason to pull my leg.'

'No William, really, truly it is the Palace. Shall I put it through to your room?' As I closed the door to my study the phone rang and as I picked up the receiver I fell backwards onto the sofa.

'Hello?' I enquired quietly. A woman's voice on the other end said 'Is that Mr Bertram? I have Lieutenant-Colonel Brian Anderson for you.'

The line went dead for a moment and then a crisp voice said, 'Mr Bertram? Ah, good to be able to speak to you. The Prince of Wales has asked me if you might find time this coming weekend to meet him at Highgrove. His Royal Highness rather hoped you weren't doing anything?'

Doing anything, I thought, Christ, would anyone ever admit that they were doing something under these circumstances?

'What sort of time?' I said, trying to sound casual.

'Sort of half past ten-ish on Saturday. Would that suit? The Prince has someone coming to lunch so that would fit in well.' I agreed to be there and asked if there was anything special I ought to know. 'Just give me your car's registration number and I'll tell the gate staff to take you round to the front door. The Prince will be so pleased that you can make it. Goodbye.'

I lay back amongst the cushions staring at the ceiling. Could this really be happening? I closed my eyes and didn't move. Suddenly the door burst open. 'Was it him?' asked Joan, eyes bright and cheeks flushed.

'Not exactly, but put it this way – for Saturday please write in my diary the following: 'Highgrove visit, 10.30 P.O.W.'

'Where is your diary, William?' she asked in a fluster, 'Oh no, I've got it', and out she bustled to the sounds of enthusiastic gossip with Yvonne Armitage and Jennifer Mahlberg, my two other secretaries. I wasn't really in a fit state to do much more, so I thought perhaps it was the moment to pack up and go home.

'Had a good day, darling ?' Vicks flung her arms round my neck as I got out of the car and gave me a kiss.

'The weekend's going to be a bit of a pig's ear, I'm afraid, I'm off to Highgrove to see Mister you-know-who.'

'Not the Prince! My God, Bert, should I go down on one knee?' She pushed me away at arms length and looked at me fiercely. 'You really are a clever boy. I'm so proud of you.'

'Hang on, old girl, I don't know what he wants and I don't even know if I can design what he has in mind, assuming he does want me to design something.'

'Oh yes you can, I know you can – you'll see,' she said and with that we went into the kitchen and made a cup of tea.

On Saturday I left in good time. I had with me my usual props: an A4 sketchpad, sharpened soft pencils, rubber, black biro and my driving licence just in case I had to identify myself. The roads on that glorious morning in late July of 1987 were unusually empty. I flew along happily drumming my fingers on the steering wheel. I pretended to look disdainfully at my fellow wayfarers. They couldn't possibly be on such a glitzy mission as me. I felt like leaning out of the window and telling anyone who'd listen. Silly really!

'In good time' turned out to be something of an understatement. I got to the Hare and Hounds Hotel at half past nine, only a couple of minutes down the road from Highgrove. I had exactly one hour to kill. I turned the car round and headed back to the arboretum at Westonbirt. I drew up in front of the new visitors centre, an attractive building with large shingle roof and Cotswold stone walls. I went into the café and tried to calm my nerves with a hot cup of coffee but without much success. Time seemed to crawl by. I looked at my watch for the umpteenth time.

'Mustn't be late, Bertram,' I said to myself, 'better be off.' And taking a deep breath, I went to see the future king of England.

I tried to remember what Luke had told me about protocol. It was quite simple. When you first met, and that applied on a daily basis, you said 'Good morning Your Royal Highness.' You only needed to do one of those, then it's straight into 'Sir this' and 'Sir that'. It would all get a bit cumbersome otherwise. Should I look him in the eye? I'd been told that you should never look the Queen in the eye. 'He is charming,' Luke had said. 'You'll find you can't help but look him in the eye.'

I negotiated the security drill at the main gate, and parked in what I hoped was a sensible place. I left my drawing stuff in the car and walked empty-handed towards the front door along the gravelled drive. The chickens which scratched and pecked at the edges of the lawn appeared unconcerned at my inner turmoil. I moved out from the shadow of the overhanging yews. The view of the east façade slowly unfolded. The architect Peter Falconer had just finished an exquisite re-ordering of the elevations. Gone was the solid parapet of the old house and in its place a delicate coronet of golden stone balustrading, with dies and urns spreading away from the sloping sides of the newly-constructed pediment. It was all most impressive, giving the old columned porch, which I was fast approaching, added grandeur.

I waited a moment wondering if I should ring the door bell. My indecision was pre-empted by a Gurkha batman who opened the door and stood there inviting me to move towards him. 'His Royal Highness will be with you shortly,' he said leaning forward in a half bow. 'Please wait here,' and with that he turned on his heel and disappeared into the house, closing the door behind him. I kept my eyes firmly focused on the front door. Quite suddenly and from behind me I heard the crunch of gravel. Before I knew it, standing by my right shoulder was the Prince himself. He was wearing blue sneakers, an open-necked white shirt, and gardening trousers.

He much appreciated my coming, especially at the weekend. He led the way into the drawing room. Inside there were cool yellow walls, a fine marble fireplace, deep easy chairs and two sofas, and those familiar family photographs. Just like home, I thought. A spread of his architectural magazine *Perspectives on Architecture* was arranged neatly on a footstool. He gestured to me to sit down. With coffee cup in hand and he sitting opposite me, we talked of Luke Rittner, whom I came to realise he'd known long before his Arts Council days, when Luke ran the Bath Festival. It appeared they were old friends and indeed much the same age. We discussed architecture. He pulled no punches.

After half an hour he thought it was time to inspect the problem that he had asked me to solve. He got up and led me through the hall, through the French windows and down four stone steps onto a cobbled terrace. Harebells and thyme, Icelandic poppies and alchemilla spilled across the stone paving and around the central octagonal pool. (I later found out that the Prince was convinced that the pool was leaking. He had it drained and checked without finding anything wrong. His splendid builder, David Palmer, topped it up, but the water level still kept on going down, much to the Prince's consternation. The mystery was solved when one morning he opened the curtains to see the gardeners dunking their watering cans!)

'What a huge cedar,' I ventured, standing beside the trunk of a massive tree[4] whose girth was half the length of a cricket pitch. It overshadowed the terrace and dominated the house itself.

He walked me up the central path, well beyond the spread of its branches. Turning back to face the house I was informed that what was wanted was a pair of little pepperpot buildings at the corners of the terrace, something to emphasise the limits of that charming garden.

There was a pause while I wondered how to play my next crucial move. When I suggested that he might like me to sketch a few thoughts, then and there, he was delighted. The moment had come. I asked if he minded if I treated him in exactly the same way as I treated all my clients. I explained that first I'd have to get my drawing kit from the car; but

4 Sadly the tree was pronounced unfit in 2008 and has been felled.

then what I needed was to be left on my own while I did some thinking. Then he asked me where I wanted to work. As it's always best to be as close to the problem as possible, and it was a fine morning, I suggested I'd sit out. I asked for a chair, one without arms. He offered to get me one. He had, he thought, just the thing; his sketching stool.

This was all too much. I had woken up that morning as a normal human being and by elevenses here I was with the Prince of Wales attending to my every need.

He roared with laughter, and still chuckling to himself he disappeared towards the cool recesses of the servants' wing. But he turned and came back just as he got to the house, and offered to show me the kitchen garden.

We walked side by side while he expanded upon his vision for the garden as a whole. I was expecting tentative ideas but it rapidly became clear that all the main structural elements and a good deal of the detail were firmly established in his mind: enclosing yew hedges to form the south garden; pleached limes and more yews to enclose the vista toward the dovecot on the western boundary. Pools, topiary, gates, outbuildings and pavilions. They were all just waiting to be brought forward as sparks which would inspire those with whom he chose to share the design of his garden.

Already he had sought experienced advice from the well-known landscape architect Lanning Roper, but he sadly died before being able to contribute. Lady Salisbury and Rosemary Verey were both deeply involved by then. I felt very honoured to be in such exalted company and not a little daunted. We walked through an oriental-style archway of the prince's own design. This opened into a long narrow gravelled walk bounded on one side by a five-foot Cotswold stone wall and on the other by a long lawn in the shadow of the enclosing high brick wall to the kitchen garden itself. Two large terracotta pots filled with hydrangeas flanked a bright pink gothic doorway into the garden. I commented on the colour.

He looked quizzically at me and asked me if I liked it.

'Unusual I'd say. Do tell me the story. The gloss finish tells me that it isn't just undercoating.'

He explained that the pink was the favourite colour of his grand-mother, with whom he'd spent many happy times in Scotland at the Castle of Mey. The Queen Mother had all her gates painted this colour, so he'd done the same. It reminded him of her and, of course, gave her such pleasure when she came down. I said nothing but looked at him and he looked back at me. Here I saw someone who I felt would under-stand and would encourage and support me in my support for him.

'Come on,' I said, 'I'd better get back to business.' We left the confines of his beloved geometric walled garden, full of its fruit tunnels, apple arbours, dwarf box edgings and diagonal brick paths. He suggested he came back to me in half an hour. I thought it best if it were indeed an hour, to give me sufficient time for a bit of inspiration.

True to his word a little later he reappeared at the French door preceded by his Jack Russell terrier, Tigga, who took a shine to my left ankle. By way of commiseration he asked me if I had had any thoughts. I hadn't, yet!

Then I really was alone. A blank sheet of paper, a scheme to be designed in some detail and a Prince waiting to see what his miserable subject might suggest. My mind wandered to another Royal architect – John Nash – and the Prince Regent. I wondered what sort of relation-ship he really had with his royal patron. My adrenaline started to pump as I began to analyse what I had in front of me. I settled down on the royal stool and began scribbling. I could see immediately that the essence of the design was one of scale. Just how small could I make these beehives? They mustn't dominate the terrace nor could they afford to be too small. They also had to be set right in the corner of the enclosing low walls either side of the terrace, one right next to the great cedar, the other with its back to the woodlands. The key was the thickness of the existing enclosing stone walls which, if I wanted, might run into the side of the little buildings. Could it be that an unequal octagon or a pure square should be the shape to go for, with a little stone-tiled roof, mitred to keep it simple?

To my delight the Prince had been given two, specially-designed chairs which he'd placed where my pavilions were to stand. These became my inspiration for the detail. They had a flavour of the Gothic about them, each with two little decorative knobs on the back. I developed my sketches along these lines introducing a gothicised version of my trademark quatrefoil window to each side wall.

Just as I was relaxing, having found the key which unlocked the puzzle, Tigga reappeared followed at a distance by his master. The Prince came round behind me to see how I was getting on. I sat staring ahead of me and then with both my hands I slowly raised the sketchpad until it gently rested on the top of my head, facing backwards towards him.

'How does that grab you, Sir?' I heard myself say, and immediately regretted the informality. Not a word. He either hated it and was trying to phrase his disappointment so as not to hurt my feelings or perhaps he just didn't understand the strange squiggles that I had shown him. I held my breath. He told me that it grabbed him very much and asked me where we went from here.

I suggested that I would draw up my proposals properly as soon as I could, and get it to him that coming week. I thought I knew exactly what he wanted. I got up from the stool and turned to face him. His handshake was firm and muscular. He said he had to go and asked if I could see myself out.

I told him I just needed to pace out the ground because I had left my tape at home but not to worry, my shoe was exactly twelve inches long and that I did it all the time. I'd be about 20 minutes. He left me on my own and he strode away with his little dog scampering behind his heels, disappearing through the yew hedge into the south garden. I sat for a moment in one of the gothic chairs listening to the throb of a car's engine. His lunch guests were arriving. The wind sighed in the boughs of the cedar tree. A great tit clung upside down beneath a Chinese bird feeder which hung from one of its long dark branches. I felt drained but very happy and peaceful. The whole exercise had taken just two hours. I then drove slowly home.

Vicks opened the door of the car and I staggered out. 'How did you get on, darling? What was he like?'

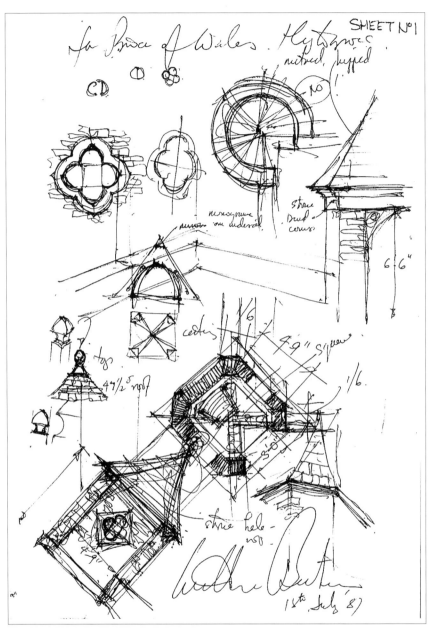

I slowly raised the sketchpad until it rested on my head.
'How does that grab you, Sir?' I heard myself say

'He's absolutely splendid. Great fun and so easy. Lots to do. I think I've cracked it. I need to put it down on paper before I forget what I've thought of. Love some sandwiches for tea. I'll just set up my board and get my head down, if it's all the same.'

I kissed her and she hugged me. 'I knew you'd get on all right. Are you going to ring your parents?' I did, but only after I had drawn the scheme up by hand, in meticulous detail. I annotated the elevations, shaded in the walls, drew in the border and signed the finished drawing with my usual flourish. It had taken me six hours. It was ten o'clock in the evening, and I wasn't in the least bit tired.

On 20 July I wrote to the Prince enclosing the three original sketches which I'd discussed with him, my setting-up drawing and the final design. The letter explained what had occurred between seeing him and finessing the detail.

The design matured in very much the way I anticipated, but you will see from the sketches that my endeavours to create a square roof on an octagonal base were unsuccessful and I have therefore reverted to an octagonal roof. If the right sized slates are used I think it the most appropriate and certainly the most elegant solution. I have raised the inside of the building by five inches. This is not in order to make the Gothic chair into a throne! more to relate the inside space to the window position.

The outside dimension of the building is slightly smaller than I suggested on Saturday because I wanted to keep the scale down to the minimum. On the set-up drawing, I have highlighted a plan which was a foot wider in size, 4'6" as opposed to 3'6". This I found produced too large a building, both in footprint and height. The smaller plan provides all that is necessary I think, with adequate window cills to hold a cup of coffee or a stiff whisky!

I waited anxiously for his reply, which came on 6 August. He liked my design but wondered if the bobbles on top of the roofs weren't just a bit too small! I had further thoughts on the way the low walls might join to

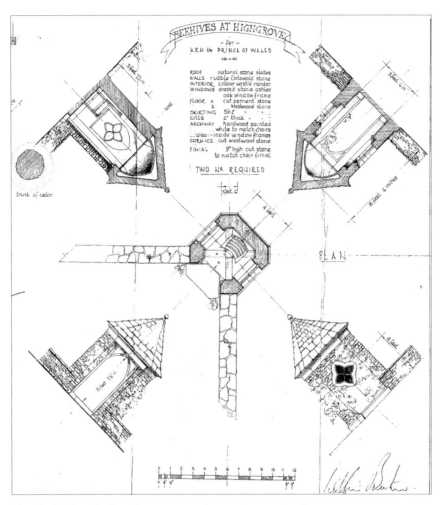

The design for the beehives prepared over the weekend

the beehives. I wrote to him a week later with a sketch. And thus the matter was concluded. All that remained was to build the two little structures within a reasonable budget. That has always been a problem for any self-respecting architect. Never mind, these two little postilions were the forerunners of many other projects which we conceived together and which cemented a happy working relationship which maintains to this day.

It was only a matter of weeks before I could arrange for the signature on the contract at an acceptable sum between the Duchy of

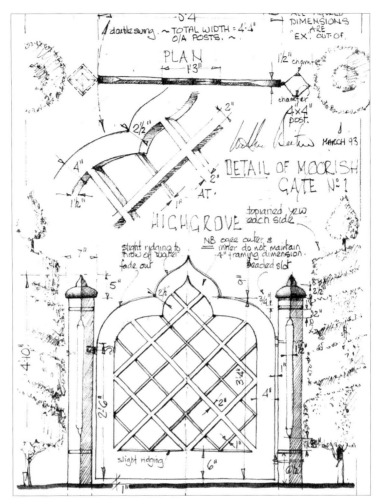

One of a dozen gates I designed for the Prince of Wales at Highgrove

Cornwall, the legal owners of Highgrove, and David Palmer, the resident building contractor whose office was close by in the village of Luckington. The first call I had from Mr Palmer (I refer to him formally because at this stage I was very much the new boy), was to ask me how I had calculated the setting-out dimension for the buildings. He pointed out that there was a discrepancy of some 1'6" overall. I had to admit, much to his amusement, to my unconventional method of measuring and that perhaps I'd miscalculated the exact length of that particular pair of shoes!

The building went without a hitch. The little roofs took shape and became far more elegant than in my original drawing. Traditionally the largest stone slates are placed at the bottom of the slope and diminish in size as they go up until right at the top they are no bigger than your hand. When applied to a constant pitch the result is to form a gentle concave sweep to the profile of the roof. When finished it looked charming.

To satisfy the Prince's concern to get the right size 'bobbles' I asked David to make three different sizes of finial in wood. One weekend when His Royal Highness was about, we arranged to offer each up and for him to choose the one he liked best. Quite rightly, as it turned out, he chose the largest one, but not before he had canvassed a number of opinions amongst the workmen and the rest of the team. Then it just remained to have Trevor Dring, the master mason, select an appropriate piece of Bath stone and faithfully reproduce two exact copies.

What visitors at Highgrove see today is the result of all these influences upon the design. It was fun to do and seemed to give His Royal Highness a great deal of quiet satisfaction. So much so that Luke, who had been in constant touch with the Boss, rang me to say how much of a success the beehives were. I thanked him for introducing me to royal patronage. Typical of Luke, he merely chuckled.

'You did it, Will. I really didn't do anything.' No, I thought, you merely put your head on the block on my behalf. You had no need to do it and yet you did. Had I not come good it was you who, unfairly, would have suffered.

Perhaps the comforting lesson to be drawn from this anecdote is that there are steadfast and very kind souls like Luke who are prepared to risk their hard-earned reputations to support those they believe in. For some that belief can change their world as it did for one inexperienced young architect who set up in Bath those many years ago.

The Merry-Go-Round

There is no knowing where one commission will take you and what set of coincidences may surface from the most unlikely set of circumstances. Those to whom you are recommended tend to hand you on, a little bit like the children's game of pass-the-parcel.

IT WAS IN 1965, JUST AFTER I'D QUALIFIED AT THE AGE OF 25, THAT I happened to be shooting with my uncle Henry Micklem at Rosehill, his home just outside Henley-on-Thames. Among the guns was Jimmy Mason,[1] a Jorrocks-like figure who sat on various boards in the City of London, as did my father. At lunch, never a meal to be hurried even when the autumn light was fading and there were still two long drives to come, I found myself sitting next to him. 'I hear you're working in Bristol, young man. Your father tells me you're quite good at this architecture stuff. D'you feel like coming up to Town and having a look at the Portland Club for me?'

'Now? The Portland Club?' I said trying desperately to remember what sort of club it was.

'Yes, you know, the bridge club.[2] We've got to move from our place in Charles Street. Been there ever since I can remember. The blighters have put up the rent from a peppercorn to something rather more commercial and we've decided we can do better elsewhere. Bit of a wrench, but there we are.'

'Where are you thinking of going?' I asked, hoping to broaden the conversation, but just then Jimmy took up with a pretty girl on his other

1 Later Lord Blackstone

2 Back in 1966 members were playing for £35 a hundred. God knows what the going rate is in 2009!

wing. However, before the day was out I had agreed a date when I would meet the Club Secretary. I needed to find out what they wanted from their move into rooms offered to them by the Committee of the Naval and Military Club[3] just down Piccadilly from the Ritz Hotel.

On the appointed day I took the initial brief and was given a roll of blueprints of their new quarters which, after going to see the rooms for myself, gave me a good idea of what I was up against. Back at my drawing board I settled down to convert my notes into what I hoped would be a well proportioned and workable layout. I was helped in this task by Rose Underdown, the steering committee's splendid choice of interior designer, with whom I kept in weekly, if not daily, contact by phone from Somerset. Eventually I was ready to present my scheme.

Carrying my roll of precious drawings I climbed aboard the express from Bristol to Paddington and within a couple of hours I found myself knocking on the impressive front door of the Portland Club in Chelsea. A tailcoated butler answered the door. 'Mr Bertram? Please come this way.' He walked slowly and purposefully through a dark hall and ushered me into an oak-lined library heavy with cigar smoke. He bowed with great deliberation and withdrew.

Jimmy Mason got up from the large table and introduced me to Quintin Hoare[4] the chairman, and the other three members. Mr Hoare made his way over to the mahogany sideboard and lifted the stopper of a Waterford decanter. 'You'll stay for a spot of lunch, I take it, Bertram, and you'd like something to whet your whistle now, I shouldn't wonder?' Out of the corner of my eye I saw him take a cut-glass tumbler, half fill it with gin and splash a thimbleful of tonic over it! He slipped it beside me as I unrolled my drawings. I took a sip, looked round the table and, with what I hoped was professional authority, began to explain what I had been up to. As I went through my scheme I was blissfully unaware of the effect the gin was having. The more I drank the less focused I

3 Known colloquially as the 'In and Out' because of what was written on the gate piers. At that time many London clubs were amalgamating or letting rooms, to make ends meet. The club itself has now relocated to Nancy Astor's London house, 4 St James's Square.

4 Senior Partner of Messrs C Hoare & Co Bankers, of 37 Fleet Street, London, founded in 1672. Beau Nash, that old roué and undisputed master of ceremonies of Bath had an account with them in 1749.

became. Only distantly did I hear Quintin Hoare say, 'Well, I think that's all very splendid, Bill, but there are one or two things we need to iron out,' and proceeded to turn my thoughtfully prepared scheme upside down. He looked over at me holding the corner of one of my drawings. 'Now then, young man, how long do you think it'll be before you can come back to us with some fresh ideas?'

Notwithstanding the gin, I had indeed taken to heart all the changes that had been suggested and if asked could, I prided myself, have recited them verbatim. However, it's curious how you think you can be quite lucid even when half cut! I fumbled with my diary and flicked over two or three pages to give the impression that I was in charge.

With studied concentration, I told him I could make it in about a month's time. 'How would that be?' I said cheerily, looking round the table for confirmation. Silence! No one uttered a word. The chairman leaned forward and in a very soft voice said, 'but my dear fellow that takes us well past the Twelfth and by then we'll all be up north giving the grouse a run for their money. Couldn't you possibly do a little better? Say, sometime next week?'

As he said this I was thinking to myself, 'Have these people no idea what goes into something like this?' But I soon realised there was only one way out of my dilemma if I was to retain the commission.

'Look, I simply can't do next week, or for that matter the week after. What I could do,' I heard myself saying through the fog of gin, 'is to ask you all to re-assemble here this evening, at say six-thirty, when I shall present to you the revised scheme. Make no mistake I'll have to redraw the whole thing, but that's my problem, not yours.' There was a stunned silence. This was finally broken by Jimmy Mason who was only too well aware that my failure would reflect badly on him. 'Well it's the members' dinner tonight,' he said, 'so I think that should be fine. But my dear fellow, do you honestly think you can pull this off ?'

Did I hell!

I now had to make some split-second decisions. 'I'm afraid, Mister Chairman, your very kind offer of lunch will have to go by the board. What I need right now is a taxi.' I stood up feeling decidedly light-headed and asked, as coherently as I could, how to get to the lavatory. I navigated myself along the edge of the table and set a course across the carpet for the door. I stood for a moment, my head spinning, and steadied myself by hanging on to the door knob. Only then did I vaguely begin to appreciate the magnitude of the task I had set myself. But, there was to be no going back now; I simply had to come up with the goods because I was not about to let down a friend of my father.

I climbed into the back of a cab with my now crumpled set of drawings, flopped down onto the wide seat and wearily asked the driver to take me on the 20-minute journey to the Architectural Association (my alma mater) in Bedford Square. When I arrived at that elegant Georgian front door I bounded up the stairs to the first-year studio at the very top of the building. I asked the first student I met if he minded my commandeering his board. I also wanted to borrow his drawing equipment, his adjustable set-square, paper, scale and T-square! There wasn't much time for pleasantries; I had only one objective in mind to the exclusion of all others. My hands simply flew across the drawing board as I traced over my original scheme reworking the plan as I went. After a period of intense concentration the new scheme had miraculously fallen into place. I lettered it up and signed the drawings. Fortunately for me there was a large printing machine in the school's basement. Courting disaster I raced down the narrow back stairs two at a time to secure my place in the queue.

It was just after six o'clock when, exhausted, I climbed into a taxi and made my way back through the evening traffic to Chelsea. I was ushered straight into the library where the atmosphere was just as impenetrable as before. None of the committee gave the slightest impression of having moved since I'd left them at lunchtime. Quinnie Hoare got up and held out his hand. 'Ah, Bill, welcome home!' Feeling a little less unsteady than when I had left, I managed to unroll my plans without mishap.

'There you are,' I said proudly, plonking them down on the table. 'I hope I've managed to get it all in.' I explained how I'd replanned the gaming room, the kitchens and the position of the loos, in fact just about everything.

Before I'd even finished a much relieved Jimmy Mason got up and patted me affectionately on the shoulder. 'That looks fine, dear boy. I don't think we have any more comments at all.' He stopped for a moment and looked for support from his fellow members. 'All we need to do now is to get on with it! We've got to be out of here in six months. Think you can you manage that?' I rather felt I'd been quite dynamic enough for one day and told him I would answer that question when I got home.

Quintin waved a glass in front of me. 'To be honest, old boy, none of us thought you'd do it; by way of congratulation I think you deserve the other half.' But that was about the last thing I needed!

The plans I drew on that remarkable day never changed. I worked up the detailed drawings which the builder would need to carry out the work. Architects can sometimes find that interior designers, however talented, get under their feet, but Rosie Underdown was the very model of discretion. We both got what we wanted and became firm friends. The job itself went well and as a final flourish Oscar and Peter Johnson provided the pictures. The whole project was brought in on budget but, as is so often the case, with only hours to spare.

Some years ago I went back to see how our work was holding up. The members were in session, with groups of well-heeled bridge fours enjoying an afternoon of deep and silent concentration. The place was, to a picture, exactly as we had left it those forty years before.

It was not long after finishing my work for the Portland Club that I got a call from Robert Boscawen[5] who, with his wife Mary, had just bought the dignified stone-mullioned Manor House at Ivythorn tucked away below a wooded hillside near Street in Somerset. Rose Underdown, with whom I'd had such a happy working relationship in London, had recommended me to the Boscawens as someone who might be able to help transform the historic house into something a little more practical.

On my first visit we got on well. Mary's uncle, the well-known latter-day Reptonian landscape architect, John Codrington had been invited to

---

5 The Rt Hon Robert Boscawen is related to Anne Warrender, née Boscawen (see *Dry Run*)

meet me. The idea was that he would deal with the site and its 'capabil-ities' before I got going on the house itself. This was one of my first commissions after setting up my practice in Bath. Having spent the first six years of my working life in the office of Kenneth Nealon in Bristol, an architect-surveyor who specialised in building low-budget schools for the Roman Catholics, I was eager, but largely unprepared, for a new world where anything seemed possible, and free and expansive thinking was positively encouraged.

Bob Boscawen, Mary, John and myself marched across the lawn in front of the fine south façade and came upon a little building perched on the edge of a small escarpment which defined the edge of the garden. The outlook from this semi-derelict cottage over the Somerset levels was magnificent but the cottage itself got in the way of the view from the Manor. We all looked at it wondering what could be done. John Codrington announced that he couldn't possibly think about anything until he'd attended to a call of nature. Without a hint of embarrassment he walked forward towards the view and stood, hands on hips, gazing out with his back towards us. 'I hope you don't mind? Only the English find this sort of thing odd,' he shouted over his shoulder, 'I love the French, so much more relaxed.' He returned to our little group looking much happier. 'Right now, where were we?'

Bob pointed at the cottage, 'What to do with this?'

'Why, knock it down, of course. I'm sure William, here, will be able to build another one somewhere else; round the back of the house, perhaps, out of the way.' He turned to me with raised eyebrows. 'What do you think?'

I joined in, casting off the last of my inhibitions. It was a moment of liberation after so many years of wearing a financial straight-jacket. 'Absolutely.' I said enthusiastically, 'just the planners to deal with, but I think I may be able to bring them round.' In those halcyon days such self-confidence was a good deal easier to justify than it is today, espe-cially as the Manor was listed.

And so it turned out. Mr Coombs, a local builder, was engaged, the house was given a new oak staircase (I still can't resist a staircase, as any study of my commissions will attest) and a fine new double-height stone bay window to the drawing room incorporating the principal bedroom above. A new line of garages and the replacement staff cottage were indeed built at the back of the house as had been suggested. And in 1970, while all this was going on, Robert fought his corner to overthrow the old Labour Government and succeeded in winning the Wells constituency with a healthy majority of nearly 9000. In due course he took his seat as a new member of Parliament on the Conservative benches.

Using Humphry Repton's well tried technique of 'before and after' watercolour overlays John Codrington convinced his niece how best to re-landscape the garden. The main drive was redirected to give greater privacy from the lane and the lawns were laid out with mowing lines to focus the eye towards the now spectacular and cottage-free view out over the Levels and beyond.

Apart from the inevitable shock of Mr Coombs's final account for all the extra work he'd undertaken, everything in the garden and in the house was lovely! Indeed, on this occasion explaining to my client the overspend on the contract (a tough moment for any architect) was made slightly easier than it might otherwise have been. On the very day I went down to Ivythorn to talk to Robert it was reported that the new under-ground car park at the Palace of Westminster had cost about three times the original budget. Our final account, by comparison, was a very modest affair!

I HAD KNOWN CHARLES AND BARBARA ROBERTSON, WHO LIVED AT COMBE Hay Manor near Bath, as the people behind the revival of the Bath Music Festival. When they married in 1935 Charles and Barbara (née Fry) brought together two of England's most successful merchant families. The Robertsons, under their famous gollywog trademark, were repre-sented on practically every breakfast table in the land, and the Frys produced some of the most famous chocolate bars in the world. When I entered their lives in the '80s they had been at the Manor for half a century. By then they had transformed it into a work of art. The house itself is a mixture of the seventeenth and eighteenth centuries with Bath freestone façades, each one carved and embellished in celebration of the phases of the day. The east face, which catches the weaker morning sunrise, is quite plain; the south, when the midday sun is high, has finely detailed window cases and subtle niches, and the west façade is pedimented, cartouched and heavily modelled to gain maximum impact from the oblique angle of the setting sun.

The fabric had been carefully restored both inside and out and a fine collection of paintings and furniture gathered over the years to embellish the beautifully proportioned rooms. This labour of love developed their interest in both architecture and the history of art. The Robertsons regularly attended lectures at the Courtauld Institute and, with encouragement from their friend Anthony Blunt and others, they established the Courtauld Summer School aimed at introducing the young to the glories of fine art.

By the time I arrived on the scene they felt they had completed all the things they believed needed doing to the house and Charles, a quiet, introspective man who was blissfully content with his lot, vowed that he would only be willing to leave the Manor feet first. However, his ever-practical and energetic wife, Barbara, was conscious that it would be far more sensible if they let their elder son Neil and his wife Diana and their family take it on. The proposition, put forward by Barbara, that they should build a new house for their retirement, was sufficiently intriguing to convince Charles that they should get hold of an architect who would be sympathetic to what was wanted and would tolerate a good deal of input from both of them!

Not surprisingly I felt very honoured that this cultured and high-brow couple chose me to help them rather than one of my architectural peers.

They decided to build in the walled kitchen garden some distance from and well out of sight of the Manor, concealed behind some mature yew trees and shrubs. Charles didn't think it a particularly good idea to simply plunge into the project without doing some research. Both he and Barbara wanted to create a place which would form the backdrop to some of the best pieces from their collections. And what collections!

There was furniture by Marjorelle, paintings by Van Dyck and the Pre-Raphaelites, Roman glass, medieval sculpture and a fine collection of Art Nouveau. They had a veritable storehouse of treasure.[6] They also told me that the architectural flavour they were looking for was a mixture: of the Italianate; an acknowledgement of Bath's Roman origins; and a soupçon of French Provençal (they also had a house in Provence). A somewhat daunting prospect, but an intriguing challenge nevertheless.

Barbara was clearly going to be the driving force. 'I know what we should do,' she announced, 'why don't we all meet down at the Moulin in a fortnight's time. We will have such fun and it'll give you, William, a chance to see where we've drawn our inspiration from.' Only days later, having been collected from the airport at Marseille, my wife and I found ourselves being driven between endless cherry orchards in a battered 2CV with the roof open and the sun beating down.

Our destination turned out to be a converted windmill some distance from the town of Roussillon, perched among pine trees on its own little knoll, high above a heat-shimmering plain. It was a rough place, thrown together in that off-hand Gallic tradition which results in a shabby kind of charm. Barbara showed us up a spiral staircase to our bedroom in the tower. We flopped down exhausted onto the bed and looked up at the ceiling of rough-hewn beams which supported a roof of clay tiles. Through the small cracks we could glimpse the deep blue of the sky and red kites circling high up on the thermals. We quickly changed and, barefoot, joined Barbara and Charles outside. He gestured towards a couple of large hand-woven hammocks slung between the fir trees in the shade behind the house. 'You might find those quite comfortable if you feel like putting your feet up.' So we climbed into them and gently rocked ourselves to sleep, caressed by the warm breeze off the plain, by the nutty smell of resins which oozed from the bark and by the creak of the branches moving overhead. It was a far cry from grey old England. We woke in time for tea, our faces taut with sunburn and our bare feet prickling from pine needles.

As the sun went down we took advantage of the cool of evening to

6 The 'Robertson Collection' was sold at Sotheby's in 2002.

explore. We passed the local quarry with its famous multicoloured layers of red and yellow sands, and made our way up through the narrow streets into the main square. Even as mist gathered across the fields in the plain below, we could still feel the day's heat radiating back at us from the medieval walls and beneath our bare feet.

I looked up at the roofs and made a mental note of the pie-crust eaves. Here, unlike England, builders had no need for timber fascias which had to be painted every four years; just simple corbelling out would do, made of the same half-round clay tiles they had used for the main roof. It had been done like that for a thousand years. Double-leaved doors and fancy glasswork to fanlights were set deep into simple, but elegant, stone surrounds. Windows, with decrepit and blistered shutters half closed, had their inner casements half open to reveal dark and mysterious rooms within. These were just some of the details which my generous hosts hoped would inspire me, and in my mind's eye there was already a design for their new house beginning to take shape.

Saturday was market day in nearby Apt with the promise of yet more fun. We bundled into the car and bounced down the hill away from the Mill in a cloud of yellow dust. We stopped on the way to marvel at a bridge over the river Coulon. It looked much as it must have done the day the Romans built it, which was surprising as no cement had been used, just carefully placed interlocking stones. And so to Apt. Barbara had given us some inkling of the charm of this walled medieval town with its fortified gateways and narrow cobbled streets, but what came as a surprise was that the entire centre of the old town was taken up with one huge street market.

The alleyways were lined with canvas stalls tenanted by flamboyant French traders dressed in bright colours. They were in marked contrast to the ageing grandmothers in black shawls who sat quietly behind them hugging their shoulders. There was bustle and shouting all round and in one corner, where the café beneath the tall plane trees spilled onto the pavement, a birthday party was in full swing with someone blowing a trumpet and another banging a drum. The sun glinted through the heavy canopy of leaves dappling the shade over the trestle tables which groaned with an amazing array of goods. If you wanted cheese or a church pew, the market at Apt would oblige. If you needed dried tobacco leaf or door furniture, Apt had got it. Cars could be seen leaving with antique doors and armoires roped casually to their roofs. A child being pushed in a pram by her mother clutched a basket of day-old chicks. Everywhere was good cheer and good conversation. It all made for relaxing and we enjoyed the privilege of being part of it. The Portobello Road in London's Notting Hill had a lot to learn!

We wandered around the ironmongers' stalls and came away with hinges and handles, locks and shutter clasps. It didn't matter that I knew not how many windows and how many doors there might be in the new house. What it did mean was that when, eventually, I got home and settled down to designing, all these things, with the fond memories I brought away with me, would give my creative juices something to feed on. Eventually we grew tired and found a café with a terrace just above street level overlooking the marketeers. It was cool in the shade beneath the trees and out of the burning sun. We spent an hour just watching the world go by. It was absorbing and quite as much fun as shopping itself.

When we got back to England I started on the design in earnest. At my instigation I took all my drawing equipment over to Combe Hay Manor where Barbara had thoughtfully set up one of the bedrooms as my studio. Each day we would review what I had done, first at elevenses and then again at tea time. The collaboration worked well although at times I got the impression that my progress was considered rather slow! We agreed that the best place for the house was at the bottom of the three-sided walled kitchen garden, where one had a good view through the trees and out over the valley. Eventually I was satisfied that my design had successfully combined both the Italian and French vernacular on which Barbara and Charles Robertson had so particularly set their hearts. When all had been detailed and the drawings finished we let the contract to Ken Biggs, a local builder, who put together a very talented team of craftsmen. One sunny afternoon, soon after the building work had started, I joined the builders for a day in the capacity of stonemason. I wanted to put a bit of my own character into the new walls! Barbara

A mixture of the Italianate and French Provençal; an intriguing challenge

engaged her very considerable artistic skills by inlaying all the internal doors to her own designs with wild flowers, cow parsley and butterflies. Her commitment rubbed off on the rest of us as we strove to create a beautiful setting in which they could enjoy their treasured possessions. The end result was a magical house and very much to their taste. By way of appreciation Barbara arranged for all the men's names to be etched onto one of the window panes near the front door.

When the house was furnished and decorated Charles again turned to me for help. This time it was to double the size of a tiny thatched one-up-one-down lodge situated on the Wellow crossroads next to the original gate down to the Manor. I approached this commission much inspired by the work of the early-nineteenth-century architect John Nash who built Blaise Hamlet.[8] I suggested to Charles that a wing should be added in the picturesque style, to complement the original.

It would double the size of the cottage and nestle under an extended thatched roof. My design was in marked contrast to previous efforts submitted to my client. These had taken the form of uncompromisingly modern extensions which, had they been built, might well have pleased the architectural cognoscenti by retaining the original integrity of the

8 Nash built a group of nine cottages around a village green for JS Harford, Bristol in 1811. They were copies of ornate cottages he had designed for a variety of clients elsewhere.

'I suggest that a wing be added in the Picturesque style'

cottage unaltered, but would also have ruined the quaintness and charm of the little building. However that's as may be. Charles took one look at my drawings and asked me to put the work in hand immediately. In the end the extension was so beautifully integrated that it even confounded the architectural historian Dr Tim Mowl who simply could not believe the whole place hadn't originally been built all of a piece. Was that a good thing or a bad thing? I simply don't know and now have little interest in worrying about it. What I do know is that it is not only stylish but makes a very pretty picture indeed; I recently saw it, heavy with geraniums, featured on the lid of a biscuit tin!

IN FEBRUARY 1983 I GOT A CALL FROM BARBARA. SHE BROKE THE SAD NEWS that Charles had died. Would I consider designing an obelisk as a memorial to him? A month after the funeral, I took out my sketchpad and began to draw. Barbara looked over my shoulder as the design developed, just as she had done before with the house. It took me just ten minutes to sketch out the design, but I had been thinking about it for days beforehand. When I'd finished she took the drawing and studied it carefully. 'Instead of a pointed stone on top, William, do you think we might have a reflective tip so it catches the sun?' The top, we agreed,

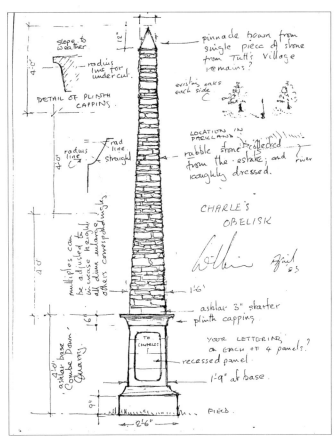

The following annotations appear on the drawing:

slope to weather

radius line for undercut.

12"

4'0"

DETAIL OF PLINTH CAPPINGS.

= rad line.
radius line C   straight.

4'0"

multiples can be adjusted to suit exact height all dims corresponding.

6'

1'0"

'ashlar base Coombe Down Quarry.'

TO CHARLES

4'0" ashlar base Coombe Down Quarry.

9"

2'6"

pinnacle hewn from single piece of stone from Tutt's Village remains?

existing oaks each side

LOCATION IN PARKLAND

rubble stone collected from the estate; and roughly dressed.

river

CHARLE'S OBELISK

William   Paul '83

1'6'

ashlar 3" starter
plinth capping.

YOUR LETTERING on EACH of 4 panels?
recessed panel.
1'9" at base.

FIELD.

Charles Robertson's memorial obelisk

would be a little pyramid of polished stainless steel so that, now, every day, at around eleven o'clock, it can be seen twinkling like a jewel when seen from Stradling House, the name they had given to their new home.

For once I didn't need to apply to anyone for permission to build the obelisk, although I did ask the Wansdyke Planning Department. Apparently you can build memorials, on your own ground, wherever you like! When it came to the question of positioning it Barbara asked me to carry a long white pole across the valley until a spot was found that could be seen from both the Manor and the new house. Ken Biggs was again commissioned to build this little structure and in due time a short ceremony was held before committing Charles's ashes to the foundations. George V Williams, a well-known firm of Bath masons, 'banked' the stone and carved out the four oval recesses on each face of the plinth.

When the obelisk was finished Charles's slate tablet was fixed into position and we reaffirmed its dedication to him.

WHILST ENGAGED ON THE ROBERTSON COMMISSIONS I WAS ALSO WORKING for Michael Codrington, Mary Boscawen's (of Ivythorn Manor) brother, at Ware Farm in Wiltshire. I had completed one of my regular site visits to ensure the building work was going as planned when Michael offered me a cup of tea. The conversation inevitably got round to what other interesting jobs I was doing. I told him that I was in the process of building the Robertson obelisk. Michael sat up. 'Would you care to see something I have not shown anyone since my grandfather died?' I must have looked a bit taken aback, because he got up, walked into his study and brought out a sealed envelope. He took a kitchen knife and slit it open. Carefully he tapped out the contents onto his newspaper. All I could see were some pink fragments of stone ranging from one to three inches in length. He leaned back in his Windsor chair, beamed and proceeded to tell me that they were chips from the base of the Egyptian obelisk which stands on the Embankment in London. I leant forward and peered at them intently. 'How do you know they are actually from that obelisk, Michael? They could be any old granite chips for all you know.'

'I'll tell you how I know, William. My great-grandfather was asked to be present in the September of 1878 when the obelisk was placed into its bronze holder on the balustrade running beside the Thames. To make sure that the operation went smoothly, especially as half London had turned out to watch, a mason was on hand, armed with bolster and chisel to make any last-minute adjustments to the bottom of the stone if, by chance, it didn't sit comfortably. Well, it didn't. When the bits had been chipped away the old man asked the stonemason if he would let him have some as a keepsake. And these pieces are the very ones!'

'Well, Michael, I really wouldn't have believed what you've just said unless I had heard it from you, at first hand.' And indeed I was rather taken by the story. So I went on, 'as your great-grandpapa was given a chip or two would you, perhaps, consider it impertinent if I were to ask you for one or two pieces for myself?'

'Not at all, William. They'll only sit in my desk drawer until I die and the children, as likely as not, won't give them a second thought.' So with my precious stones carefully tucked into a pocket I decided to drive home via Combe Hay. When I got there I rang the bell at Stradling House. The hall light came on and I saw Barbara through the glass of the front door. 'William,' she exclaimed, kissing me, 'how lovely to see you.'

'Not half as lovely as what I've got for you, my dear girl; just you take a look at this,' and I opened my fingers to uncover the little chips nestling in the palm of my hand. I explained their extraordinary provenance. I could see from her expression that she knew immediately what she was going to do with them! I bade her farewell and thought no more about it. But, the next time I visited the obelisk I saw, to my surprise and delight, that one of those little chips had been placed into the stone just above the oval plaque commemorating the life of Diana, Neil Robertson's wife, who sadly had died young, some time after the death of her father-in-law, Charles.

But there still remains in my mind the nagging doubt that Michael, in spite of himself, could have been misled as to the origin of that handful of granite. I well remember the story of Ned Lutyens who was caught by his secretary cutting some horsehair from one of the sofas in his office. He got to his feet holding the tuft, placed it carefully into an envelope, and sealed it with red wax. On the front he wrote in copper-plate lettering 'A lock of Marie Antoinette's hair, taken on the 16th October 1793, on her way to the scaffold'! 'That'll fox 'em' he said, with a boyish twinkle, and popped the envelope into the middle drawer of his desk.

I rather agree with Sir Edwin: life is a merry-go-round, never meant to be taken too seriously!

Full Circle

IF YOU ARE IN BUSINESS PRESUMABLY YOU'RE IN BUSINESS TO MAKE SOME money. After all, there's no point in working your socks off if you go bust in the process! The fact that you practise architecture often gives the misleading impression that artistic flair may suffer if you are business-like in financial affairs.

It was with considerable foreboding, therefore, that I responded to my bank manager's suggestion that we meet for lunch. It rather put me in mind of my friend Askari (see *Never Give Up*) whose answer to my own request for lunch taught me a good deal about human nature. 'Why would you offer me lunch, William? If I'm asked out for a meal it is usually because somebody wants something from me. I do not want to give you anything and therefore I do not want your hospitality!' Well, that told me!

As the firm's account was overdrawn, and had been for many years, it didn't need a genius to work out what he wanted to discuss. I declined lunch, arranged a meeting instead and walked the couple of hundred yards down George Street and through the impressive portals of my bank, at the smart end of Bath's main shopping thoroughfare. I was shown up to the first floor where Mr Bank-Manager was waiting for me. He took up station behind a large desk while his pretty secretary placed my papers in front of him.

'Now, it's about a year ago that we discussed your account, William. On that occasion I was rather generous in extending your overdraft facility. I may say this was done on the understanding that you would treat it as a safety net – not, as seems to be the case, a Christmas fund. Outgoings still seem to be running ahead of income.' He looked down at me with raised eyebrows, 'Problem, William, or am I missing something?'

'No,' I said cautiously, 'you've not missed a thing. I'm glad to say the firm has a full order book and is growing, but work-in-progress is taking an ever larger slug of our fee income. However, the difficulty we do face is that some of our long-standing clients are not at all keen to stump up when fees are properly due to us: and we don't seem to be able to do much about it.'

He walked over to the sideboard and poured two cups of coffee and came over and sat down beside me. 'My dear chap, that's just too bad. Do you think there's anything I could do?' No doubt he expected me to ask for yet further provision for our mounting overdraft.

'I'll tell you what you could do' I offered, shifting onto the edge of my chair. 'One of my creditors is a certain Christopher Cardew. If he paid us what's due then you and I wouldn't be here discussing my finances.' When I had bearded Christopher some weeks previously about the overdue account he rather disarmingly confided that his own bank manager had told him that there was no need to pay us yet and urged him to clear some of his more urgent bills. Apparently the fellow, in a light-hearted moment, suggested that 'A gentleman never pays his tailor'. Well, in this case, Mr Bank-Manager, I'm the bloody tailor!'

He shifted uneasily in his chair. I proceeded with my narrative with gusto. 'When I asked Cardew who might this bank manager be, to my surprise he mentioned your name. Perhaps you could explain to me when it was that you became an expert on when professional fees are due?' His cheeks began to redden and he got up and returned to the safety of the far side of his desk.

'I can appreciate your predicament, William, and yes, perhaps I was a trifle hasty in the advice I gave the other party. I'd best have a word or two.' The conversation stuttered to an embarrassed silence, which I broke. 'Mr B, over the years you've given me some very sound advice. Sending out bills in good time, chasing up the late payers and so on.' His demeanour brightened. I went on, 'Taking your advice at face value I know you'll be impressed if I start now.' I gently pointed out that he was lucky that I didn't have miles to drive to see him; just a minute or two from door to door. 'My hourly rate is one hundred pounds an hour. This meeting has taken two hours and I hope the invoice I shall send you for my time will be credited to the firm's account.' I also suggested that if he could persuade his old friend Cardew to cough up then that would put us both on the right side of the line. He looked at me with a half smile. 'I'll see what I can do William,' he promised.

True to his word the following week two most welcome envelopes fell through the letter box at 5 Gay Street. The first held a cheque and an apologetic letter from the reluctant Mr Cardew for the full amount he owed. The other a bank statement, with no covering note, showing that our overdraft had been generously reduced by the princely sum of four hundred smackers.

The Luck of the Draw

To ACHIEVE ANYTHING WORTHWHILE IN A PROFESSIONAL CAREER YOU HAVE TO find ways to break through the vicious circle of not being considered for a commission because you have no experience of the subject in question. Sometimes one can gain such experience by design – in every meaning of that phrase – but more often by chance. I have to tell you, dear reader, that if ever Lady Luck shone her beneficent light upon anyone, then that person was me. Let me tell you how it happened.

I'd set up my practice in Bath in the late '60s and, after a year of struggling to cope with the everyday business of running a new and thriving firm, had taken into partnership an old friend and colleague, Peter Fell, a building surveyor. As an architect I prided myself on being rather good at the arty bits but was conscious that I was a poor administrator and at that stage quite hopeless at the technical side of building buildings. Peter, amongst many attributes, was good at both, having cut his teeth in the London office of Cluttons, one of the oldest surveying firms in the country, under the watchful eye of Jack Wix, a senior partner. Peter joined me after a year, leaving the Bristol-based firm of Nealon, Tanner & Partners[1] where I too had been employed for six years. Not long afterwards we took on our first employee, J S Mill (no, not the author), who was a bright young building surveyor with a good eye and the ability to produce clear and coherent pencil drawings. With all of us working away, perched in our little garret under the roof of 14 Queen Square, the commissions which came our way were, I like to think, skilfully and efficiently dealt with; so much so that one morning in 1978 I came into the office and realised that I needed to generate rather more work if, like the

1 The partners were Kenneth Nealon, Ivor Tanner, James (Ronald) Leask and Christopher Marsden-Smedley.

shoemaker in the fairytale, we were not to become destitute.

I cast around for inspiration and in so doing the bound volume of my fourth- and fifth-year's work as a student at the Architectural Association (AA) caught my eye. I pulled down the book and quite by chance it fell open at my design for Reid's Palace Hotel in Madeira. That old hotel had a long-established reputation for providing excellent facilities for those Edwardians who wanted to escape the dreariness of the English winter. Why not, I thought, create such an establishment in Bath? Not, you understand, to avoid the winter so much as to provide that same level of comfort which was available to the discerning traveller in other parts of the world.

After a congenial lunch with friends at the Bath and County Club, which was a hundred yards or so from my office, I went down to the Citizens Advice Bureau where I asked for a list of all the hotels and guest-houses in central Bath. The friendly lady behind the counter handed me a brochure and asked if she might help me find lodgings. Not wishing to divulge the reason for my request I bid her farewell and returned to my desk.

I flicked through the pamphlet which confirmed what I already knew, that there was not one single five-star hotel in the place. Yes, there were good run-of-the-mill establishments, like the Lansdown Grove and Francis Hotels, but nothing to entice the London *glitterati* to come down as once they did to that wonderful architectural extravaganza which is Georgian Bath. So, taking each entry one by one, I settled down to write a critique on each, designed to help anyone who was interested in understanding what the city's establishments had to offer, and perhaps more importantly, what they lacked. The conclusion I drew from my research was that a hotel of excellence was not only required, but indeed vital, if the city was to hold its own in what I confidently predicted would be, at the very least, a decade of prosperity ahead. At the back of my offering I attached a design for the sort of luxury hotel I thought might be appropriate. Looking back on this suggestion I have to admit that my choice of a site next to the river, which was prone to flooding, was not ideal. At the time I imagined that by removing the inner ring road (not a realistic option) my new hotel might gain from being on the banks of the Avon, which would allow me to introduce some fine landscaped gardens with terraces and steps leading down to the water's edge; perhaps even a mooring or two for longboats which could be taken on to the Kennet and Avon Canal through some lockgates, just up river. In a foreword to the pamphlet I expanded upon my considerable experience in the commercial realities of both building and operating five star hotels. This was rather cheekily based on my recent success as a student in redesigning that famous hotel in Madeira and was central to my pitch. In fact I left the reader in no doubt that, if there was to be such a development in Bath, then I was the man to do it.

Some hope!

The whole process, designing the hotel and writing the report, took only a couple of days. When I had finished I chose a nice stiff cover, had six copies rolled off and then wondered what on earth I should do with them! I managed to get rid of three to hoteliers in Bath, who most probably didn't want them, and I took another up to Alistair Parry, an old friend, who was then working at the Churchill Hotel in Portman Square, London. Unsurprisingly I heard not a squeak from any of them. I had just one copy left, apart from my own. These last two sat on my desk gathering dust. It was a week or so later, armed with the report that, on my way down to collect a pair of shoes, I called in on a chum with whom I had recently had some dealings. John Cowley ran, and still runs, a well-to-do estate agency situated in a charming building that incorporates Ralph Allen's town house, overlooking Abbey Churchyard.[2] He invited me up to his room which looked out through the most flamboyant Corinthian façade, and asked if he could help. I simply handed him the last copy of my report and asked him to look at my conclusions. I like to think he was impressed. Anyway he congratulated me on taking such pains to make my point, but gave no commitment to promote the idea.

2 Allen came to Bath as a boy, after spending his youth in St Columb in Cornwall where his mother was postmistress. Allen became rich from organising the first comprehensive postal service in England. He also made it his business to provide the freestone from his own quarries to build much of eighteenth-century Bath. He used this town house and his mansion, Prior Park, to show off the versatility of his stone. He was a good and kind man who became the inspiration for Henry Fielding's Squire Allworthy in *Tom Jones*.

Thinking no more of it I sauntered out into the warm sunshine and stopped at the Pump Room for a cup of coffee and to listen to the string trio before making my way slowly back through the town to my office.

It was two days later that I got a phone call from Cowley. He sounded very matter-of-fact. 'I've just spoken to a client from London who is in the process of buying a couple of houses in the Royal Crescent, numbers 15 and 16. I think you may have described them in your report, William, as 'one up from a boardinghouse. Anyway,' he went on, 'a Mr Tham might possibly give you a ring. I hope it's all right, but I've given him your folder. He seemed quite interested.' I thanked him profusely and for a week I waited anxiously. And then, to my surprise, I got a call.

'I've been given your name, Bertram (I rather like that authoritative public-school form of address), as someone who knows a bit about hotels?' John Tham spoke languidly, finishing in what I assumed was a question rather than a statement of fact.

'I know as much as anyone who has made a detailed study of such things, and I like to think, rather more than most.'

He suggested we meet in front of the Royal Crescent the following day at 11.30; 'I shall have with me my solicitor. After we've had a look round, perhaps some lunch together?' I was already getting quite used to his rhetorical questions.

The next day as I walked slowly round the majestic sweep of the Crescent I spied a black Mercedes parked a little way ahead. The car had obscured windows and two figures were standing by it, looking up at the buildings. One was tall and dark, the other rather shorter. Both wore wrap-around dark glasses. For a moment I rather hoped that they weren't my prospective clients, but circumstance suggested otherwise.

'Hello there,' said the tall one offering me his hand, 'John Tham.' His colleague introduced himself as John Lewis. They both turned to gaze again at the massive honey-coloured ionic façade which, like Bernini's giant colonnade in the Piazza San Pietro in Rome, curved away in both directions. Neither of them took off their glasses, which was slightly unnerving. I determined that if John Cowley had unwittingly introduced me to what might turn out to be family members of the London Mafia

I would let him know all about it. But to my great relief such anxiety as I might have had was short-lived. We strolled over to the white front door of number 16, which marks the very centre of John Wood the Younger's elegant composition. The owner ushered us into a gloomy marble-flagged outer lobby beyond which I could see the inner staircase hall, which was generous in proportion and full of light. The elderly lady informed us that she and her husband had run the hotel for about 20 years. She then asked if we wanted to have the building to ourselves or would like her to show us round. Without waiting to reply John Tham strode up the fine stone staircase, stopping for a moment on the quarter-landing to peer through a grand Venetian window which overlooked an uninspiring garden divided by stone walls and large trees. He then turned his gaze up to what Andrea Palladio would have known as the piano nobile and eagerly proceeded on his way to the first floor. John Lewis and I followed with Madame patronne in tow.

The house itself was in a poor way. For all its fine features and southerly view over Victoria Park, it had been run as a 'bed and break-fast' for the penny-wise brigade; the sort of place where you couldn't be sure of getting a gin and tonic! Clearly the rates being charged were never going to match the amount of cash needed to keep it in good repair. If there was work to be done then it had been carried out on very limited budgets. This was exemplified by the way number 15, the next-door building, had been linked to number 16. If there is one feature of a house in Bath which sets it apart, it is the staircase. Some of course are more lavish than others; it depended on the wealth of the commissioning owner. However, all of them, in their own individual way, are grand pieces of design and invariably occupy fine stairwells. During our inspection we came across the most beautiful horseshoe stair sweeping up, apparently unsupported, to what should have been an open and gracious first floor landing. Number 15's staircase, however, went nowhere. Right across the front of the top step there was a full height wall, constructed entirely from glass blocks. Our owner was most apolo-getic. 'I'm afraid it was the only way the fire officer would allow us to link the two buildings.' By way of vindication she argued that it may not have looked very pretty, but it did the job!

We explored the two houses from top to bottom; up into the cramped attics, down into the dark and peeling cellars and out into the narrow gardens behind. We discovered the old mews buildings, which were hidden from view behind tall stone walls at the bottom of the gardens, with cobbled coaching yards approached from Julian Road at the back.

'I think it's about time we had some lunch,' announced Tham, rubbing his hands and thanking the owner for her help. So off we went to find the Hole-in-the-Wall restaurant in George Street. The 'Hole', as it was affectionately called, had never quite recaptured the excellence of its hey-day in the late '50s under the doyen of all fine restaurateurs, George Perry-Smith. But some of the character that he had created still hung in the arches of its vaulted cellars. We settled down by a window and ordered some drinks. 'Well, do you think we can make anything of it?' asked John Tham, pushing his wine glass across the tablecloth and fixing me with his eye. Lewis sat back and watched my reaction.

'Most certainly,' I said, 'but it rather depends on what you mean by 'making something of it.'

Tham became a little more reflective, 'You'll soon come to realise, William, that we are not in the business of half-measures. What we want to do here is create a world-class hotel.[3] It's got an unbelievable position, but can it be altered to achieve a viable business? That is really the question. Maybe this is where you come in.'

I asked them what exactly their brief was. John explained that he must know, as soon as possible, how many bedroom suites could be achieved when the two buildings had been properly joined. That was the crux. He poured a second glass of wine, leaned back in his chair and mused. 'I really don't know much about you, except what I've read in that report of yours, and what Cowley has told me. John here and I have talked over what we would like you to do, and if you agree, it is to prepare a philosophical study of the way you would approach this conversion. For that we will pay you a flat fee of 250 guineas [I liked that gentle-

3 The Royal Crescent Hotel became the venue for talks prior to 'Black Wednesday', 16 September 1992, when the European financiers forced Britain's Chancellor of the Exchequer Norman Lamont to leave the ERM (Exchange Rate Mechanism).

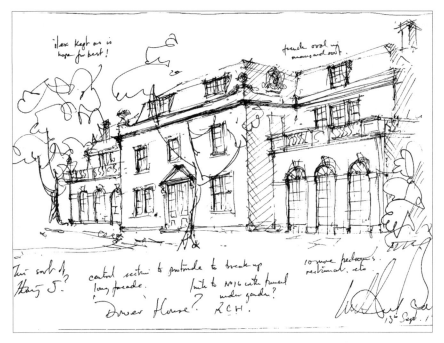

The Dower House in the garden of the Royal Crescent Hotel, Bath, which was the first of the college of buildings

manly sum], plus of course your travelling expenses to London where, in due course, I hope you'll be able to convince us that you're up to it.'

John Lewis took up the conversation by making it abundantly clear that there would be no obligation on their part to commission me once I had delivered my report. I supposed that if they were going to be unreasonable they could simply take my recommendations, pay me off and choose someone else to do the work. A bit of a risk, perhaps, but I was acutely aware of the opportunity that was being offered; and by complete strangers. So I took the bait and set-to with a will. I spent days up at the Crescent walking the corridors, climbing the stairs, and sitting in the garden deep in thought wrestling with a rash of ideas.

What, I wondered, would make this hotel like no other? It soon occurred to me that with two adjacent gardens there might be the possibility of uniting them to produce an oasis of calm in the busy city. A bit like the tranquillity found in the quadrangle of a university college. To my way of thinking I had found the key I was looking for. I proposed that number 16 Royal Crescent should act as the gatehouse to a large central garden bounded by its own college of mews buildings. The fact that my client didn't own many of the next-door mews was of no concern; these could, I suggested, be added to the collection as and when they came to market. I drew up a plan for removing the stone dividing walls, allowing the mature trees, which had been planted along them a century or so before, to stand on their own in generously redefined landscaped gardens.

In addition to this I demonstrated how the layout of these fine Georgian houses could be opened up to provide far more elegant spaces, with a good deal more light and airiness. I determined to keep most, if not all, the important upstairs rooms intact, whilst sacrificing the rooms in between to bathrooms. The historic plan of the buildings was so strong that the answer to John Tham's question of numbers became inevitable. I would create 29 good bedrooms each with its own traditional bathroom, some of course being smarter and larger than others. When I was satisfied that I had properly covered the subject, and with some misgivings, I sent my illustrated document up to London, and anxiously waited for a reaction.

'Got your report William,' said Tham when he rang a couple of days later. 'Can't agree with half of it, but I think we may be able to work together. Any good you coming up tomorrow?' This early presumption that all other commitments I might have were to be rescheduled to fit in with him eventually became second nature to me!

'I'll be with you at ten o'clock,' I said, trying not to sound too eager.

I saw him in his office just off Sloane Square. After discussing what he saw as the shortcomings in my report I realised with some concern that my client had never before done a hotel, let alone a luxury one. Although neither of us was prepared to come clean, it appeared we were both novices learning from one other as we went along. When eventually we finished our discussion I asked John how he had got wind of the Crescent Hotel in the first place. I admitted that, even though I kept my ear to the ground, I hadn't been aware that it was up for sale.

'Well now, there's a tale, William. You'll not believe this, but my hairdresser in London was talking to one of his clients, who owned the hotel. In the course of the conversation he asked how things were going down in Bath and the fellow admitted it was all getting a bit too much for them. They were, he said, seriously thinking of selling up.' Apparently only a week after that conversation Tham had found himself sitting in the same chair discussing his next venture with the same hairdresser. He happened to mention that he was looking for a place to convert into a very smart hotel. His hairdresser simply put two and two together and suggested he got in touch with the owners. Within a week Tham had agreed, in principle, to buy the pair of houses, subject to looking over them with his architect.

It was, said John with a broad grin, quite as simple as that. 'I suppose we could blame it all on my barber!'

'And what persuaded you to come to me, John?'

'Well, it was only the week after I'd made contact with the owner that I rang John Cowley, who was selling the place. It looked as if there might be a deal and I wanted some background on the two houses in question. As a long shot I happened to ask him if he could put me in touch with a local architect who knew something about top-end hotels. He mentioned that, quite by chance, he'd been talking to you only the previous week and suggested that you and I ought to meet. The rest you know, William.'

Through such unlikely events lives and careers can, and are, greatly influenced. Was it pure luck, coincidence, or perhaps just fate that brought us together? I like to think it was fate and that, somehow, it was pre-ordained. But whatever the reason, I not only carried through my designs for the Royal Crescent Hotel,[4] much along the lines of that first philosophical study, but I worked with the two Johns for the best part of a generation. Being their architect opened up a world of opportunity. We had our successes and our failures, but above all we had fun. It involved re-ordering some of the best-known buildings in this country and abroad. Earlier worries about the flow of work through the office

---

4 The original conversion was carried out by Ernest Ireland Construction, organised by Les Dymond, as was the subsequent work to convert the college of buildings, including my design for the new Dower House.

were eased. The commission to convert Cliveden, the Astors' country house in Berkshire, into another astonishing hotel [see *Dry Run*], and winning the competition to convert the Salm Palace in Prague, the old Swiss Embassy, into yet another [see *A Sting in the Tale*] were the highs in a portfolio of work which held some pretty 'high' highlights. Of course these commissions did not come our way by pure luck, like the Royal Crescent. By then the work came to us because we were genuinely experienced in our chosen field. Thus we were able to break that frustrating 'catch-pinch' which hobbles and benights the young architectural practice.

Over lunch recently I was discussing, with my erstwhile accountant David Taylor, the fluctuating fortunes of various businesses we both knew. During the course of our conversation he asked if I knew the definition of the word 'luck'. 'Luck,' he said, 'is what occurs when a business opportunity encounters ambition.' Remembering the worrying situation I'd found myself in when I first started out, with staff to pay and a dwindling order book, I might be forgiven for suggesting that 'luck', is encountered when 'opportunity' meets desperation!

Without the arrogance of youth and the often ill-founded confidence in one's own ability, opportunities are hard to come by. And even then there is still no guarantee that circumstance will chance your way. No, my experience tells me that in the end it is – and perhaps always will be – very much the luck of the draw.

The House in the Woods

'AH, WILLIAM. I'VE JUST SPOKEN TO A MR BILL PORTER,' SAID MY SECRETARY Joan, as I struggled with briefcase, rolls of drawings, car keys and my overcoat. She handed me his telephone number. 'He rang about half an hour ago.'

'D' you know what he wants?' I asked as I dropped my stuff onto my drawing board.

'Not really, but I think he got your name from the estate agents, who've just sold him a stretch of woodland near Bruton. Probably wants you to use your charm on the planners to put up a house there,' she replied, watching me grimace. In truth I was beginning to get worried that my reputation for achieving planning consents on difficult sites was becoming a burden. I thought, probably unjustly, that the easy commissions were going to my colleagues in the profession and I was being left with the really tricky ones. The authorities were alert to the fact that if Bertram was involved they were not going to make things easy for me. My approach has always been to do what I think is right where design is at issue, and to hell with bureaucratic negativity. To be fair to them, what I applied to do was invariably against government policy and as such was all too easily dismissed by a simple refusal. My track record of winning planning appeals, however, was very good; and they knew it.

It was against this background that I agreed to meet Mr and Mrs Porter on site, at their recently acquired wood. On a glorious, sunny June day in 1981 I drove up across the Mendip Hills, down through rolling valleys on the other side where the early morning mist still hung in the hedgerows, through the weathered stone walls of Bruton and left the town behind me as I made my way up the gentle slope towards Redlynch.

They were waiting for me, the two of them, standing by a wooden five-barred gate set back from the verge, framed between two fine old oak trees. I wound down my window and introduced myself.

'Stay in your car, Mr Bertram, and follow me,' said Bill as he swung himself into his Landrover. His wife, Angie, closed the gate after us and joined me in the passenger seat. 'Thought I'd come with you in case you got lost,' she said. 'It's rather thick in there and the track's a bit overgrown.'

We pulled up in a clearing a couple of hundred yards into the plantation surrounded by a mixture of mature larch, beech and oak. My client walked over to me as I got out to stretch my legs. 'Fantastic spot!' I said, 'is it all yours?'

'All twenty-five acres of it, I'm delighted to say,' said Bill, 'I've been looking for something like this ever since I sold a fir plantation, the size of North Wales, to the Trustees of the National Coal Board Pension Fund. This one needs a bit of forestry but the bones are here.' He looked at me with a wry smile and waited for me to say something.

'What exactly do you mean by the bones?' I asked, intrigued to hear what he had in mind.

'Well, I thought that if you wanted a decent setting for a house it was easier to buy a wood, cut down the trees that you didn't want and leave the good ones with a bit of space about them. I had it in mind to create a traditional parkland with perhaps a herd of deer to graze it: the possibilities are endless. I know it looks a bit of a mess at the moment.' He waved his arm in the direction of particularly impenetrable thicket. I looked carefully at where he had pointed and my heart sank. I didn't want to be a spoilsport, but I did think the time had come, perhaps all too soon, to acquaint Mr Porter with a few home truths.

'I'm not at all sure that the planners are going to look very kindly at building in this fine old wood of yours, however much you may want to thin out the trees.' As I spoke, the smiles never left either of their faces. I went on, 'it's just the sort of place, outside the village, all on its own, that they will want to keep just as it is. The chances of getting planning permission on this, even at appeal, are zero.' I thought there was no point in mincing my words: better to wrap up the meeting without wasting everyone's time and money.

'Ah, but there is a house here already;' said Bill turning away from me as he spoke, 'and you, William, are standing within twenty feet of it.' He stopped talking to study my expression. Then he slowly raised his left arm and pointed to a large pile of ivy some 15 foot high. 'Get your boots on, and I'll show you something you'll never forget.'

And so it was that on this gentle afternoon, with the sun squinting through the heavy canopy of leaves, I stooped beneath the overhanging bundles of ivy to find there, in the middle of it, an entire cottage. Not, you understand, a ruin, but a complete house with tin kitchen cupboards, a rusting cream Aga, stained bath, cracked loo and a disintegrating staircase. Gingerly we pushed open a flaking panelled door of the simplest design, its hinges protesting against unaccustomed use. Bill led the way upstairs. Using the very outsides of the worn treads we found ourselves in a small bedroom.

'My God, this is unbelievable. Who knows this is still here?'

Bill grinned at me. 'Well, if the agents did, they certainly weren't telling us. Mind you, if one looks at the OS map it's all there: shown quite clearly as a house. Perhaps no one bothered to check up that it hadn't fallen down, can't blame 'em. Fooled you, didn't it?' He chuckled, obviously pleased as punch with his find and much enjoying the moment.

'When you bought the wood had you no inkling that this was here?' I asked, pressing my palm up against the sagging ceiling.

'No, we hadn't. Initially we just wanted a project, you know, something we could sort out. Thought perhaps we could buy a cottage nearby, and then we discovered this.' He undid the catch and pushed open the small window which still held traces of cream paint. He paused, peering out at the tangle of ivy just outside, lost in thought. Then he snapped the window shut and said, 'I think we've probably seen enough. Let's go into town and have some elevenses and talk about it.' I followed them back to Bruton thinking carefully about what I'd been shown. There was so much of the house still there that, with a bit of making-good and

There in the middle of overhanging bundles of ivy was an entire cottage

renewal, the place would scrub up pretty well.

The little tearoom was full of sunshine and the tablecloth crisp and white: just the sort of cosy place where one can think clearly. Over hot buttered toast, orange marmalade and large cups of coffee, a way through the problems which had been presented by the little place would unfold. I thought it was probably up to me to start the ball rolling.

'The first thing I'd like to say is that I don't think we need to approach the Planning Department at all. As I understand it if we change nothing and just put back together the cottage as it was, no one can prevent us from doing so, nor for that matter, you from living there when it's finished. Now, do we know anything about its history?'

'Not a lot,' said Angie as she refilled my cup. It was at that moment the waitress approached our table to asked if we had everything we needed. On the off-chance that a local might know more than we did, I asked if she happened to know anything about the old cottage in the ivy bush up the road in Redlynch wood. She thought for a moment and then said slowly, 'Well, no, I don't, but my mum has lived hereabouts ever since she were a little girl. Perhaps she might be able to help you.'

It was only days later that I was on my way back to Bruton to meet her mother, a Mrs Belcomb. She lived just above the town in a line of modest terraced cottages with long, well-tended front gardens. 'My daughter's already told me what you're after,' she said as I sat down in her low-ceilinged front room. She went over to a highly polished mahogany sideboard, pulled open the top drawer and picked out a bundle of old photographs. She brought them over and sat down beside me, spreading her apron over her knees to hold the pictures. She peered at each in turn muttering to herself as one by one she held them up. 'Ah, here we are,' she said and handed me a sepia print of a small cottage standing on its own with not a tree in sight. It showed a charming thatched cottage with an old brick path leading to a wooden front door beneath a rose-covered porch. A decorative white gate set in a wicket fence enclosed the tidy garden. I looked at it intently, trying to remember what Bill's place looked like under all that vegetation. Then reassuring herself as much as me she said purposefully, 'Yes, that is the place, I'm sure of it. If I'm not mistaken it was the keeper's cottage. Old Percy Fox lived there till he died, and they just abandoned it. Don't suppose there's much of it left now?'

'Rather more than you might expect,' I said, thinking of the unusual protection that the ivy had offered. 'Perhaps I could borrow this and let you have it back when I've had it copied? It could prove rather helpful.'

'No, you take it, Mr Bertram. If you don't have it, then it will just stay along with all the others at the bottom of the drawer, and not be seen again. I'm just glad that it's been worth me holdin' on to; nearly cleared out the lot last Christmas.' I looked at her as she bundled up the rest, got up and put them back in the drawer. 'Any of the Fox family left in the village, do you know?' I asked, hardly expecting to 'strike gold'.

'Well now, let me think,' she said turning towards me and leaning back against the sideboard. 'Old Perce had a nephew who worked with him as an underkeeper. I have a feeling he moved up to Wells. Timmy Sampson, that's right: nice young man. Took up keepering on his own account at one of them big estates up there.' She paused and pushed in the drawer. 'I don't suppose that's much help, is it?'

THE HOUSE IN THE WOODS

'I'll look him up.' I pulled myself out of her deep armchair. 'You've been very kind.' That evening I ran my finger down through the phone book, and there to my surprise was TR Sampson's name. I dialled the number and waited.

'Hello,' boomed a deep, resonant voice, the voice of someone who had done his fair share of hollering at beaters and dogs.

'Is that Mr Sampson?' I asked tentatively, 'I'm afraid you won't know me from Adam but I rather think you may be able to help.' I explained that the Porters had bought Redlynch Wood and all about the cottage. Did he remember it?

'Couldn't forget it, could I? Pretty little spot and nicely placed for keeperin': good shoot too. All gone now – such a shame,' he said wistfully.

'Yes,' I said interrupting him, 'but you don't just let a cottage like that fall to pieces. Surely the family at the big house would have wanted to keep it up?'

'Good Heavens yes,' he replied defensively, 'but they fell on hard times and had an awful lot of other calls on a dwindling estate. That's why the shoot went. After they'd paid the death duties there wasn't much left, other than for essentials. They couldn't hardly keep up the maintenance of the Park let alone all the other places. 'Course,' he said, 'they'd have loved to have been able to; always had it in mind, but you know, never got round to it.'

I asked him whether he could write to me, and put down in his own words what he'd just said? I explained that it would make what I needed to do so much easier. I gave him my address, and true to his word by the Friday week I had in my hand a letter which provided me with the second vital piece of the jigsaw which would enable me to resurrect the little building: the proof of intention to rebuild.

Without further delay I wrote to Bill Porter and explained that now there seemed to be nothing to stop him from proceeding with the refurbishment of the cottage. 'But, William, don't we need to involve the planners at all?' he asked. I again reminded him that we didn't, so long as we made no changes whatsoever to the footprint of the dwelling nor any modifications to the elevations. 'I have the photographs which tell me all I need to know about the original design and I am about to embark on a set of drawings which will show the cottage just as it was.' I went on to tell him that I had got from Tim Sampson written confirmation that there had always been the intention to save the house from dereliction and that the letter would lie on my file until we needed it; which I was quite sure we would.

'Well, to be honest with you I think the place, as it is now in its unaltered state, won't really be big enough for us. Couldn't we stick on a small extension?' Bill sounded agitated, 'I mean surely, just a modest extra bit wouldn't upset the applecart, would it?'

'It absolutely would, Bill,' I countered. 'The only way you are going to get this thing off the ground is to do as I say. If you give the Planning Department any excuse to get involved at this stage we'll have Hell's own job. If you follow my way it keeps them at arm's length, and even if they hear about what we are up to they have no reason to get involved. Mind you, they will find out, sooner or later, and they'll try it on. Applying for planning permission is not necessary for lots of things. It is known as Permitted Development, all part of our civil rights.' I went on to explain that the time to apply for any modification was at the stage when the cottage had been put back together; when there could be no opportunity for anyone to argue that it wasn't a bona fide dwelling.

So over the next six months builders were engaged, ivy stripped away, roof rethatched, floors strengthened, and doors and windows mended. Even the old post holes of the wicket garden fence were located and the lines of the original flowerbeds unearthed. As the last bits were being finished off, there, for the first time in decades, stood the little cottage, just as delightful as it had been forty-five years before.

There was, however, one flaw in my strategy. It so happened that I could not avoid asking the electricity board for a new power supply. This was to be brought through the wood on poles, the last hundred yards or so being buried under the new line of the drive. It didn't surprise me that within a few days of my making this application I received a letter from our friendly local planning department asking me, very politely, to explain what was going on.

In a phone call to Bill early the next morning I told him that we needed to meet them on site without delay. 'I've prepared a scheme for your extension and I think we should try to head them off by being positive and discussing those proposals,' I suggested.

'Do we have a problem, here, Will?' he inquired, sounding anxious. I reassured him that we didn't and were well within our rights. 'Just hold your nerve,' I said.

In the afternoon of the following day the chief planner, looking very stern and accompanied by his enforcement officer, strode purposefully onto site. Mr and Mrs Porter and I were there to greet them. Under my arm I held the file and in my hand the roll of drawings. They merely nodded their acknowledgement. I anxiously followed their eyes as they took in the scene. Not a word was said. They walked round the cottage, popped their heads inside the front door and looked up the new flight of stairs. 'Hmm, this all looks pretty new to me, Mr Bertram,' said the planner addressing me over his shoulder. 'Perhaps you would be good enough to let me see details of any planning approval you might have.' He turned and looked me straight in the eye. He knew perfectly well I had not one single sheet of paper to satisfy his request. Bill stepped forward to field the question. He pulled from a buff envelope the Ordnance Survey map on which the outline of the cottage was clearly shown. 'This may help,' he said, pointing to the plan. 'The dwelling was built, we think, about a hundred years ago, and if you were to ask your rates department you will see that the last occasion that your council received a payment was in 1948.'

The planning officer looked unconvinced. 'Well that's all very well but it's thirty years ago,' he said testily. 'You can't just go around rebuilding things without the necessary authority.' He turned to his colleague for support, but failed to get the response he expected. It was time to avoid further confrontation so I suggested that it might be the moment to look at my drawings. I unrolled them on the bonnet of Bill's Land Rover, holding them down at each corner with a stone. I pointed to my design for an extension which provided a scullery and kitchen. I explained that these were inadequately catered for in the diminutive structure as it stood. The chief planner ran his eye over the sketches and made what I took to be constructive criticism; a good sign I thought. Feeling slightly less inhibited I went on, 'in due course I will let you have the documents which support our work here, some photos, and a letter proving that there has always been the intention to rebuild. I think you will find that there's nothing to stop essential maintenance from being carried out on the place: we have done nothing more than that, and this,' I said waving my hand in the general direction of the building, 'is the quite splendid result.' I hoped that my enthusiasm would carry the day.

I then, somewhat obsequiously, requested their help and advice on what would be needed to obtain planning approval for the small extension. 'Before I deal with that,' said the chief planner looking round, 'and you may find this odd, but I must say that you should congratulate your builder on the quality of his work.' To my relief and astonishment, and with just the faintest hint of a smile he handed me an envelope which contained all the application forms I needed for the next phase.

Turning to my client he said, 'I shall much look forward to receiving your architect's letter of explanation, Mr Porter, but it may be, and I give no promises here, that if we can find a way to support your new application it could put this whole tricky matter to rest.' He turned again to his enforcement officer, who had remained silent during the exchange and smiled. They shook our hands and walked slowly back down the drive to their car, deep in conversation. We stood looking after them, much relieved.

'Phew,' said Angie, 'Do you think we're going to be alright?'

'Well,' I said, 'if we were for the high jump we'd know by now.'

And that, I am glad to say, was the last we saw of officialdom. Nothing more was said or written by the authorities except to grant us planning approval for the extension. Then the specifications were written, detailed drawings prepared and a fresh set of instructions given to our builder. I encouraged him to keep up his standards and to use all his skill to build in as traditional a way as possible. He reassured me that he would do his best.

The walls went up. The new clay-tiled roof over the extension took shape and the place was soon ready for plastering. As we were getting down to the finishing touches I found myself at the Singleton Open Air Museum in Sussex.[1] For those of you who have never been there, and are interested in early forms of old buildings, it is a treasure trove. Rather in the same way that Clough Williams-Ellis found a home at Portmeirion for structures which would otherwise have been broken up, so the museum has acquired a remarkable collection of buildings. These are set out in an informal grouping making up the heart of a settlement with its very own village hall. In the furthermost corner of the site there stands a half-timbered, jettied farmhouse.[2] I was immediately attracted to this fine example of the medieval carpenter's art. As I entered the gloom of the central hall I noticed a man sitting at an oak refectory table writing with a quill pen on some parchment. Light flooded in from a glass-less oak window beside him. I thought the museum curators might be taking authenticity a little too seriously!

A log fire set in the middle of an earth floor crackled and sizzled sending wisps of smoke drifting upwards through the timber trusses into the open air through a small rectangular hole at the ridge. Surprisingly this majestic double-height hall was remarkably free of smoke. I asked if the fire had a special bed under it or was it just sitting on the earth floor. The man at the table put down his quill, leaned back in his heavy armchair and replied, 'Well, it isn't just an earth floor; not earth which is packed down as dried mud. That fire is laid on some baked clay bricks which are set flush with the floor. We let the ash build up into a mound to protect the bricks from the heat.' I bent down and tapped the surface of the floor by his desk. It was rock hard.

Still puzzled I said, 'What's the secret then?'

'We found an old recipe for earth floors: ordinary topsoil and oxblood mixed to the consistency of mincemeat. It is laid down and compressed; goes off pretty quickly and makes a dust-free, hardwearing surface; it's been used for centuries.' Then he got up and stamped his

1 Now The Weald and Downland Open Air Museum

2 A traditional Wealden house originally from Chiddingstone in Kent and re-erected at the museum in the late 1960s

Bill and Angie Porter's house in the woods, restored.

sandalled foot on the floor to emphasise the point.

As I drove back to Bath I wondered whether the floor in the extension to Keepers Cottage might benefit from such a charmingly traditional approach. I discarded the idea of asking the builder to forget the concrete slab in favour of an earth floor, principally because the slab had already been laid. What hadn't been laid, however, were the clay floor tiles which I had asked to be grouted with sand and cement. In a fit of enthusiasm I rang Angie Porter to let her know what I had in mind. 'I think it would be great fun to grout the new floor between the tiles with a mixture of earth and oxblood.' I heard an exclamation the other end. 'Good heavens, William, isn't that taking things a bit too literally; won't it be terribly expensive?'

'I can't see why,' I said beginning to feel that perhaps this might be one idea too far. 'The cost of the earth is nil and the oxblood can hardly be the same price as cement. I reckon its six o' one and half a dozen of t'other.'

'Well if you are sure,' she said with her voice drifting into silence. So to put her mind at rest I told her all about what I had seen at Singleton, and after a bit she agreed. 'Alright then I think we should do it, don't you?' And so the next day I instructed the builders to proceed.

When the house was finished there was a grand tea party to which the Porters invited their friends and relatives and all those who had been involved in the project, including Tim Sampson the underkeeper, and dear Mrs Belcomb. In the course of the afternoon Ted Green, the builder, and I walked round the building. He showed off proudly the little details which had been incorporated, and which he felt I might not have noticed. We got to the scullery and I showed my satisfaction as to the quality of the finish. 'Bet you've never done a floor like that before?' I said turning towards him and smiling.

'No I haven't, and I jolly well hope I don't 'ave to do another one, neither,' he replied in his deep Somerset brogue. 'Bloody nightmare, if you'll pardon the expression, sir.' I was made aware of his frustration some months later when I received the final account for the building work. I'd been keeping tabs on the general level of expenditure and religiously reporting back to my client as the contract progressed. So it came as a bit of a shock when I turned to the last page and found that the figures showed an unexpected four-hundred pounds overspend. Four hundred, in those days, was a very significant sum. I analysed the build-up of the figures and narrowed down the overrun to an explanatory note which read, 'The omission of grout as specified and the addition of earth and oxblood in lieu'. I wrote to Mr Green thanking him for his account and for a job splendidly well done. I also asked him to give me some explanation for the discrepancy in the cost of the grouting. About a week later I received a blow-by-blow commentary on what had been entailed in carrying out what I thought had been a modest instruction. His letter ran as follows:

Dear Mr Bertram,

We allowed in our price for mixing-up and trowelling-in the grout for which we estimated one man for two days to do the floor in the kitchen, scullery and cloakroom. On receipt of your 'Architect's Instruction' we immediately identified a patch of earth down by the big elm tree which we thought would do as the 'earth' bit as described in the revised specification. We also found that the closest source of ox blood was the local abattoir which was some fifteen miles distant. They were prepared to let us have, at no charge, as much blood as we needed, so long as we collected it. My firm doesn't have a great deal of knowledge about fresh ox blood and although we hoped to use only one can to finish the job, we found that by the time we had transported it to site and opened the tin the blood had already started to congeal. This made it difficult to mix and we could only use about a fifth of the contents. We therefore needed five cans to complete the work together with the additional cost of transport.

To further complicate matters the time it took to grout the tiles was increased due to the consistency of the mix. It proved impossible to work it into the joints using trowels as originally priced. We found, by trial and error, that the only way was to take a handful of the mixture and press it in with fingers and thumbs. After cleaning-off and wiping down this took four times longer than we had allowed for.

I hope that the above explanation gives sufficient detail for you to approve the extra cost incurred in carrying out your instructions. I remain, Sir, your most obedient servant.

It was signed by Ted Green himself.

I put down the letter, sat back in my chair and roared with laughter. It wasn't everyday I received such a gem and I thought it was well worth the extra four hundred quid he was asking. But then, it wasn't my money! So I wrote to Bill enclosing the final account and appended to it Mr Green's splendid letter and offered my own relaxed view on the matter.

The next day my telephone rang. Bill didn't sound too angry, unlike some clients I could mention. He began by pulling my leg about the cost of the blood recipe, but he wasn't prepared to let that spoil our relationship. 'The builders have done a most marvellous job and, if I may say so, without your help in those early stages, William, we might never have had a cottage, let alone a floor to grout.'

Never Give Up!

IT WAS 1974 AND THE PRICE OF OIL HAD JUST QUADRUPLED.[1] SHEIKH YAMANI, the spokesman for the oil producers of OPEC, had come to the conclusion that the West was becoming increasingly wealthy at the expense of the Arab nations. The decision was made to shift the weight of economic muscle away from London and New York towards the Middle East, particularly Saudi Arabia, Iran and Iraq. The first impact of the new order was not long in coming. Petrol rationing cards were printed and distributed. Sunday motoring was limited, and the price of petrol doubled overnight. Teheran became one of the centres for banking in the Middle East and the focus of a building boom the like of which hadn't been seen since the height of the Persian Empire two thousand years before.

To be able to enjoy the fruits of this boom western construction companies were obliged to enter into partnership with Middle Eastern businessmen. One such was Omeed Askari, second cousin to the finance minister. In short order he became one of the 'Mr ten percents' of the new regime taking a healthy commission from the contract to construct the new sports stadium – ostensibly for the Asian Games, but really a carrot to secure the Olympics for Teheran. On one of his frequent visits to England Mr Askari discovered the town of Cheltenham and liked it enough to buy a house there. It was a classic freestone villa situated on the southeast slopes of the town. Once ensconced with his young family he decided to build a swimming pool and in so doing to re-landscape the gardens. Through his solicitor, George Dawkings, a well known and much-loved Cheltenham figure, he asked me if I would help him to realise

1 From $3 a barrel to $12

his ambitious plans. Little did I know what I was letting myself in for.

Mr Askari felt that, before entrusting me with the commission, he needed to get to know me, so I was invited for coffee at the house. I drove up the long hill out of the centre of Cheltenham and turned sharp right between two imposing stone gate posts. The drive curled back on itself and wound up through a mass of overgrown shrubs to the late eighteenth -century villa. I parked in a wide bit of the drive level with the main lawn. As I eased open my door, to my consternation, the first word I heard was 'kill'. At that moment two very large and angry Rottweilers came bounding across the grass towards me. Clearly they had eaten little for some days and gave the unwelcome impression of seeing me as their next meal. The impressive figure of my client, grinning broadly, was to be seen casually sauntering towards me behind the dogs. 'Mr Bertram, do not worry about them,' he said nodding towards the two beasts, 'they are quite harmless. Welcome to Leckhampton Villa.' I made sure the dogs were well out of the way before gingerly stepping out to greet him. He threw his dog leads into his left hand and clasped mine in a vice-like grip. 'George tells me that you're my man; perhaps we should look round before we go inside.'

The house was perched on the side of the Leckhampton Hill with a very small stone terrace in front of it. The road was some 30 feet below and although mature trees and shrubs shielded it in the summer it was clear to me that in winter when the branches were leafless the noise of traffic grinding its way up the hill would be intolerable. I immediately suggested a much larger terrace in front of the main façade, with enough width to cut out the foreground and concentrate the eye on the fields and open meadowland in the middle distance and on to the Black Mountains of Wales beyond.

'You will of course take some notes of our conversation, William, and then perhaps we can agree what is to be done,' he suggested as we walked to the far end of the garden. We sat down inside a little stone folly with four identical keystoned arches framing the northerly view back towards the house. 'I'd rather like to build a covered swimming pool up here, but there isn't a lot of room,' he said, getting up and marching around purposefully. I followed him and looked back at the charming little summer-house.

'You're right, there isn't much space, but perhaps we might incorporate this building into the new pool structure,' I ventured, turning to watch his reaction, 'Cheltenham planners can be pretty awkward about such things, but I think if we fuse contemporary design with the classical like some of the best Italian designers, then they might have less to complain about.'

'I'm told,' he said, 'that you often sketch out your thoughts while you are on site. Do you think, perhaps, you could draw the sort of building and terrace you have in mind?' Over a cup of coffee I sat quietly and marshalled my thoughts. Within half an hour I had done enough to present my client with the first impression of his pool and how it might link into the new terracing. I slid my drawing pad across to him without saying a word, took a sip of coffee and settled back into the deep cushions of the armchair. Omeed studied my sketch, nodded slowly and, in silence, handed it to Elnaz, his wife. 'Now perhaps we should talk about money.'

He got up and wandered round the well-proportioned room, then abruptly turned to face me. 'William, I could ask you how much you think all this will cost, but let me tell you that I have a budget in mind for everything we have talked about. That figure is one hundred and fifty thousand pounds.' I jotted down the sum and without looking up said slowly, 'That I take it is for the building work only; fees will of course be on top?' I meant my remark to be more of a question than a statement. I should have realised that, when negotiating with someone from the Middle East and especially if one had not studied carefully their method of doing business, this approach might have been a mistake. Given the choice, they'll always take any benefit of doubt, which I suppose is only sensible when you think about it.

'Oh no, no, no, William, you misheard me, I think. There's no 'of course' about it. My figure is to include everything. The job is yours as long as you can confirm that you can do it on my terms.' I really didn't feel comfortable with this all-or-nothing approach. I told him that I would first have to discuss it with my colleagues and then come back to him. He quite understood and announced that he was off to Teheran the next day. He asked me to fax the minutes of the meeting over to him and confirm my decision one way or the other.

We shook hands and I departed. The following day I compiled from my notes an accurate record of our meeting, the decisions taken and the scope of the work. I read and reread my text before sending it off to Omeed. By return I received a long facsimile which pumped its endless ribbon of paper all over the office floor. It was covered in alterations. Not one sentence had been allowed to remain as I had written it. More worryingly the text had been adjusted to omit my caveats, and work which I understood to have been excluded from the contract had been reinstated; and to add to all that he wanted everything to be undertaken within his original budget. Not something I'd come across before! So I rang my client in Teheran.

'Ah William, so you got my fax,' he said cheerily, 'I think we can now go ahead on that basis?'

'Well actually, no. You asked me to write the minutes for your approval and to the best of my memory I did just that. I really didn't expect you to rewrite them in a way that simply doesn't reflect the meeting we had.'

There was a long pause before my client responded in a very quiet voice. 'William, are you calling me a liar? I can remember everything we discussed and what we agreed. Now that it is recorded properly and you have it in your hand, I really don't think we need to discuss this any further.'

There's not a lot you can do when such occasions arise, particularly in the first throes of a relationship. You could walk away from it on the pretext that you were dealing with an unscrupulous client, but in so doing you might miss out. I thought it would be more fun to go along with the game and see if I couldn't outplay my opponent.

A dangerous course of action!

I knew of only one firm, whose headquarters were in Bath, whom I could approach with an unconventional proposition. Ernest Ireland

Construction,[2] under the skilful and charismatic managing directorship of David Evans, had just completed the refurbishment of the Royal Crescent Hotel for me. During this challenging operation I had built up a strong relationship with members of his staff and in particular with Terry Gardner, his young senior finance director against whom I played squash every Monday evening. Now perhaps was the time to test the strength of that friendship.

I walked down from my office in Queen Square to the headquarters of Ernest Ireland. I was shown up to Gardner's office which overlooked the old Midland railway station with its impressive stone-columned façade.

'And what can I do for you William?' he said as he lifted a couple of large files off his desk and on to the floor beside his chair. He leaned forward and offered me a seat.

'Leckhampton Villa in Cheltenham, the client is Iranian, indoor swimming pool and re-landscaping steep garden,' I said trying to be as succinct as possible. 'I've done a few sketches of the principal things to be built and I've got a brief schedule of the works to be done.' I tossed the papers across to him. He gathered them up, put his feet on the edge of the desk and pushed himself back into his chair. He absorbed the information by flicking through the pages in quick succession.

'I take it you haven't yet got Listed Building Consent for this, William. How long will it be before we could start?' He continued studying the pages without looking up.

'It's early days, Terry,' I said not wishing to sound too optimistic, 'and if you and I can't agree on a sensible contract figure there won't be a planning application and there won't be a start either.'

'What figure have you in mind?' he asked, as any good negotiator would.

'Look Terrence, my boy,' I said, at my most schoolmasterly, 'before we talk money I'd like to impress upon you, and your board, that the essence of this contract will be the contract figure itself. Unlike any other arrangements you may have entered into, this one will be unique in that

2 Part of the Mowlem Group, now Carillion.

whatever instruction I shall give you during construction will merely be deemed as assistance to you in the building process. It will not carry any monetary value whatsoever. You will receive, at the end of the job, the agreed figure – not a penny more, and not a penny less.'

'Thanks for warning me.' He sucked the end of his pencil. 'You're dead right. No one in their right mind would contemplate such a one-sided deal.' He stopped to think for a moment. 'All depends, I suppose, on what the figure is to start with,' and he looked at me from his deeply reclining position. 'What about contingencies?'

'None,' I said, 'You've simply got to take a view.'

He dropped his feet and rocked back into a seated position behind his desk, opened a drawer and took out a sheet of paper onto which he wrote down half a dozen numbers. 'How are we going to do this – get to the figure I mean?'

I knew from experience that professionals like him, who dealt with valuations every day of their lives, got a feeling for a job as soon as they had read the papers. For Mr Gardner it was a matter of pride that he could assess pretty accurately what the likely cost to his firm would be and the margin of profit to be made. I thought I would put his pride to the test.

'I'll tell you what,' I said, 'I'll write on this piece of paper the figure and you do the same on yours and then we'll exchange them and see what the other has written.' I'd learned this technique from John Tham who successfully used it to determine my own fees! We duly exchanged our respective estimates and placed them face upwards on the desk. Terry's read £125,000. Mine, £130,000.

'Okay,' I said, 'let's do it the Italian way. Take the average of both figures, which by my reckoning is one hundred and twenty seven thousand, five hundred and for good measure add seven and a half grand of contingency. That brings the total to a hundred and thirty five. Now, can you live with that?'

'What happens if the client wants to add something significant to the job?' asked Terry, who by now was looking decidedly uncomfortable.

'Well, what if the client omits something significant – would you expect still to receive the full contract figure?'

'Depends what it is,' he countered looking a little more relaxed.

'Let's agree, Terry, that we put the word 'significant' into the documents and in the spirit of reasonableness both you and I will have to agree what constitutes a significant change if and when it arises, and hope our mutual client agrees.'

I got up and we shook hands. 'Just put your initials on this paper,' I said as I was leaving, 'with a note to the effect that one hundred and thirty-five thousand pounds is the figure.' He signed the appropriate page and handed it back to me.

Later that day I rang Omeed Askari in Iran. I told him that as far as I was concerned the deal was on at the figure of £150,000 which included the contractor's costs and my fees. And thus the deal was sealed.

I'm not inclined to give a blow-by-blow account of the works, which were admirably organised by the significant presence of Terry Lee, the contract manager, who each morning, when Omeed was in residence, was summoned to a meeting at eight sharp. Not, you understand, to discuss the niceties of the contract but to hold a wide-ranging review of world events over a copy of the *Daily Mirror* and, with varying luck, a small cup of strong coffee. However, there were one or two incidents of note. Like most clients he felt that the speed of construction was woefully slow and compared unfavourably to the major projects he was involved with in the Middle East. On one of his visits to Cheltenham to inspect progress Omeed appeared on site just as the men were settling down to their lunch break, which is taken around half past ten in the morning. Small knots of men were to be seen gathered in sunny corners of his garden munching on sandwiches and reading the more salacious tabloid newspapers. It presented a relaxed scene, not unlike a lull at Henley Royal Regatta on a fine summer afternoon.

Askari beckoned to Jack Battle, master foreman and product of the old school, to join him on the terrace. 'Why aren't the men working? They all seem to think they're on holiday,' he said rather irritably.

'They are having their morning break, sir,' said Jack politely, 'it's one of the traditions we like to observe in the construction industry over here, apart from the fact there would be a mutiny if I told them to work through.'

'Why can't you employ Korean workers like we do in Iran? They don't need all these stoppages. They work all the time, on a three-shift basis. It gets things done much more quickly.'

'Mr Askari, we don't work all hours God gives for the simple reason that in England we like to think we're civilised!' replied Jack with just the slightest twinkle in his eye. And to give him his due Omeed threw back his head, roared with laughter and affectionately clapped the burly Battle across his broad shoulders. For a time, at least, a truce existed between client and contractor. Until, that was, the tail-end of the job when we were overrunning by at least a month.

Perhaps ill-advisedly I had specified that the travertine stone surround for the indoor swimming pool was to be obtained from the famous quarries just outside Rome. The supplier had been paid and was all set to pack the slabs into the container when disaster struck. That year the Italians were hosting the 1982 World Cup and for the third time in their history had made it all the way to the final. I watched on television as the three tenors, Placido Domingo, Luciano Pavarotti and José Carreras opened the proceedings with an emotional rendering of Puccini's *Nessun Dorma* performed under the floodlights of their National Stadium. Their team fulfilled every Italian's dream when the leading goal scorer, Paolo Rossi, held up the golden trophy to an adoring crowd. I was genuinely delighted for them.

My delight in their success, however, was short-lived. On the following Monday, I rang through to the Italian quarries to be greeted by an answerphone whose message had clearly been dictated by a member of staff who had seriously entered into the national celebrations before making the recording. I gathered that normal service for the delivery of stone was on hold for the foreseeable future. The impression given was that I shouldn't bother to ring back for at least a fortnight! The message ended with a hiccup and a descent into uncontrolled giggles. Instinctively I knew this was exactly the sort of news which my client Omeed would appreciate!

Oh yes, he understood it all right. The work had gone well. The pool was all but complete, with its gold mosaic and artificial night sky reflected in its dark waters from a ceiling studded with pinpricks of light. The formidable new terracing in front of the house had, to my mind, successfully anchored the building into its hillside and a newly surfaced driveway swept gracefully up to the front door beyond which I had designed a large classically inspired garage. I was quietly please with the way it had all come together.

A jovial Omeed rang me to invite me up to see him. He wanted, he said, to settle up. I took with me Ted Brewster who had looked after the contract, armed with all the files, ready to fend off any criticism and answer any queries. We found Omeed in the drawing room dressed in his white kaftan with no sign of any worry beads. Perhaps I should have taken mine! As we entered the drawing room he got out of his chair and clasped my outstretched hand in both of his and eagerly directed me into one of three sofas. 'You have done well, William, and the family and I are all very pleased with the way everything has turned out. I know you have had your troubles but we must forget, if we can, how long it has taken to finish.' He gestured towards a bottle of champagne, three glasses and a pot of Beluga caviar and raised his eyebrows.

'Yes,' I said, 'how very kind.'

'To you,' he said, raising his glass. 'Before you go today you must not forget to take your cheque for the outstanding amount.' I could hardly avoid noticing his pen and bank book sitting neatly in front of him on top of the glass table. 'Now, I believe I have paid you a hundred thousand pounds,' he said pulling the cap off his fountain pen. He scribbled on the back of a newspaper to make sure the ink was flowing and opened the cheque book. With a few deft strokes he made out the figure, turned the cheque face down on the table and flicked it across towards me. I let it lie in front of me for a moment.

'Thank you Omeed, it has all been the greatest fun.' Then I picked up the cheque and looked at it. The figure was not for the £50,000 I was expecting, which would have taken the total up to the agreed figure, but some £15,000 less. This represented the entirety of my fee.

'Omeed, I think there may be some mistake,' I said, keeping as calm as I could under the circumstances, 'this surely isn't the right amount.'

'You have a very satisfied client, William, who will be recommending you to all his friends. That surely is worth a great deal to you? Apart from that I shall be leaving for the Middle East early tomorrow morning and I shall not be back in England for at least six months. If you are not satisfied perhaps you would like to discuss the matter when I return?' I sat there wondering what to do next.

'My dear friend,' he went on, 'don't be silly. Think how easy it is to fold up that cheque, pop it in your breast pocket and shake my hand. If you do,' said Askari waving his hand in my direction, 'then I will take that as confirmation you accept the amount as full and final payment of all that is owing to you. My money is good.'

'Don't you ever give up?' I folded the cheque and tucked it awkwardly into my wallet. 'I mean, for heaven's sake Omeed, a deal is a deal.'

'No, no, William. In business, you never give up – you should know that, especially when you are dealing with people like me who apply an international perspective to such things. Remember what one of your own businessmen, Mister Tiny Rowland, says: 'There's no better basis for negotiation than an agreement.' It's not personal, my dear friend, but business is business. You, perhaps, still have a lot to learn.' Indeed I had and I was learning fast. I got up, shook my client by the hand, wished him well and Ted and I took our leave. As I left I thought to myself 'well, if it works for him it might just work for me!'

The following morning as my client was boarding his plane for Iran, my office telephone rang. It was Terry Gardner who wanted to know how I'd got on. I told him I was, at that very moment, on my way to see him.

He was looking slightly ill at ease. The papers and file boxes surrounding him on this occasion were to do with the Askari account – clearly he'd spent an hour or two before I arrived analysing the figures. Before I could sit down he said, 'William, I've got variations to the contract amounting to ten thousand pounds.' Clearly the comment was offered by way of getting in the first negotiating blow!

'I know you'll be glad, Terry, that we have a very satisfied client. I have with me my cheque book and I've come to settle the final account.' His eyes widened as did his smile. He watched me carefully. I wrote out the amount then turned the cheque, face down, and flicked it across his desk towards him. Eagerly he turned it over and then with mounting concern lifted his eyes and looked at me long and hard.

'Good grief – Will, this is fifteen grand short. You're not seriously expecting me to accept one hundred and twenty thousand are you? I mean we're ten grand adrift, as it is.'

'Well,' I said, 'the cheque is good; it won't bounce. You've done a splendid job, but I'm afraid that is it.'

'What options do I have?' he asked, looking crestfallen.

'The only sensible option open to you is to fold up that cheque and put it into your breast pocket. If you do, then that will be the matter concluded. If you don't, I won't be able to help you for at least six months which is when our mutual client will next be back in Cheltenham.'

Terry sat for at least a minute looking down at the numbers, picking at the corner of the cheque. Then a slow smile spread across his face and without looking up he said, 'William, you bastard!' Then he folded the cheque, put it carefully into his breast pocket and patted it affectionately.

The Lady at No 13

Bath, Friday, 26 January 1984

THIS MORNING I REDESIGNED THE LAYOUT FOR THE GROUND FLOOR FLAT AT number 13 the Royal Crescent. I sprinkled the margin with soft-pencilled cameos of interesting bits of the design which I hoped might make it a little easier for my new client to understand what I had in mind.

After lunch I went to see her, an aristocratic lady of eighty-six who presently lives in a second-floor flat in the Crescent. I rang the bell and waited. After a while the front door was opened and there stood the imposing figure of Leigh-Helmer Peterssen. She shook my hand, turned and with me in tow limped along a gloomy passage and slowly up the stairs to her drawing room.

'Do sit down, Mr Bertram,' she said waving me towards an old armchair. 'This is such a terrible flat.' Still apologising she guided herself carefully onto the sofa. 'I hate it; you see I had to take it so quickly when my husband died, when everything was so upside down.'

She spoke with an attractive Swedish burr which camouflaged some of her words. 'I can't tell you how kind Mr Tham is to let me take the ground floor, and at such a very low rent [£300 a year, all in]. It could be made very attractive and you, you are so clever William; your rumour goes before you. I'm sure you will be able to improve it. Now do show me the plans.'

Leigh-Helmer took the drawing and laid it on her lap. Then carefully she looped her glasses over her ears and cupped her grey hair back into place. 'Ah yes, you haven't done quite what I thought.'

I didn't mind what she said. I was quite expecting criticism. 'I would have made the bedroom there,' and she placed an unsure finger on the room marked 'study'. 'Could I, do you think, have my bedroom there, instead?'

She leant back as if the effort of discussion was too much for her. 'I was nearly ready to leave for Denmark when I was offered this new flat – so nearly gone, but now I shall stay and I will die in my beloved Crescent. John is *so* understanding.'

I wondered why she had ever thought of leaving.

'Oh I have had a tragedy in my family – so sad. My daughter, she died four months ago. She was frozen to death; it is all too terrible.' She used an arm to push herself back into the sofa, then changed the subject.

'I shall sell all this awful old junk and get some really lovely bits to put into my new flat. Do you think that is a good idea?' She leant forward and placed a hand on my arm. 'William, the flat will be beautiful, won't it?'

I got up from my chair still holding her fingers, and walked round behind her. I placed both palms gently on her shoulders and leaned forward towards her ear. 'Oh yes, Leigh,' I said softly, 'it will be really beautiful,' and then brushed her cheek with mine.

'I'm so grateful,' she sighed, squeezing my hand, 'so very happy. Everything is going to be all right now, you know. Everything is going to be quite wonderful.'

Dry Run

I WAS AT A LOOSE END ONE DAY IN LONDON'S KNIGHTSBRIDGE, WHERE MY long-standing client John Tham shared offices with his business and legal partner John Lewis, and their colleague Gerald Pell, so I thought I'd look in. I climbed the wide stairs and knocked at the door. One can never be sure how welcome such unscheduled visits will prove, but on this occasion I needn't have worried. I found Gerald in relaxed mood, leaning back in his chair, phone trapped between shoulder and ear, with the sun streaming across his cluttered desk. He acknowledged me with a raised hand and mimed to his secretary to give me a cup of coffee.

Having signed off the telephone conversation Gerald leant towards me and threw a glossy booklet across the desk. 'What do you think of that?' he beamed. I picked up the deep blue brochure and casually studied the cover. There in all its majesty was a picture of a house I knew well. It had hosted kings and queens, princes and princesses, dukes, duchesses, politicians and prostitutes. In large gold letters it bore the one word, 'Cliveden'.

'Good grief, Gerald, that's like being asked 'what do I think of Buck-ingham Palace'. What on earth are you doing with this?'

'Quite simply their agents, Debenham, Tewson and Chinnocks, have been asked by the National Trust to find a tenant for the place. It's on the leasehold market for eighty thousand quid a year for twenty-five years, a bit short, but perhaps we can persuade someone to be a little more generous.' Jamie,[1] the two Johns and I are thinking of going down to Taplow to take a look. Want to come?'

I was, at that moment, in the process of designing the Dower House

1 The Lord Crathorne, a director of Blakeney Hotels, was responsible for buying many of the paintings and prints which adorn the walls of Cliveden.

for John Tham's Blakeney Group. It was a bottom-of-the-garden, pavilionesque extension to the Royal Crescent Hotel in Bath. It added to the 'college' of buildings which we were developing from the old mews yards which formed the backdrop to the connected private gardens behind numbers 15 and 16. I enjoyed working with John. He was one of those rare clients who commissioned work calculated to inspire; and if not inspire, then to offer, at the very least, a most enjoyable diversion. A visit to Cliveden, I thought, would prove to be one of those jolly outings when the prospect of doing more than poking one's nose into the glitz of the really big time was wildly improbable. I believe it was Sir Hugh Casson who suggested that architects didn't look for commissions, they looked for opportunities. He might well have enjoyed this particular jaunt.

On the morning of 21 October 1983, our black Mercedes turned left off the Maidenhead road opposite the Feathers pub and passed through a set of magnificent deep-blue iron gates which reminded me forcefully of those at The Breakers, that opulent Italianate 'cottage' of colossal grandeur designed for Cornelius Vanderbilt in Newport, Connecticut. Not surprising really, for the house which we were about to visit had once been owned by the leading light of that millionaire set, William Waldorf Astor, an anglicised American and one of the richest men in Britain. He had set about embellishing Cliveden and its gardens with much of the extravagance of that gilded age.

We were not to be disappointed. As the long gravel drive emerged from the woods, there before us stood the most exotic fountain I had ever seen.[2] The centrepiece, a carved marble shell of massive proportions weighing 30 to 40 tons, was supported on a bed of rocks and fresh green ferns. Marble nymphs and winged angels stood guard over the gentle trickle of water which ran lazily down the ribs into a large circular pool. Tham flicked excitedly through the brochure. 'That's quite something; if the rest of the place is anything like this, then it's my sort of place.'

We left Waldo Story's romantic fountain behind us as our car turned

2 Designed by the Italian sculptor Thomas Waldo Story for the first Viscount Astor. He was responsible for an equally flamboyant fountain at Ascott, de Rothschild's house in Buckinghamshire.

'If the rest of the place is anything like this, then it's my sort of place.'
Waldo Story's fountain at Cliveden

up the gravelled drive between an avenue of limes taking us straight towards a majestic house. This enfilade was wide, generous and positively Versailles-like. If the designer had set out to create a sense of theatre, then he had succeeded beyond measure.

As we drew to a halt Robin Evans,[3] the National Trust's land agent, was there to welcome us in front of the imposing main entrance. Before going inside I had a moment to take in the atmosphere. The early morning sun shining from a clear blue sky fell obliquely across the mellowed walls, enriching the classical detail of one of the most gracious houses in England. The mansion itself was built on three storeys and nine bays wide. Stuccoed piers punctuated the Italianate façade, teasing the eye up to a balustraded roof terrace peppered with urns. This ensemble formed the focus of the composition. Two-storeyed pavilions on both east and west sides faced one another across a large gravelled forecourt. These in turn were linked to the mansion by balustraded single-storey curved passages. Impressive as all this undoubtably was, it

3 Robin Evans later left the NT to run the Landmark Trust, the brainchild of Sir John Smith.

'Stuccoed piers punctuated the Italian façade teasing the eye up to a balustraded roof terrace peppered with urns'

wasn't nearly as striking as the one-hundred-foot-high clocktower set to one side. It had a faded gilt face, and an Eros-like figure balanced precariously on tip-toe provided a flourish to the very top. Little did I know it then, but that tower, and what was inside it, was to present me with one of the most uncomfortable moments of my whole career.

'I'm afraid the inside doesn't quite match the grandeur of the outside,' said Evans subtly increasing our anticipation. We passed beneath Henry Clutton's handsome *porte-cochère* and walked into the gloom of the oak-panelled hall. A battered sofa, of such monumental proportions that two families could quite happily have enjoyed it without the need to engage in conversation, faced a heavily carved stone fireplace the size of a small cottage. Behind us, and beyond three panelled arches, a generously proportioned carved oak staircase rose to a first-floor gallery beneath a frescoed ceiling.

'Not sure about this not living up to the outside, Robin. It looks pretty good to me,' commented Tham. 'Now, what have we in here?', and he gently pushed at an ornately glazed rococo door. Beyond it lay a large saloon full of light, decorated with the most lavish French boiserie. Robin walked over to the French window, 'I know what you mean, but this, I'm afraid, is about as good as it gets.' The panelling was bought by Waldorf Astor in 1897 and came from the Chateau d'Asnières near Paris where Louis XV housed his mistress Madame de Pompadour. Robin Evans walked out onto the long belvedere terrace, the only remaining feature of William Winde's original 1670 house which had been built by the then richest man in England, the second Duke of Buckingham. We stood looking over the balustrade out across the giant parterre below. 'And that,' he said pointing down at the grass terrace below the house, 'is the balustrade which the first Viscount Astor bought back with him in 1896 from the Villa Borghese in Rome. Sort of *objet trouvé* on a Grand Tour scale.' Twin stone figures, perched elegantly on top of two sentinel pillars with fountain basins carved into each of three sides, led the eye towards an exultant statue of *The Rape of Proserpina* at the far end of the garden.[4]

'You may be relieved to know, John, that the Trust intends to keep the gardens out of any lease. We have every intention of letting the public have as much freedom to enjoy the place as they do now. If you are thinking that Cliveden might make a rather exclusive hotel,' and Robin looked round our little group for confirmation, 'then you will have to accept that they'll probably want to see inside the house itself. That, I believe, may prove a little difficult for you.' Tham and John Lewis looked at one other, but said nothing. They had already hatched a plan to allow just that. If they decided to bid, what may have proved a stumbling block to others would, they hoped, play to their strengths.

Evans led the way back into the house. 'I'm afraid this is where things get a bit more institutional,' he said, pushing at a large oak door flanked

---

4 This very valuable statue was removed by the National Trust and replaced with a convincing replica. So as not to damage the garden the original was lifted from its plinth by helicopter, but not without incident!

by a pair of antique suits of armour, with a backdrop of Field Marshal the Earl of Orkney's war tapestries. The long room, overlooking that spectacular view of the parterre, had been set up as a library. The books, however, had gone, and with them the English outpost of Stanford University. The National Trust had originally responded to the terms of the second Viscount Astor's bequest in 1942 that Cliveden should be used for promoting friendship and understanding between the people of the United States and Canada and our other Dominions. Stanford may have filled the bill from that point of view but the students who studied there found it too far from the bright lights of London and others of their own age. The decision to move to nearby Oxford had been taken and the keys handed back. This left the National Trust with a dilemma as the property was not considered ideal to open as a Trust property because of the differing dates and styles of the rooms created by the first Lord Astor. The dilemma was, should Cliveden be one of the first of their properties to 'go commercial'? Only by inviting interest would they find out what viable future there was for the place.

I decided that I'd do best to explore on my own. I left the party and walked round to the East Wing where I came across the heavily panelled billiard room, which sported an ornate Victorian full-size table. I pulled out a drawer of what, to my surprise, turned out to be a chest full of plans. There I found a set of scale drawings of the house and all its outbuildings. They were exactly what I would have asked of my fairy godmother, had she given me a wish. And to make matters even more intriguing the name of the firm who had prepared those plans was none other than the long-established firm of architects, Bertram and Bertram of Reading. Even though the two are not related to me (at least I don't think they are!), it was, I hoped, a good omen. Anyway, at the time the coincidence did feel rather reassuring.

I pulled out the faded yellowing sheets which showed the layout of the main floors and used them as my guide. Then I proceeded to explore the rest of the building. First I took the gently curving steps down to the basement. Below stairs I found a warren of arched passages, vaulted cellars and narrow staircases which enabled staff to scurry about unseen and to pop out through a host of secretly placed doors strategically positioned on the ground floor. The lie of the land also made it possible for delivery vans to unload down at this level. These would pull up outside the kitchens where provisions and fuel could be directly unloaded. Narrow-gauge railway tracks had been set into the basement floor which allowed a miniature train to link with a series of coal bunkers and wood stores in the vaults under the forecourt, making it easy for staff to push little trucks along access tunnels to the extremities of the house. Here they would be unloaded into scuttles and baskets which allowed the 'tweenies' to make up the many fires, well before breakfast, so the house was nice and warm when Lord and Lady Astor got up.

I climbed halfway up the back stairs to the first floor. This gave a fascinating insight into the way Sir Charles Barry, one of the leading architects of his age, had determined the scale and proportions of the mansion block itself.[5] This staff staircase, tight and pinched as it was, held the key. Each flight consisted of a three-sided stair with a full-width landing on the fourth. This provided access to low-ceilinged staff rooms set exactly half way between the ground and first floor. Once Barry had established the turn of the staircase and then doubled it he had the ceiling heights of all the grand rooms.

Up on the first floor I came across Nancy Astor's bedroom. It was situated on one corner of the house and was large and full of daylight. The room itself had been sub-divided, rather inelegantly, to provide living quarters for the National Trust's caretakers, Don Kennedy and his wife, Pauline. The massive carved surround to the fireplace had been removed and was later found in a rather distressed state at the back of one of the many garages. I found Mrs Kennedy busy with her washing in a makeshift sink in one corner of the room. 'This all looks very cosy,' I said by way of introduction. 'I know I'm being a bit nosy, but tell me, what happens out there?' and pointed towards the French window which lead out onto a flat roof enclosed by a stone balustrade embellished with

5 Charles Barry designed Cliveden in 1850 ten years after winning the competition to rebuild the new Palace of Westminster. When Nancy Astor took her place in the House of Commons in 1919 she had the unique distinction of both living and working in buildings designed by Barry and JL Pearson.

a pair of impressive urns.

'Oh you really must come out here,' she said, leading the way. 'This is still known as Lady Astor's terrace. Well, it was also used by his Lordship, but he only slept out here.' She walked over to a low wall and pointed down at a dilapidated framework of poles and fragments of cloth still attached to the wall of the East Wing. 'Bill Astor had a weak heart and didn't like being inside at night. He had his bed moved out here in the summer and kept the rain off with that contraption.'

We turned back and looked out over the formal gardens. The view was magnificent. In the distance the river Thames shone like steel. It was framed as if in a nineteenth-century watercolour with woodland to the north and a majestic line of blue cedars to the south. 'She certainly had some fun up here, did her Ladyship,' confided Pauline. 'She was a very keen golfer; well she would be, wouldn't she, being the sort to take on the men at their own game?' She turned towards me. 'I suppose you saw that nice portrait of her by Mr Sargent[6] hanging in the hall by the fireplace? She was really quite pretty when she was young. Now, where was I? Oh yes, anyway, the poor gardeners had to look out for themselves when they were working down there in the flowerbeds. Her Ladyship liked to practise her swing and she'd hit golf balls off this terrace and, I'm told, she wasn't much bothered where they landed!'

It was good stuff and I was revelling in the whole idea of turning this wonderful house, with all its historical connections,[7] into something very special indeed. A place which might, in future, be enjoyed by countless people and not just a privileged few.

I came down the main stairs two at a time, and walked purposefully out through the front door, across the sun-filled forecourt, along a generous herbaceous border, and through a large oak door in a high brick wall. On the far side I found myself looking at an open-air swimming pool, an innocent stretch of blue water with a little stone-pillared

6 John Singer Sargent (1856–1925) an American painter who was born in Florence. He came to London in 1886 and lived in Whistler's studio in Tite Street, Chelsea. He was famous for painting dashing portraits of the American and English social elite until 1910, when he decided to stop.

7 See *Cliveden, The Place and the People*, James Crathorne (Collins and Brown, 1995)

gazebo at the far end. I ambled along the side and sat down on the curved wooden bench in the shade of its rose-covered roof. It was a moment for reflection. A passenger jet growled its way slowly overhead from nearby Heathrow, momentarily breaking the spell. What stories this particular place could tell. How intrigued guests would be to experience the setting of what had become known as the Profumo Affair – although I wagered none would care to admit it.

I eventually caught up with my group, who were by then enjoying lunch in the National Trust restaurant, close by but well out of view from the main house. 'Well,' said John looking up at me, 'and how did we get on?' I proudly unrolled the plans and laid them out on the table and asked if he thought Robin might let me take a copy of them; they'd be invaluable if I was to make a quick start. John promised to get them down to Bath and failing that suggested I might be able to blow up the small-scale plans at the back of the brochure.

'Ah!' I said, 'so I take it you've already made up your minds?' They just smiled. 'Well,' I went on, 'from first impressions the main house will be comparatively easy – there are lots of closets strategically placed next to bedrooms which can be turned into bathrooms. The only difficulty will be sorting out the West Wing. The staircase is in quite the wrong place which makes a sensible layout of rooms almost impossible.' I was later to find out that this unremarkable stair was one of the few bits to survive the fire which had consumed the previous house in 1849. It featured on the plans drawn by Colen Campbell in the second volume of his great work *Vitruvius Britannicus* of 1717 and was designed, as were the wings themselves and the exedras,[8] by no less than the celebrated eighteenth-century architect Thomas Archer. These were early days, however, and none of us was prepared to be deterred by such trivial concerns, especially as this had all the makings of a grand adventure.

When I got back to my office a message was already waiting for me. John Tham, always anxious to maintain momentum once his imagination had been fired, was suggesting a meeting with the South Bucks Planning Authority to discuss what, at that point, were my non-existent

8 Curved links.

plans. 'Good God, man,' I remember saying to him, 'my feet haven't touched the ground since we left Cliveden. How in the name of fortune do you expect me to have produced anything worthwhile by this Tuesday?'

'William, I don't need a fully worked-up scheme. Just an indication of the number of bedrooms we might achieve so I can calculate staffing levels. I really only want to talk about general principles and make my mark with the chief planning officer.'

Over the weekend I worked feverishly on the layouts. If by shifting the Archer stair I could achieve five suites from the West Wing then the total complement of rooms would be just under 30. Early the following Monday I called John with the news. He sounded concerned. 'Oh dear, I thought we might have done better than that. It does rather look as if the West Wing's going to prove crucial. If we can't get those bedrooms I doubt if I can make the figures work.'

I tried to reassure him 'Look, John, I haven't done any proper drawings yet, at least not ones that I'd be prepared to share with anyone but you. With a bit more time I may be able to squeeze the plans to get a few more rooms. You never know.' But as it turned out he wasn't unduly worried and went and discussed the fundamentals of our bid on his own. I idly wondered how many other syndicates would be doing the same exercise in the next couple of months. We had already heard from the agents that interest was being expressed from all quarters.[9] Time would not be on our side.

A week later Tham was eager to let me know how he'd got on. He began by telling me of an amusing meeting he'd had with a Mr Sydney Jobson. 'He's not only the chief executive of South Bucks but, rather oddly, he's also chief planning officer too. So he holds all the cards and, if I'm honest, he's a rather charming 'card' himself.' John was warming to his subject. He enjoyed an unparalleled ability to embellish even a good story. 'My main pitch was the welcome increase in employment

---

9 Our competitors were: ICL as their head office – they withdrew because there was insufficient headroom in the basement for their computers; Jim Sherwood's Sea Containers, owners of the Orient Express; The Roux Brothers, a restaurant with rooms; John Mowlem & Co's head office (on which subject Mr Tham had words!) and a Johnny-who-came-lately, a Mr Sykes, who tried unsuccessfully to out-match the Blakeney bid.

A magazine cover announces the proposed transformation of Cliveden by John Tham

we'd bring to the area. I thought the idea of sixty to seventy new jobs would be something he'd like to hear and might get me off to a good start.' Rather surprisingly it hadn't struck the right note at all.

'Now, Mr Tham,' Jobson had replied, 'we're a bit over-endowed with people down here, so we don't need any o'your fancy job creation schemes; got more employment than we know what to do with, as it is. Any rate, we can't provide enough schools nor housing to meet the demands of folk already here, let alone what you're talkin' of.' John, never a man to be fazed by such an unpromising reaction, merely roared with laughter. He then steered the conversation towards what the chief executive of South Bucks did think might be best for a building such as Cliveden. 'Oooh,' growled Jobson, 'I've seen all sorts in the past. Mind you, if I had only my planner's hat on, I'd say it'd be one that does least damage and makes fewest changes to the fabric of the place itself.'

'Ah,' interjected Tham, 'there is just the little matter of bedroom numbers. Without being able to do a bit to the small wing on the right hand side, as you drive up to the house, I fear we may not be in business.'

'I like your style, Mr Tham,' said Jobson, warming to my client. 'Up north we don't beat around the bush. Tell me now, what does your 'doing a bit' mean, exactly?'

'Well, my architect, who I've worked with on a similar project in Bath, tells me that he really does need to move the staircase across the plan into the middle of the building. You see it's presently in one corner. Now if we can do that then we can definitely get another three bedrooms. If we can't get those extra bedrooms, then I'm afraid the whole thing's off.'

'What about the rest? Much change there?'

'Not really, Mr Jobson. Just the usual fire precaution stuff, but that presumably has already been covered under Stanford University's use of the building.' Syd Jobson looked into the middle distance clearly undecided whether his rapport with John had been sufficiently developed to give some level of encouragement.

'I'll tell you what, John, my people will meet your architect on site to see what's entailed in moving that stair. No guarantee what they'll say, mind, but I'll make clear that this is serious. Best leave it to me.'

John was full of it. On the strength of Jobson's apparent support he had already arranged for a meeting with the architectural committee of the National Trust. It had been scheduled for 17 May 1984. But one thing bothered me: I couldn't understand why he'd asked me to prepare all my drawings to a very large scale. Wouldn't they be a bit unwieldy?

'Not a bit of it, William, I want the drawings to fill the table, and any notes about 'changes' to be written as small as possible. I rather hope it will give the impression that we can achieve all we want without appearing to do too much!'

The day came. Our team was led by Tham and supported by John Lewis, who would deal with any legal niceties, Lord Crathorne and myself. We convened at Cliveden around a long trestle table set up for the occasion across the windows in the main hall. I invited John Daniels, and my team leaders Ted Brewster and Alan Hardiman, who would organize the bulk of the work, to sit with me.

Across the table sat those we needed to impress. Julian Prideaux, the Regional Chairman, was supported by Robin Evans, Richard Haslam and Christopher Wall, the Trust's architectural representative. Flanking these three were Philip Jebb, the National Trust's consultant architect, and Julian Harrap the architect who had been entrusted with the maintenance and restoration of the outside of the house. Ian McCallum, yet another trained architect and the director of the American Museum in Bath,[10] had been invited to look after the interests of the Astor legacy. They presented a formidable group who quite clearly knew their stuff – or so I imagined.

In the middle of explaining how I proposed to resolve the layout by introducing late twentieth-century facilities to what we all hoped would become one of the great hotels of Europe, I was interrupted by one of their number. 'You say, William, that you have to move this wall to achieve a bathroom,' and he pointed to the offending area on my plan. 'I would have thought that was wholly unnecessary when you could so easily have put it here,' and he placed his finger on a space which I realised was a built-in wardrobe (next to two lines indicating the inner and outer faces of the external wall of the mansion) and only two and a half feet wide. He was probably confused by the unusual size of the drawing, but from the corner of my eye I sensed the unease of his colleagues.

'I have to admit I hadn't thought of that,' I said diplomatically, 'it might prove a bit of a squeeze, but I'll look into it.' Fortunately he did not pursue the point and John Tham tactfully moved the conversation towards other, less technical, matters.

When the time came Jobson, true to his word, steered our planning applications through the labyrinth of his committees, and approvals were issued for all that I had applied for. However, included in those permissions was a condition that the Archer staircase should not be altered in itself. Thankfully it was agreed that it could be moved, en bloc, to where I wanted to put it. Shortly after this we got a call from the office of the then recently-formed English Heritage who felt the need for a

10 Claverton Manor (now the American Museum in Bath) was the setting for Winston Spencer Churchill's first political speech, delivered on 26 July, 1897.

meeting to discuss our proposals. All those involved dutifully foregathered at Cliveden and assembled in the French dining room to hear what their representative, a small man dressed in a strangely baggy tweed suit, had to say. Mr Jobson sat at the head of the table and listened patiently to a stream of hand-wringing criticism with special odium reserved for what was seen as my cavalier handling of the West Wing. 'Have you finished young man?' inquired Jobson politely when he detected a suitable lull.

'Yes, I think so,' said my critic, 'but I have to tell you that we at English Heritage are opposed to the whole idea of a hotel. Much better to let Mowlem take over the house as their headquarters. At least they would be able to use the place without all this upheaval.'

'Well, if I might say so, you're just a bit late on the uptake,' retorted Jobson, 'and anyway we never wanted Cliveden to become a builder's yard. I don't know who's been keeping you up to the mark, but we've already approved the hotel scheme – so you can say what you like – we're going ahead with it, no matter what!'

Our friend looked around the table as if he'd been pole-axed. 'In that case I fear I'm wasting my time.' He got up, stuffed his papers noisily back into his briefcase, wished us well, which I thought showed some style, and left the room never to cross our paths again.

However, the person who did cross my path was Mr Barry Bradford, the head of South Bucks Technical Services, whose support I needed to be able to implement what had been approved by Mr Jobson's committees. In mid-April I drove up the gravel drive, swung left into the forecourt and parked in front of the East Wing. It was the building where Rudyard Kipling had once stayed, as had the Italian patriot Garibaldi. I found it increasingly difficult to come to terms with the fact that the place was so steeped in historical association and could not help feeling a tingle of excitement to be so intimately involved. It was all beginning to feel a little surreal. However, the spell was about to be broken. I entered through the portals and found Mr Bradford, from the council, waiting for me in the hall, somewhat lost in the massive sofa. He got up and walked towards me clutching a roll of drawings. 'Ah, Mr Bertram,' he inquired tentatively, 'you, I take it, are responsible for these plans?' He went over to the window where the light was better. 'I've spent some time studying them and there is one thing that worries me.'

'Oh, Mr Bradford, and what might that be?'

'Well, I'm sure you've thought of it, but how are you going to tackle the spread of flame over all this panelling?'[11] He waved his hand airily over the vastness of the room.

I was dumbstruck. 'What have you in mind?' I asked, playing for time. He suggested that perhaps some sort of varnish might do. Now, one of the glories of Cliveden is the magnificence of that hall with its stone-flagged floor, soaring height, intricately moulded oak panelling and carved staircase created by JL Pearson,[12] one of the late-nineteenth century's most accomplished architects. You can imagine my horror at what was being suggested and it was rapidly dawning on me that if anything was going to break the yet unconsummated deal with the National Trust, this was likely to be it. Mr Bradford would have been blind not to have sensed my dismay.

'Well,' he ventured trying to be a little more helpful, 'you could always install some sort of sprinkler system; that would probably do. They are used to great effect in multi-storey car parks.'

'Look,' I said pointing out of the window, down towards the Fountain of Love, 'that is the only sprinkler we're going to have here!' I needed to think quickly to quash any more ideas he might have. 'Clearly, Mr Bradford, Stanford University were not required to undertake anything as drastic as covering this beautiful panelling with something that has the consistency of marmalade. Surely they made greater demands on the house as an educational establishment than we will as a hotel.'

'That unfortunately is just where you are wrong, Mr Bertram. Before coming out to see you this afternoon I did some research of my own and found, much to my surprise, that Stanford never did apply for a change of use, nor did the National Trust on their behalf. So, to put it

11 'Spread of flame' is the term used to indicate how readily a substance burns and thus how rapidly a fire spreads across its surface.

12 John Loughborough Pearson went on to design, amongst many fine buildings, Truro Cathedral.

simply, I have to treat your application as the conversion of this fine house into a hotel from the private home of Lord and Lady Astor, with all that goes with it.'

Why, I wondered, did I get myself involved with such things when I could so easily have been an ordinary sort of architect, doing ordinary sorts of things. I resigned myself to the fact that it was just one more challenge and one which, with a bit of clear thinking, could and indeed must be resolved. We'd all invested far too much time and enthusiasm in the project for it to turn sour.

My colleague Alan Hardiman rang Mr Jobson who was helpful as always. He thought that a chap who ran a firm called Firecheck Consultants might be able to help us, and kindly gave Alan their number. I met Mr Parnell at the house a couple of days later and explained the problem. 'Oh, that shouldn't be too difficult,' he said comfortingly, 'These council officials are really only interested in one thing: shifting responsibility onto someone else should anything go wrong. With a report from us to say we're happy with your proposals, as far as fire precautions are concerned, you should be home and hosed.' I was surprised and delighted to hear such a confident approach to what a moment before had appeared insuperable. 'How the hell will you do it?' I asked, 'Rules, surely, is rules.'

'Depends whose rules you're talking about, Mr Bertram. The advantage we have is that my colleagues and I actually wrote a fair bit of the fire regulations. You really shouldn't take them as gospel.' He was marching round the hall sizing it up while I tagged along behind. He explained that he would make a calculation of the time it would take for the iron girders supporting the brick vaults above the panelled ceiling to collapse onto the hall floor if all the carpets, curtains, sofas, tables and chairs were stacked up like a bonfire and set alight. 'At a guess I can't see that happening in under about three hours, and you need less than half that time under the regulations – so I think we should be able to convince the powers that be.'

'You're quite sure? Because I'm about to tell the good news to my rather worried client, not to mention the people at the National Trust.'

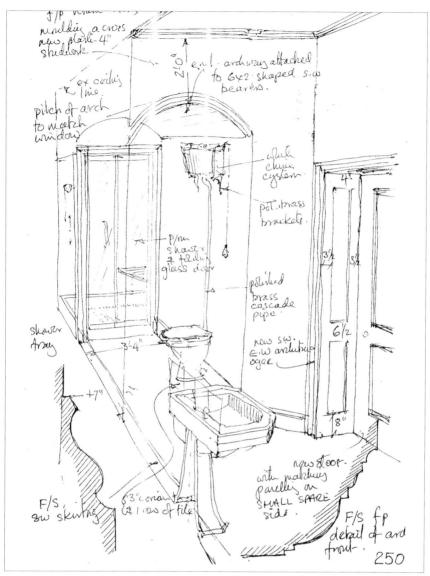

A page from the 'Cliveden Bible'

He put out his hand and gripped mine. 'All in a day's work, Mr Bertram. If only your profession called on us a little more often they might save themselves a good deal of heartache.' And thus the last major hurdle was cleared and the way lay open for the hard slog of refining the detail of just how I and my team were going to set about the transformation.

We'd done it before in Bath at the Royal Crescent Hotel, and so I

Alterations to the billiard room panelling

started writing what would become the reference book for all one hundred and fifty rooms in the place. Each was given a code followed by a detailed description of what was to be changed, where things would go, how pipes were to be concealed, the profiles of the new joinery and so on. It ran to many pages, each one illustrated with a freehand sketch, quickly done, to bring it to life. I christened it the 'Cliveden Bible' and it was issued to everyone from the National Trust and John Tham to his new recruit as General Manager, John Sinclair[13] who had been persuaded to leave the Lancaster in Paris to join the team. I distributed it to Robert Bowles of Alan Baxter, the structural engineers, and to Brian Harris and Maurice Vieceli of E.C. Harris, the quantity surveyors, and of course to my own team. Our appointed contractor was Ernest Ireland, a subsidiary of John Mowlem & Co who had been our main rival for the Cliveden lease and who very nearly outflanked us. My old friend

13 John Sinclair inherited the title Lord Thurso on the death of his father in 1995. He sat in the Lords on the Liberal Democrat front bench and in 2001 became the first, and so far only, hereditary peer to become an MP in the Commons where, once again, he sits on the front bench. He is grandson of Archie Sinclair, a lifelong friend of Winston Churchill.

Terry Lee, the contract manager, distributed copies to his surveyors who immediately nicknamed it 'Willie's Waffle'! I gave a copy to Rupert Lord, one of two interior designers whom John Tham had engaged. Rupert had been appointed on the recommendation of the National Trust. They had been impressed by his work at Sledmere in Yorkshire and promised Blakeney that they would not interfere with his proposals if John was prepared to take him on. And lastly I gave a copy to my dear friend Mary Home, the other designer who was to be responsible for the West Wing and was at that very moment preparing schemes for the interiors of the new Dower House in Bath. Everyone used the 'bible', but not necessarily always in the spirit that I intended.

It certainly wasn't meant to absolve the consultants from thinking for themselves. I don't know why it is, but mechanical and electrical installations have been the Achilles heel of the architectural profession for as long as I can remember, and I fear 'twere ever thus.[14] We had been recommended a firm to help us. They were asked to analyse what plumbing had been installed in the house and how they proposed to service our new bathrooms and heat the place. They reported that in the roof voids they had found lots of redundant cold water tanks which, to simplify matters, they intended to remove. Large calorifiers would be strategically placed to provide hot water for baths, all of which we stipulated must be capable of being drawn simultaneously. They didn't see a problem and reassured us that they had done it many times before and were quite happy for us to leave it to them. And so, rather foolishly, we did. It proved to be a fraught and uncomfortable relationship. Their team was quickly christened 'Why Oh Why!' And it didn't end there.

The main contractor's staff also came in for some stick. They developed a tendency to inundate my team with letters, schedules and applications for extensions of time and demands for more information, much of which in my view could have waited. I wouldn't have minded if their work rate on site had matched their prodigious output of paper. One morning when a particularly heavy mailbag hit my desk I penned

14 In 1852 when trying to complete his work on the Houses of Parliament, a frustrated Charles Barry had no option but to dismiss Dr David Reid who was responsible for electrical and heating installations!

a smart rebuke to David Evans the managing director. 'If we are to remain friends I think I need a little less of the 'Ireland' and a bit more of the 'Ernest'!' The following afternoon a magnum of champagne landed on my drawing board. The note which came with it read 'William, we do not underestimate the Importance of being Earnest!' It was a stylish response from David and one which reflected the true spirit of our relationship.

In January 1986, as the works were drawing to an end, John Tham flew into Heathrow following one of his many trips to America to drum up support for this, his most ambitious venture. He had invited my wife and me, my team and a host of other friends to join him in what he termed a 'dry run'. This was to be an opportunity to test the systems and to monitor how the staff coped; what sort of food the chefs could produce out of the spanking new kitchens and to expose other short-comings before paying guests were invited to enjoy the place.

The public relations machine had moved into top gear. As we arrived in the fading light a Lufthansa helicopter carrying German press corps was preparing to lift off from the forecourt, whipping the fresh powdery snow into a blizzard and blowing it through the front door right into the hall. It clattered into the sky, circled above the house and out over the 400 or so acres of formal gardens and parkland. Back it came swooping low to take the pictures which that night would be beamed worldwide.

Friends and family of the Blakeney Hotel directors continued to arrive. All around there was a sense of excitement and anticipation. Lord and Lady Astor,[15] who had been staunch advocates of our scheme from the beginning, were among the guests, so too was Robin Warrender and his wife in nostalgic reminiscence of his ancestor Sir George who had bought Cliveden in 1824.[16] Michael Holiday had been installed as head butler, stepping seamlessly into old Edwin Lee's shoes, the last butler to run the house for Lord Astor's father. All was prepared as if for a

15 Lady Astor is mother-in-law to Conservative politician and party leader David Cameron. It was after the 3rd Lord Astor's death in 1966 that the family decided to depart Cliveden and hand it back to the National Trust to whom it had been gifted by the family in 1942.

16 In 1810 Sir George Warrender married Anne Evelyn Boscawen, sister of the 1st Earl of Falmouth (see The Merry-go-round). Robin lived in the pretty Widcombe Manor, Bath.

1 The Prince of Wales's pavilions in their formal setting, seen from the drawing room at Highgrove

2 The pavilions showing my trademark, gothicised version of the quatrefoil window

3 left, a hideaway for a prince

4 below, the cedar has gone, the enfilade has grown and the beehives are hidden. My quatrefoil pool with William Pye's centrepiece stands proud

5 *left*, Hollyrood House in its original habitat and 6 *above*, in its new, 'grounded' position

7 Bath
1: Somerset Place; 2: End of Cavendish Crescent; 3: Cavendish Road;
4: Marlborough Buildings; 5: Cavendish Lodge; 6: St James's Square;
7: Lansdown Crescent; 8: The Dower House; 9: Royal Crescent

8 The Royal Crescent, Bath with the Royal Crescent Hotel as a discreet interloper – identified by its paired columns

9 The Dower House in the grounds of the hotel

10 Cliveden, designed by Sir Charles Barry in 1850 and home to William and Nancy Astor

11 The clocktower at Cliveden

12 The Great Hall at Cliveden with John Singer Sargent's 1908 portrait of Nancy Langhorne, later Viscountess Astor, hanging by the fireplace

13 Nancy Astor's bedroom with the fire surround salvaged from the garage and returned to its original position

14 Cavendish Lodge and the lodge houses

15 The south façade of Cavendish Lodge with the unfortunate ashlar freestone panels

16 *Top left*: Detail on the Lodge

17 *Above*: The west façade which I had set back *behind* 11 Cavendish Crescent

18 *Bottom left*: Andrea Palladio's influence can be detected in the design of the west façade

19 *Above*: The church of St Martin's, Bladon. In 1965 Sir Winston Churchill was buried here next to Lady Randolph Churchill, his mother, and his father, Lord Randolph

20 *Left*: The word 'Churchill' carved in bold letters, facing the path, suggested by young Winston. The stone was re-dedicated on 8 May, 1998

21 *Opposite*: the family plot showing the steps to resolve the problem of the sloping ground

22 The oriel window at All Saints Long Ashton, near Bristol. A testament to the single-mindedness of one man who managed against the odds to inspire those around him: Reverend Beverley Tasker

23 Charles Robertson's memorial obelisk. On top is a little pyramid of polished stainless steel so that every day, at around 11am, it sparkles when viewed from Stradling House

24 Prague: the still-deteriorating Salm Palace broods in the winter gloom

weekend house party from the *belle époque.*

The ubiquitous 'Jennifer', in the shape of Betty Kenward, arrived with her Diary. She drifted effortlessly through the assembled company garnering social gossip. Later she would share it with the world at large through the pages of Jocelyn Stevens' society magazine *Queen.*

Bob Webb, an old school chum and client of mine got terribly excited when he read Jennifer's glowing tribute in which she also mentioned me. I on the other hand was concentrating on making sure everything was tickety-boo and was oblivious to the fact of having spoken to her at all! The place looked wonderful. Every window was aglow. The fire in the great hall was ablaze; the library and Nancy Astor's boudoir were warm and cosy, and the staff could just be heard putting finishing touches to the tables in Rupert Lord's sumptuously decorated terrace dining room. Down in the basement the men's loo had been hung with two original portrait sketches by the osteopath, Dr Stephen Ward:[17] one of Christine Keeler,[18] the other of her friend, Mandy Rice-Davies. Beside these two flirts were photographs of other rather more distinguished folk who had stayed at Cliveden. Amongst them were George Bernard Shaw standing ramrod straight beside his over-worked bicycle; a smartly suited Charlie Chaplin; and the dashing Hollywood actor, Douglas Fairbanks Snr. Next to them was a large sepia print of Queen Victoria, plus entourage, enjoying tea under an awning on the belvedere terrace.

It all made for the stuff of dreams but, as I was shortly to find out, the stuff of nightmares too.

The evening gong had long faded and I was just getting ready to go upstairs to join my wife to change for dinner. As I sat contentedly beside the hall fire I used my time to jot down one or two things which I thought could usefully be discussed the following day after the excite-

17 In 1963 Dr Stephen Ward took his life towards the end of his trial for unsubstantiated charges of 'living wholly or in part on the earnings of prostitution'.

18 In 1961 Christine Keeler met John Profumo at Cliveden, which led to a brief affair. Profumo was Secretary of State for War in Harold Macmillan's Conservative Government. Yevgeny Ivanov, the Soviet Naval Attaché and a known spy, was also seeing Keeler. The fact that the Secretary of State for War and a Russian spy both had relationships with the same woman enabled the Labour opposition to make much play of the security risk. The 'Profumo Affair' led to the downfall of the Macmillan Government in 1963.

ment of that first night. Then out of the corner of my eye I became aware of a tall, good-looking figure walking slowly down the main staircase wrapped in a white towelling bathrobe. John Tham stopped on the lowest quarter landing and beckoned me to join him at the foot of the stairs. He held firmly to the oak handrail and leaning forward said very quietly 'There's no hot water, William. The bath and basin in my room have no water at all. I've asked Gerald (Pell) and he hasn't got any either. The place is dry.'

My heart began thumping. 'Dry run' be damned, this was absolutely ridiculous. 'That cannot be so, John,' I protested rather feebly, 'we've got stacks of hot water all over the place.'

'I really don't mind what you say, William, just bloody well get it fixed, will you?' This was my moment of truth. That fine clocktower which I had admired all those months before would now prove my nemesis. I have to admit I'm not at my best at such moments, but instinctively I knew who would be. I rang Alan Hardiman, who knew everything technical there was to know about the place. He was already dressed in black tie for dinner. 'Al,' I said in as level a voice as I could muster, 'I think we may have a problem with the water supply.' There was stunned silence.

I waited for his reply. 'It might be worth having a look at the tanks at the top of the tower, William. Let's first make sure they're full?' Some 20 minutes later he reported back. It felt like a month. By the light of a torch, he and John Sinclair had climbed the outside spiral steps and then onto the narrow metal ladders inside the tower right to the top. With their fists they had thumped the sides of the iron tanks only to be greeted with an ominous hollow boom. 'There's barely enough water left to clean your teeth, Will. If we haven't got enough water down here, we sure as hell aren't going to get any from up there.'

'Where's Sinclair?' I asked with mounting concern.

'I rather hope he's getting on to the local fire brigade to see if they can send someone to pump water straight up into the tanks, but it's a hell of a height. We have no option; we simply can't rely on the supply from the one-inch main. It'll take for ever.'

He was too damned right! Some of our long-suffering guests might soon start to complain if they found they couldn't have a bath. Then to my great relief I heard the first of what would be a succession of fire engines, rumbling down the gravel drive with tanks full of fresh water and heavy-duty pumps.

I never did know how much the other guests knew of that 'dry run' near-debacle, but John Tham seemed remarkably unconcerned the following morning. With a broad grin on his face he opened the meeting. 'Well, I thought that all went off pretty well. Better get the water sorted, William.[19] Now, what's next on the agenda?'

If I'd been him, I would have killed me!

After lunch, as I was making for my car, a rather large and formidable guest collared me. 'Mr Bertram,' she said in a loud voice, 'you may not remember me, but when you first showed us your plans, the National Trust members I mean, I remember saying to you in no uncertain terms that I thought it a disgrace that you were intending to use baths made in, of all places, Germany; particularly as this is the most English of country houses. Well, I must tell you that last night I had a perfectly glorious deep, deep bath before dinner in one of your new sumptuous 'Dukers', or whatever you like to call 'em. I just want you to know, I take it all back. Well done you!' And with that she affectionately slapped me across the back, momentarily knocking me off balance. She would be the first of the many appreciative guests to visit Cliveden, from Her Majesty Queen Elizabeth the Queen Mother and Her Royal Highness Diana Princess of Wales, to dukes and duchesses, lords and ladies, deal-makers and deal-breakers, politicians and paramours. Humbler folk too, as was the intention; the likes, perhaps, of you and me.

Fate decreed that the two hotels for which John Tham was the inspiration, Cliveden and the Royal Crescent in Bath, were to be linked romantically. Jenny Agutter, the darling of the British film establishment and 'national treasure' had been invited to open the 1989 Bath Music Festival. The opening ceremony was held on the lawns in front of the great sweep of the Royal Crescent. Before the evening was out John had

19 To solve the problem, the cold water tanks in the roof of the house were reinstated.

taken Jenny under his wing and, as a couple, they never looked back. They were married in 1990 in the little church of St Nicholas, at Remenham near Henley on the banks of the river Thames, at the far end of that famous mile-long reach. Their wedding reception was held at Cliveden on a warm summer's evening with the celebrity worlds of cinema and theatre coming together to wish them well.

In the middle of dinner John called for our attention and suggested we might like to drift out onto the belvedere terrace to enjoy the evening air. From that high vantage we were then witness to the most spectacular firework display many of us had ever seen. As the last of the glitter faded from the velvet sky one by one the guests filtered back to their tables. My wife and I, and John and Jenny, were the last to leave. We stayed, in silence, looking down the moonlit gardens, towards the silver ribbon that was the Thames, with the soft glow from the lights of London in the distance. It was as if Cliveden itself had breathed a lingering sigh. At long last the great house lived again, setting course across another century to match, no doubt, the intrigues, the romances, the reputations lost and gained, and the scandals which had, for so long, enriched its glorious past.

The Battle for Cavendish Lodge

Opening Shots

BATH, A CITY OF DAZZLING CLASSICAL ARCHITECTURE, BUILT FROM THE sublime honey-coloured limestone on which it so perfectly rests, has provided the battleground for many a hard-fought architectural campaign. None more so than when, without too much thought, I accepted the challenge to design a new building in the very heart of the most sensitive part of this beautiful city. Over the previous 20 years many designs had been proposed but they had come to nothing. I should have been warned, but then I suppose I'm a warrior at heart, and I reckoned my chances of success in this particular skirmish were rather better than evens.

It really all started with the present my wife gave me on our wedding day in 1963, a pair of original copies of John Wood's 1749 *An Essay Towards a Description of Bath*, beautifully bound in leather by George Bayntun, a firm of fine bookbinders with a long history in the city. You cannot read those books without realising that here was a young man who had a passion for both architecture and mythology, mingled with an overriding self confidence. This might be seen as arrogance, but I know from experience that the real motive behind such arrogance is self-preservation.

His story is well told. When he returned to Bath from Yorkshire where he was still working at Bramham Park under the tutelage of the Venetian architect Giacomo Leoni,[1] the young John Wood fell into the company of property developers and land and quarry owners. He needed to impress them with his ability to make them money by building fine

1 Giacomo Leoni published the first complete English translation of Andrea Palladio's *Four Books of Architecture* in 1715.

John Palmer's watercolour of my proposed development. I'd watched many schemes for this particular site come and go over the years.

houses for the visitors who were flocking to Bath to take the curative hot mineral waters in the wake of royal patronage. His was the original vision of an enlarged medieval city adopting Palladio's refined understanding of proportion, scale and embellishment to give his architecture poise and grandeur. His 'New Bath' would reflect the splendour of its Roman past and a good deal else besides.[2] I knew that Wood, the aspiring architect, was only 21 years old when he started out on his own account. Here was I, twice his age; if he could do it then so, I thought, could I.

On 24 September 1986 Peter North, a young and enthusiastic property developer, came to see me. He told me that his firm, Hammercrest, had bought a piece of vacant ground on the south-facing slopes overlooking the city. The old Cavendish Lodge site was situated immediately below John Pinch's Cavendish Crescent, a fine late Georgian sweep of eleven dwellings the end of which towered above the impenetrable undergrowth of what once had been the well-tended garden of the demolished Lodge. The site had been derelict for over 20 years. The hill

2 *John Wood: Architect of Obsession*, Timothy Mowl and Brian Earnshaw.

rises steeply behind that crescent, up to the subtlest of all Bath's architectural set pieces, Lansdown Crescent, designed by John Palmer in 1790. Its refined detailing and sinuous curves and counter-curves respect the contours of the bluff on which it is so majestically perched.

In the other direction, down the hill, is the much underrated St James's Square, also designed by the busy Mr Palmer, with its own delightful symmetry: a square with, as it were, neat hospital corners. And all this elegance nestling behind the charismatic sweep of the Royal Crescent itself, started in 1767 and built in only eight years by John Wood's son in celebration of his father's vision. All these fine crescents and squares represent the greatest concentration of Grade I listed buildings in the kingdom. The speed with which they were built was to be in stark contrast to the bureaucratic assault course on which I, unwittingly, was about to embark.

I realised none too soon just how fiercely Bath was guarded by a veritable army of conservationists. They quite rightly made it their business to protect the character of these fine buildings and their settings. They did this as fiercely as the squares of infantry employed by the Duke of Wellington on the battlefield at Waterloo, and I use the word 'battlefield' advisedly!

On a brisk sun-filled day in late autumn with the leaves just beginning to turn Peter North and I walked up the hill and pushed open a forlorn wooden gate half hanging from its hinges. He took from his pocket a plan with a red line indicating the extent of the three-acre plot. It encompassed two very different bits of land. The forward part was lined with some wonderfully mature trees, but essentially it remained the scrubby, over-grown former garden of the Lodge backing onto the pavement of Cavendish Road. This was approached via 'in' and 'out' openings each flanked by gate posts in the tall freestone wall through which we had just entered. The other adjoining piece of ground was situated at the back of the site, beyond a tumbled down rubblestone wall. This was a large flattish area which, from early photographs, had once been open grassland with its own separate field access.

We pushed through the brambles, climbed over walls and made our way through the thick undergrowth to explore the back of the site. The convenience of this abandoned piece of waste ground as a general rubbish tip for those living close by in Park Street was evident. We tripped over iron bedsteads and rusting bicycle frames and choked on smouldering debris. In one corner, well out of sight, we came across a secret den with its tell-tale assortment of burnt spoons, silver paper and hypodermic needles.

'Bit like the back-end of nowhere,' said Peter picking burrs from his jersey. 'Seen enough, William?'

I had. The site depressed me just as much as I believe it did Peter although neither of us was prepared to admit it. Over lunch he showed me the architectural brief for the place, which Peter had been told by the selling agents had been drafted and refined over many years by the city council's Planning Department.

For my part I'd watched many schemes for this particular site come and go over the years. A generation before, when as a young architect I had been a trustee of The Bath Preservation Trust, I recalled a partner from Towning Hill and Partners, a well known and much respected firm of architects from Bristol, coming to see me. He had designed a long, curved building of forty-eight flats made in concrete and rendered the colour of Bath stone. It was a rather brutish piece with little acknowledgement of the surrounding classical architecture apart, perhaps, from its shape. Before submitting his detailed design to the planners he needed reassurance that the Trust would support his scheme. Reluctantly I could not offer him that confirmation. Instinctively I thought that such a large and overtly modern building on this, of all sites in Bath, was not appropriate. Although I was only voicing a personal view on behalf of the Preservation Trust it was enough, apparently, to scupper the scheme even though the city had previously granted outline permission for residential use on this colossal scale. It only highlighted just how delicately balanced the future of the site was.

As we settled down to our meal I couldn't help asking Peter what had persuaded him to buy it. 'You do realise, I suppose, what you're taking on here?'

'I think I bought the site because I like a bit of a challenge.'

'Some challenge,' I said and he laughed and looked at me quizzically.

'Why, having second thoughts? Don't you think you can do it?'

'Perhaps,' I nodded, 'but before committing myself I'd just like to study this development brief thing in a bit more detail.' It wasn't lengthy and having read it once, I felt I had to read it again to try to get the full gist. Even then I simply could not understand what the authors were trying to achieve, and I wasn't at all sure they knew either. It was all words, no drawings ... nothing to inspire one.

I thought very carefully how best to phrase what I wanted to say next. 'You know, Peter, I can't possibly produce a decent piece of architecture if I follow this rubbish, and I doubt if any self-respecting architect could either.'

'What's bothering you, William?'

'Just about everything. Listen to this: it says here that the main building should be no more than four storeys high and it should not be built appreciably in front of the southern end of Cavendish Crescent.'

'Problem?'

'I should jolly well think there is a problem. For a start the site slopes about ten feet from one side to the other. Where, may one ask, is one supposed to take the four storeys from, the top of the slope or the bottom? Then there's that bit about not being 'appreciably in front of ... etcetera'! If you build anywhere near the end of Cavendish Crescent it will ruin its setting.'

'Don't you think the guys in the planning office might have thought of that?' he offered, limply.

'No, I don't, and if their thinking is a bit suspect on that, then how about this?' And I read out that all the garages for the flats and up to three detached houses (and presumably all the paraphernalia that went with them) could be built in the meadow behind the site – our flat field.

'Isn't that rather a good thing? I mean it makes my site more valuable, surely William?'

'It's got nothing to do with value, Peter. It's got everything to do with practicality. If you could put the garages where they suggest, then I might agree with you, but to do so would mean cutting down perhaps three rather wonderful trees, all of which have preservation orders on them; and to confuse things further the brief makes great play of not cutting down any trees. The only way it will work is to pull the main building back into the meadow far enough to allow a drive to pass between the new building and the trees.'

Peter leaned back in his chair and started folding his napkin with studied concentration. 'Well, what about those three houses?' he ventured.

'If you're being encouraged to build something in the field then why not put the main building there? It's quite the best place for it, and I would argue the only place. Anyway it's not only the three houses but the bungalow by the gate that worries me. I really don't think that this so-called brief of theirs was written by anyone who had actually studied the site in any great detail.' Warming to my subject I went on. 'What logic is there in scattering a lot of disparate buildings all over the place like confetti? Why for instance do they restrict development next to Cavendish Road to just one bungalow? Why not a pair of elegant little lodges? That would at least give a bit of substance to any composition.' Rashly I banged my fist down hard on the table to emphasise the point, making the cutlery jump. I looked round rather sheepishly to find the people at the next table staring across and frowning at us.

Peter leaned forward and said quietly, 'Maybe, William, because it's not called Cavendish Lodges,' and allowed himself the broadest of grins.

'Look,' I whispered, 'whose side are you on? Take it from me, my dear boy, if you want to follow this God-awful brief then you'll have to find another architect to do it. I simply can't help you. You never know, they might even follow that ludicrous suggestion that the building could be a modern piece or, as the brief puts it, of its time. And if that happened it would destroy the setting for every classical building in the area.'

'You'd go for the more traditional approach, I take it, Will. Do you think you can justify that to the planners?'

'Well for a start, Peter, I imagine you've come to me because I have a reputation as an architectural traditionalist. You're the client. You are the one I have to convince. Do I really have to justify such an approach? If John Wood felt comfortable in following the Vitruvius-inspired Andrea Palladio, who preceded him by at least a couple of hundred years, then I think I am quite entitled to follow John Wood's example, who practised 250 years before me. Designing buildings now is not so very different from Wood's day. In Bath we still have fine stonemasons; we still have carvers, plasterers and metalworkers, all of whom are quite capable of executing anything which I might ask of them, just as they did for Mr Wood.'

Battle Plan

PETER LEANED BACK IN HIS CHAIR, 'I CAN SEE YOU HAVE GIVEN THIS A LOT OF thought, so why don't you just design what you think is right for the site and completely ignore the development brief? Then, if I like it, let's see if we can persuade the powers-that-be to support us! How about that?'

There are very few clients who feel able to give their architects *carte blanche*,[3] but here was a man who was prepared to trust me and give me my head. I certainly didn't need to be asked twice. Straightway I went to my library to research the historical background of the site. The first and perhaps most important discovery I made was that, far from the meadow at the back of the site being a no-go area for the main building, there had been a late eighteenth-century plan prepared by Harcourt Masters to extend Park Street right up into the heart of my meadow. Yet another nail in the coffin of that ludicrous briefing document.

By now I was getting quite enthusiastic about taking this on. I knew, for instance, that John Wood had conceived his design for Queen Square, his first major excursion into property development as a great palace

---

3 However, I should mention those who have been prepared to give me some degree of independence. Esmond and Susie Bulmer at Redlynch and Poston; Henry and Sally Clive at Perrystone Court; Martin Dawes at Dinmore Manor; the Shamoons and Dr David Gabbay and family in Hampstead; Dr Dennis and Joan Gillings at Manresa Road, Chelsea, assisted by Ian Cox; Lady Herries at Angmering Park; Sir John and Lynda Jennings at S. Kenwood; Adam and Hilary Kidd at Poulshot; Hans and Eva Kremmel at Dunley; William and Gigi Salomon at Poyntington Manor; Trevor and Barbara Osborne at Combe Hay; Michael and Louisa Stone at Ozleworth Park and Michael and Emma Treichl at Parnham.

running the full length of its north side, with east and west wings forming two flanks of the new square. Although that was to be his architectural anchor it was not, of course, the reality of what he planned for *behind* those façades. This *palazzo* acted like a Venetian mask for a series of relatively simple terraced town houses and villas.[4] Why not, I thought, be equally theatrical on this occasion and design a great house with stabling (as garaging) and a pair of elegant little lodges at the entrance onto Cavendish Road, instead of all those dotty buildings encouraged by the brief? At least the composition would then have a coherent architectural hierarchy and strong visual discipline.

In a state of mounting excitement I put up my drawing board at home where I wouldn't be disturbed by my office staff and settled down to work on the design. First I studied an accurate survey of the site marked up with contours and trees. Then I carefully sharpened a soft pencil to make sketching as easy as possible. On to the plan I placed two circles representing two little lodges next to Cavendish Road. Then I drew a straight line for the drive up into the heart of the site flanked by the existing mature trees. I flicked a thick pencil across the site, well behind the end of Cavendish Crescent, to show my favoured position for the main façade, which would face the road. Behind this I would eventually design some 20 smart apartments, the majority of which would embrace the south-westerly view downhill over the rooftops of the city. I decided the whole composition should be symmetrical with terminal wings and central porticos.

Just to be on the safe side, and to curtsey to the development brief, I slashed a pencil line across the field to denote the cross-fall, then wrote the words 'three storeys top side and four storeys bottom'. A circle then appeared, as if by another hand, in the middle of the meadow, representing the carriage turn. This was placed in front of what would become the long 'secret' southern façade.

It was clear to me even in those few short minutes that this was the only sensible way to treat the site. Then, quite suddenly, a sense of calm enveloped me. I put down my pencil and glanced sideways out of my

4 'The Origin of Queen Square', William Bertram, unpublished thesis, 1963.

upstairs window at the spectacular view across to the Mendip hills which were just then melting into the purple and gold of twilight. I got up from my drawing board and stood leaning on the window sill looking out at the view. I stayed there for about five minutes, staring into the distance, lost to the world. Just as well, perhaps, because unbeknown to me the conservation fifth-columnists would soon be hard at work. Blissfully unaware of this I turned back to my drawing, pulled up my chair, adjusted the anglepoise light and with a flourish drew a long curving line at the bottom of the page to represent the garaging (stabling). This long low building would, I thought, best define the southern boundary of my site.

When at last I came to the design proper I consulted my books on French chateaux and the villas of Palladio. These established for me the scale and proportion of the piece I wanted to build. The main element, the 'Great House' as I now christened it, would I thought work best if it were both symmetrical and rectangular. This shape would of course be in direct contrast to the subtle curves of Cavendish, Somerset and Lansdown Crescents which are its nearest neighbours. It seemed to me that a curve seen against a straight line enhanced both. The relationship of the long and very straight line of Marlborough Buildings to the west of the Royal Crescent nicely demonstrates this.

Did I want to design this building entirely in sawn stone like the majority of classical buildings in Bath? No, I didn't. I would follow Palladio's *dictum*: 'If you intend to adorn the building with columns or pilasters make the bases, capitals and architraves of stone and the other parts in brick'! A clear demonstration of his acceptance of contrasting materials. I didn't want to be different just for the sake of it, but here was a semi-rural site at the very beginning of the Cotswold Way,[5] that famous one-hundred-mile footpath running from Bath to Broadway and on to Chipping Campden in the heart of Gloucestershire. The natural limestone found in the Cotswolds is quarried in thin courses, especially in the top layers which are used for drystone walling. What, I thought, could be more stylish than to mix the two; the sophistication

5 In 2006 the Cotswolds were extended beyond Bath towards Combe Hay. This decision has given even greater powers of control over building to Bath and North East Somerset Council.

and sharpness of Bath freestone for both pediments and rusticated base, in contrast to the tweediness of Cotswold drystone for all the areas of walling in between. The different textures would enhance the look of both materials and lift the composition out of the commonplace. It would also combine town and countryside in one piece of architecture which just happened to be sited where the two meet.

And so, slowly and with great care, the design evolved. The two lodges became miniature versions of the main house. This idea was inspired by reading Dr Timothy Mowl's then recently published book *Trumpet at a Distant Gate*, which studies the relationship of lodges to their parental grand houses. To give the little lodges greater impact I crowned each pyramidical roof with a large stone vase, like those on the gatehouses leading from the main road down to Dyrham Park, some six miles north of Bath. The chimneys, at opposing corners, reflected the design of that charming pair of pavilions along Queen's Parade Place which John Wood the Elder designed in the gardens behind his northside master-piece in Queen Square. And those carved dagger-like blades on the front elevations? They were designed as an act of mock defiance aimed at my potential critics; the carved stone bows intending to soften the blow![6]

The design for the Great House, on the other hand, presented me with a mass of complexities. To overcome the crossfall of the site I decided to construct a firm plinth on which to settle the building. This acted as a rusticated, full height storey to the lower side but like a mini-skirt to the elevation on the upper side. To cushion its wedge-like profile when seen from the road I created a generous flight of stone steps leading up to a balustraded terrace in front of what would be the most important façade. I widened the building to dominate the site, and intro-duced an attic storey, in ashlar, to give the impression of its being a later addition to a once lower building, in a similar manner to the Holburne Museum at the end of Great Pulteney Street.[7]

I had made a study, in particular, of Palladio's Villa Barbaro in the Italian Veneto and much enjoyed the way the *capomaestro* had broken

6 And not, as Steve Billett suggested, a material manifestation of 'get knotted'.

7 The Holburne of Menstrie Museum had been extended upwards in 1836 by John Pinch the Younger, from the original designs by Harcourt Masters inspired by Thomas Baldwin.

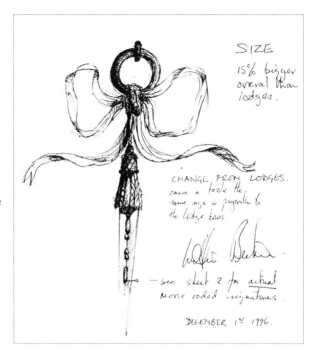

SIZE
15% bigger
overall than
lodges.

CHANGE FROM LODGES.
carve a table the
same size in proportion to
the lodge taos

— see sheet 2 for actual
Morse coded signatures.

DECEMBER 1st 1996.

The carved dagger-like blades on the front elevations of the lodges were designed in mock defiance of my critics

the architrave to pair the columns,[8] allowing the face of the central portico to drift upwards into the pediment. Although I knew Peter North's budget wouldn't run to the voluptuousness of the carved work which made Palladio's design so special, I did introduce my own rather less extravagant eye-catcher of an incised dagger-blade, down the centre of which I pretentiously signed my name in morse code.[9]

I wanted to get as much of the design onto one sheet as I could. To do this I chose to draw at the very small scale of 1:200,[10] or roughly one-sixteenth of an inch to the foot, in old Imperial measurement. This produced a series of relatively small images but they were no less powerful for that. To my delight I managed to get all the elevations onto one sheet with the ground and first floor plans on two others. I felt sheepish that, despite metrication having been introduced to the construction industry in England back in 1970, here was I some sixteen

8 *Capomaestri* – the makers of Italian buildings – ensured their detailed designs (usually based on an intimate knowledge of masonry) were carried out correctly by the craftsmen.

9 On the south façade the same artifice is used to acknowledge Trevor Dring, the master stonemason.

10 Most drawings are at either 1/8th of an inch to the foot (1:100) or twice as big at 1:50.

years later, still far more comfortable designing in feet and inches. I could much more easily visualise the spaces I was trying to create using this old and familiar rule. In fact as I write in 2007 I confess that I still draw in Imperial with the help of a conversion scale and I shall continue to do so. Not for me, now or ever, a computer keyboard and screen in place of a friendly soft-nosed pencil and a drawing board to lean on.

Within a couple of days I had put together the whole scheme. I then decided to commission Peter Challen, a talented local watercolour artist, to produce a painting which would show the scheme in context and help me convince the planners and others that at last Bath was to be offered a full-blown piece of classical architecture. And yes, I admit I was intensely proud of what I had designed. I still am!

After putting the finishing touches to the drawings I rang my client. 'I've done it, Peter,' I announced enthusiastically, 'so when you're next in Bath you must come and see me.' I didn't want to send the drawings through the post; I wanted to gauge his reactions when I first unveiled the design.

'Ah, but are you entirely happy with it? If so, I shall be down tomorrow – can't wait.'

I imagine the most difficult moment for any client is when a blank sheet of paper is transformed into a picture. For the architect there is no hiding place. The lines you draw are the lines they see, and you know within seconds if you've got it right. So the following day, in front of an excited client, I laid out my three drawings. Peter looked at them for a space without saying a word. Then he leaned back in his chair and slowly folded his arms behind his head. 'My God,' he muttered, 'wouldn't I just love to build that.' He got up and wandered over to the phone, dialled a number and waited for someone to answer. 'Do you think I could speak to Mr Sparks, the chief planning officer?' he said firmly. A moment later he was put through. 'Ah, Mr Sparks, I'd very much like to come and talk with you about my plans for the Cavendish Lodge site. I know this is rather short notice, but is there any chance that Mr Bertram, my archi- tect, and I could see you this afternoon?' There was a pause. Peter turned to me and slowly raised his thumb. 'Right, three o'clock, that's fine, how

wall to
with badger hole.

HOUSE SET BACK

'Ah, Mr Sparks, I'd very much like to come and talk with you about my plans for the Cavendish Lodge site.'

kind.' He put down the phone. 'Come on William, let's go and celebrate over a bit of lunch.'

After we ordered our meal I decided to inject a bit of realism into the situation in which we might find ourselves later on. 'You know, Peter, I wouldn't expect too much from this afternoon. In my experience there isn't much logic to any planning decision. These guys don't, or very often can't, use what you and I might call common sense. I fear they are bound by other considerations. There are just too many other factors, apart from aesthetics, to be taken into account, and they *certainly* don't talk architecture!'

'You old Jonah, William. Let's wait and see. I can't believe it can be that bad. I reckon Sparks will be knocked out by the scheme. Nobody could ever have foreseen you'd come up with something as good as this!'

Reconnaissance

THE YOUTHFUL LES SPARKS, SITTING IN HIS BRIGHT, BUT FOR A CHIEF planning officer, rather small office overlooking the magnificence of Bath Abbey, listened in silence as I explained what I'd done. When I had finished he looked first at me and then at Peter North. 'Haven't you got a copy of my council's development brief for this site?' he asked, in a way which gave the impression he'd just stubbed his toe.

Peter looked over at me for the answer.

'I have read it, but I'm not sure it's all that helpful in getting a design worthy of this particular site, Les.'

He sighed and placed praying hands to his lips. 'Well, this is certainly one way of dealing with it, but it doesn't happen to be the way our brief thinks it should be done. Anyone who seriously considers putting the principal building in the field is asking for trouble – the Town Plan specifically prohibits it. I do hope I am making myself clear?' Indeed he was, which in its way was helpful. No platitudes, just straight to the point, even if neither Peter or I liked what he was saying.

I simply wasn't prepared to let it rest there. 'Les, I've studied this site very carefully and the only place that you can put a large building, and by any yardstick this one is bound to be fairly big, is on the field; anywhere else and it will detract from the surrounding crescents and houses. You can see that, I hope?'

'Well it's not only me you'll have to convince, but our consultant architect John Darbourne and my planning committee. They will be greatly influenced by the views of The Bath Preservation Trust and The Bath Society to say nothing of The Georgian Group in London, the immediate neighbours and anyone else who feels strongly about it. We are not dealing here with some run-of-the-mill parochial little scheme. This will attract national attention. You have to remember that Bath is now a Unesco World Heritage City and we are all very jealous of that status.' As we got up he shook Peter's hand and rather worryingly added, 'Well I reckon this'll keep us all busy for a couple of years.' How wrong could he be? I rolled up my drawings and we both left. As we strolled back to the office, Peter looked pensive. 'Well, I suppose it's about what

I expected. I think, William, you'd better go and show your designs to the people Mr Sparks[11] mentioned, meantime I'll try and get a steer on what our chances might be at a planning appeal; I really can't see the scheme being approved by this lot.'

Propaganda War

A FEW DAYS LATER I OPENED MY DOOR TO A MAN DEDICATED TO HIS CAUSE, whom I would come to know only too well: one Major Anthony J W Crombie, vice-chairman of The Bath Society. Somehow he'd got wind of my scheme and had come, hot-foot, to see me, representing the views of his conservationist members and a number of architects who practised in and around the city. Crombie, a heavily built man with a shock of dark hair which fell across his large square face, appeared agitated as he entered my conference room on the first floor at number 5 Gay Street where I had laid out all my drawings. He was breathing heavily, due no doubt to the speed he had climbed the stairs. He stood leaning on the table with outstretched arms while I went through the scheme in some detail. I explained the reasoning behind the siting of all the different elements: lodges, garages and driveway, all of which made up the formal setting for the Great House which I'd placed on axis in the middle of his precious field.

When I'd finished he looked decidedly unimpressed. He scribbled something in a little book, wished me good-bye and left as hurriedly as he'd arrived without saying another word. Within 24 hours he had had time to call a meeting of his Society, write a criticism of my design, and send it down to the council with a copy to the *Bath Evening Chronicle*, which duly published a stinging rebuke on my whole approach. This episode taught me a valuable lesson. Never again would I take the diplomatic route of inviting interested parties to discuss my work. Those who are unscrupulous merely look on it as spying-made-easy, and the scrupulous? Well, they tend to listen to the arguments and after a balanced discussion most, but not all, agree. I can handle that.

11 Shortly afterwards Les Sparks left Bath and moved to Birmingham.

Perhaps in hindsight it was a mistake not to go and see my old colleagues at the Preservation Trust, housed in their elegant offices at 1 Royal Crescent.[12] They had made themselves allies of Crombie's and I knew that they were prepared to let him, through The Bath Society, do the initial skirmishing. So I didn't think it would achieve much. What I did do, however, was to arrange a meeting with the residents of Cavendish Crescent who, living so close to the site, would be most affected by what I proposed. If I was going to win this battle, their support would be crucial.

We met under the gentlemanly chairmanship of Tim Kirby.[13] The gathering was held in the Berrys'[14] beautifully proportioned first floor flat, which spread across two houses. The atmosphere was a good deal more cordial than I had any right to expect. It may have been that they already knew that it wasn't a question of 'if' something was going to be built on their doorstep, but 'what'. I was there to tell them that the 'what' was going to be a beautiful, classical, natural-stone building which would neither obstruct their view nor devalue their houses. Mary and Douglas Home, who then lived at number seven, were full of enthusiasm for my design and their support proved contagious. By the end of the evening I had won over most of the residents, so much so that I came away with the reassuring feeling that they would champion my efforts, even in the face of ridicule.

At the end of a week of presentations I met with Peter, who asked me how I was getting on, but without waiting for my reply let me know that he was doing rather well. He sounded upbeat and looked in very good feather. 'I've had a very positive response from Andrew Warner, a friend of mine who's a planning consultant. Wants to meet you, William. God knows why!'

'What does he think?' I said, feeling a little more optimistic.

'He reckons it'll take a bit of time, but your scheme is good enough

12 Given in 1968 to Bath Preservation Trust by Bernard Cayzer of the British and Commonwealth Shipping family who lived in my village of Timsbury south of Bath.

13 Tim Kirby has the enviable distinction of having been Marilyn Monroe's solicitor in England

14 AA Berry of Berry Bros and Rudd Ltd, the world-famous wine merchants.

to win the day.'

'Has he read the council's brief?'

'Yes, he doesn't think much of it either.'

At last somebody with experience was rooting for us. I began to nurse the idea that there might just be a chance we could pull this off. Then came another piece of good news, this time from the architectural correspondent of the *Bath Evening Chronicle.*

'Tim speaking,' said a clear, decisive voice on the end of the line. 'I would very much like to write a piece on your Cavendish Lodge scheme, William. I've just seen the drawings and with a few provisos I like them very much. Perhaps I can persuade the council to support it.' True to his word he then wrote a very enthusiastic article in which he made a flattering comparison between me and the arrogant Mr Wood! I took his article with me when later that week I was asked to go and see Les Sparks again.

Les opened the discussion by telling me that it would make their lives in the planning department very much easier if he could persuade me to change my design to follow the brief a little more closely. 'You do know that in its present form you have no chance at all of getting planning permission? You may not like it, William, but this brief has been the subject of intense debate over many years and isn't something which you can just dismiss out of hand.' He looked down at my plans, brow furrowed. I told him that I really wasn't there to make his or his colleagues' job any easier. I was there to argue, fiercely if necessary, for what I genuinely thought was the proper way to tackle one of the trickiest architectural conundrums in England, let alone Bath.

'Les,' I continued, 'I've canvassed some opinions, with admittedly mixed results; nevertheless on the strength of those discussions I've decided to change not one jot of my design. I still believe that what I am proposing here is right for the site. What's more my client has taken advice in London and is confident that eventually we will win this argument, and if all else fails he is quite prepared to fund an appeal.'

Sparks looked resigned. 'Well it's up to you, William, but remember I have warned you.' He knew that an appeal would divert precious manpower from his overstretched department. And for what? The whole thing to my mind was madness. Here was my client offering a fine classical building to a city made famous by the wealth of its fine classical architecture. You might be forgiven for thinking that Bath would have leapt at the chance. The system I was dealing with appeared to be designed to frustrate and debilitate people like me, by battling such applications to the death. And all this was happening while new buildings of so-called contemporary design and the weakly Georgian were replacing wonderfully elegant, but modest eighteenth- and nineteenth-century buildings that had been approved for *demolition*: destruction condoned by the very men with whom I was dealing. I'd rather hoped that John Betjeman's immortal couplet might have been in their hearts:

> Good-bye to old Bath. We who loved you are sorry
> They've carted you off by developer's lorry

At least I didn't need to knock anything down to make way for my piece.

Those who really cared about such things knew only too well that during the '70s and '80s the architectural canvas of Bath had been allowed to wear thin.[15] I genuinely felt that my building would be a worthy addition to the fine architecture of this great city and might, just might, usher in a more enlightened era. Fine words and fine sentiments indeed. No student of architecture should run away with the idea that building anything worthwhile in such circumstances is easy. Indeed I was about to find out just how difficult it was going to be.

Battle Joined

As news of my design spread through the city so the solicited and unsolicited letters flowed into the planning office. As self-appointed spokesman for The Bath Society Major Crombie had perfected his own unique style of lobbying. All he felt he needed to do was to reiterate criticism from previous newspaper articles – for which he'd been

15 See *The Sack of Bath*, Adam Fergusson.

responsible – to give the impression that there was a far greater weight of objection to my scheme than there really was. On this occasion it was taken to such ludicrous lengths that an incensed Peter Fell, my business partner, sent the *Chronicle* his own satirical fairytale entitled 'The Old Soldier and the Newspaper Chase', a story about the art of 'double grumbling'. It delighted my supporters and I'm glad to say, infuriated my opponents. (See *Appendix*)

The ground on which I decided to fight was well chosen. I felt confident in the scheme I had produced and so on 7 August 1987, just eleven months after that fateful first meeting with Peter North, I lodged the planning application. This produced a barrage of objection from Lord Raglan's Bath Society members and much unnecessarily wounding comment and ill-informed criticism (see *Appendix*). When my plans were eventually laid before the Committee on 9 September 1987 the scheme was unceremoniously chucked out. Only three 'musketeers' spoke up for it including Alderman Alleyne Berry to whom I remain greatly indebted; standing alone is never easy. The architect John Darbourne, a freelance design consultant who advised the city on architectural matters described my Great House as:

> luxurious and overblown ... No matter what you may think of this 'palace of apartments', I think you should stick to the Town Plan. This field should not be built on.

Was there a hint in that statement that secretly he found something admirable in my designs? After all, if the Royal Crescent itself wasn't considered 'luxurious and overblown', when it was first proposed then I didn't know what was. What perhaps Darbourne had conveniently forgotten was that he himself had approved the development brief back in 1986, encouraging potential developers to build those three houses and all the garaging in the field. Now he seemed to be championing the Town Plan which, although still in draft form, called for that same field to remain as open space, free from any form of development. He looked like the joker in a pack of cards who faces both ways. Darbourne's shot across my bows in the planning meeting was followed by another broad-side from Councillor Paul Buckley: 'these plans are far too bulky and ostentatious for this site. We would be the laughing stock if this goes ahead.'

Listening to all this my mind drifted back to John Wood's bitter frustration when in 1727, exactly 260 years earlier, it was his turn to submit plans for Queen Square. He wrote matter-of-factly:

> I thrust a plan for rebuilding the whole town before the Corporation ... My plan was thrown out. They thought proper to treat my schemes as chimerical (a grotesque product of the imagination!).

I was in good company.

When the planning committee's decision to refuse my application was made known, The Bath Society, The Georgian Group and the Bath Preservation Trustees were cock-a-hoop. My client, however, was philosophical. 'I never thought we'd get a fair hearing in Bath – too much emotion – too many galloping majors with nothing better to do than ride their hobbyhorses.' I too was far from downhearted. I took heart from Tim Mowl's encouraging words in an article in *House and Garden*:

> It was never easy to ignore any Bertram design any more than it was possible to ignore John Wood's Queen Square, North side, when it was first set up in palatial self-confidence on the Barton Fields outside the old medieval city. What is certain is that if anyone is to break the mould of the timidly self-effacing sub-classicism which has recently passed for good taste in our most elegant provincial city, William Bertram will be the man.

On 4 April 1988 in the courtly surroundings of Thomas Baldwin's 1778 Guildhall in the shadow of Bath Abbey our appeal got underway. The centrepiece for the occasion was a scale model of the site, which for good measure also included the whole of Cavendish Crescent. Our forces were legally represented by Anthony Dinkin, an experienced planning barrister and a man of cheerful and confident disposition, ably supported by Andrew Warner, who had never wavered from his initial view that eventually we would prevail. Nicholas Pearson, the well-known landscape architect, was there to defend his design for the gardens surrounding my building. And last but not least Mike Jenner, a perceptive architect from Bristol who had ironed out one or two of the details on my southern elevation to give it more poise. (In particular he persuaded me to abandon my small Chinese-inspired, two-pillared portico in favour of the bolder four-columned version that would match the one on the west elevation which faced the road.)

The opposing battalions were led by the solicitor to the council, supported by Major Crombie who still held the brief for both The Bath Society and The Bath City Conservation Group. Steven Parissien, who I remember wore a striking pair of red and white hooped stockings, represented The Georgian Group. My friend Nicholas Pearson remarked that it was impressive to see a man dressed like that who expected to be taken seriously on matters of architectural good taste! The National Trust was represented, so too was English Heritage in the person of Edmund Booth and also the Royal Fine Art Commission. Christopher Pound was primed to shoot me down on behalf of The Bath City Conservation Group, a task which given the choice I don't think he would have accepted had he not been ordered to do so by Les Sparks. Finally the rearguard was amply provided by Brian Barry, the council's planning officer, who was so laid back that to those who didn't know him well occasionally gave a very creditable impression of being asleep! When I looked across at this establishment line-up I have to admit I did, for one brief moment, wonder if God might not, after all, be on their side. But I'm glad to say the feeling passed!

During the appeal there were two particularly memorable moments. I was in the middle of presenting my evidence when I called for the blinds to be lowered and the first of my slides to be projected onto the screen. I had carefully rehearsed what I wanted to say. The picture was a panorama of the city taken in June from the top of Beechen Cliff, a steep hill on the opposite side of the city. Our site was quite clear and I spent some time describing the beauty of the scene. Unable to contain himself any longer Major Crombie leapt to his feet to interrupt me.

'May I respectfully suggest,' he said turning to the Inspector and pushing back a flop of hair from his reddening face, 'that we in The Bath Society whole-heartedly agree with Mr Bertram. This scene is just what we want to preserve – not to have his inappropriate and overblown building ruining it.'

The Inspector listened quietly then turned back to me and asked me to continue with my evidence. Crombie for some unknown reason remained standing, like a snooker player who thinks that the quality of his last shot will ensure that his next turn will not be long coming.

'A timely interjection, if ever there was one,' I retorted rather pompously, 'for what you are looking at, Mr Inspector, is a photograph on which the building that Major Crombie refers to has already been superimposed.'

Crombie exploded. 'Where, show me where?'

So I brought up the next slide of the very same view, but without my building, then flicked back to the original picture for comparison and pointed out where my chimneys showed just above the trees. Crombie decided to sit down.

'Mr Bertram, is that really all you will see of your new building?' asked Mr MacDonald, the Inspector, patiently. I assured him that it was indeed all one would see when the trees were in leaf and I admitted that I had cheated a bit by raising the chimneys so that they could be seen at all!

The second occasion concerned the building itself. It is not easy for a barrister to cross-examine another professional on their own particular subject. Not surprisingly the lawyer tends to know rather less about it than the expert. It is also natural to feel uneasy in the witness box, but on this occasion when it came to my turn to be cross-examined, I felt pretty confident. Usually a lawyer will ask the architect which parts of his scheme have been changed, and why did he now defend so steadfastly a design that was already compromised. The only changes I had ever made to my building were of my own choosing; not ones which I thought might commend themselves to the city planners. My inquisitor knew this and therefore needed to adopt a rather different line of attack. So he launched a withering assault on my overall ability as an architect and the inappropriateness of the architectural language I had chosen to use.

'I would like you to listen very carefully, Mr Bertram, to the following passage,' and with head down he read out an involved description of how a building should be designed; what relationship wings should have to the main body of the composition, even down to the size of the windows themselves. 'I have looked at your so-called piece of architecture, Mr Bertram, with these principles very much in mind, and I ask you now, are each of your wings indeed one quarter of the length of the whole façade as is set down with such clarity here?' To emphasise the point he waved his papers theatrically above his head.

'I don't really know, sir. I haven't measured them. Anyway it's not the way I go about things. I tend to use my eye which I may say, hasn't failed me yet.'

'Well, there's always a first time for everything,' he intoned looking down again at his notes for the next question. 'Now I'd like your reaction to this. Do your ascending windows follow the traditional rule that each one should diminish in size both in width and in height and be centred one above the other so as to strengthen the proportion of the elevations?'

'I'm not sure I quite understand the question, sir, but clearly they do *not*.' I then leaned conspiratorially towards him from my witness chair, 'but tell me, what has all this got to do with the height of St Paul's?'

He ignored my flippant remark and continued in a steady voice. 'Then I take it from your answer, Mr Bertram, that you are ignorant of the author. I find this most surprising in a man ...' and he turned to address the Inspector for added effect ... 'in a man who sets himself up as an *expert* on the fundamentals of classical architecture.'

'Go on then, tell me.'

'None other than the great Michelangelo himself, Mr Bertram. You have heard of him, I take it? Not someone whose views can lightly be ignored, I suggest.'

'Of course I've heard of Michelangelo. Bully for him, but why on earth should I be criticised by you for not following his examples when it is I who have been asked to design this scheme, not Michelangelo. If it suits me to proportion my building as I have that surely is good enough. I doubt if you, sir, would appreciate me telling you how to put a legal argument, and by the same token I don't see why I should be told how to design by you, Mister Angelo or anyone else for that matter. To those listening this may sound a trifle arrogant, but I'm afraid it's the way I do things.'

'Yes,' he said, stretching to breaking point that single syllable. Then he snapped his file closed, looked up at the inspector and informed him there would be no more questions!

In his report Mr MacDonald the inspector, an architect in his own right, commented on my building in the following terms:

> The design has been criticised for being incorrect within the grammar of classical design or, at least, idiosyncratic in its use of classical elements. The architect has certainly used elements of the classical vocabulary in a free, and in some respects, non-traditional way, but the resulting building is not unpleasing nor out of character with its setting. The proposed building would be appropriate to its site and setting. It represents a successful attempt to design in harmony with classical principles, but without slavish adherence to precedent.'

Pyrrhic Victory

TO THE ASTONISHMENT OF CITY COUNCILLORS, THE PLANNING DEPARTMENT, not to mention The Bath Society, it happened that on 30 November 1988 I received the welcome news that my scheme had passed muster with Nicholas Ridley,[16] Secretary of State for the Environment and the government minister directly involved. The reaction to the announcement from the chairman of the planning committee, Martin Hemmings,

16 I like to think that the decision to approve the Cavendish Lodge scheme may have had something to do with the fact that Nicholas Ridley was Sir Edwin Lutyens's grandson!

was typical of many: 'I am almost speechless. I condemn the decision in the strongest possible terms.'

His astonishment was fuelled by the apparent success of Major Crombie and his cohorts who only a month or two earlier had successfully persuaded the Local Plan inspector to exclude the field from any development whatsoever and to formally have it designated as open space. All this had been going on while our own Inspector was formulating his approval of the fiercely argued aesthetic points which surfaced during our long and testing appeal.

Peter North who had been sitting shoulder to shoulder with us in the trenches was of course delighted by the news. Andrew Warner commented that he wasn't in the least bit surprised by the verdict. He thought the scheme '…was of exceptionally high quality in terms of design and its use of materials, and was one of the best he had ever seen.'

However our euphoria was to be short-lived. Those in The Bath Society, encouraged by a favourable opinion from their barrister, were determined to carry on. And so just before Christmas, while festive lights twinkled their goodwill message down the length of Milsom Street, Major Crombie and his foot soldiers were not engaged in writing their Christmas cards, as one might have hoped, but preparing their High Court case. Indeed they had already unsuccessfully tried to persuade Bath City Council to take up the cudgels and fight on, but when Crombie found that they had neither stomach nor ratepayers' cash for continuing the struggle, he decided to ride once more to battle bearing the standard behind which objectors could rally. Between Boxing Day and 1 January 1989 he applied for Judicial Review to the High Court in the hope that Mr Ridley's recent decision to approve the scheme might be quashed.

Outflanked

THE BASIS FOR THE BATH SOCIETY'S LEGAL CHALLENGE WAS WELL-FOUNDED. Whilst we had all been concentrating on the merits and disadvantages of building in the field and studying the quality or lack of it of my Grand

House, there had been an interesting development in the way planning applications for new development in the United Kingdom would thereafter be assessed, particularly in conservation areas. Two redoubtable ladies, Professor Hannah Steinberg and Dr Elizabeth Sykes, had successfully argued in the High Court that preserving could also be interpreted as not harming a situation. Although this lowered the bar over which we had to leap this important aspect also needed to have been properly considered by the Inspector. Lord Justice Stocker in his later judgement in the Court of Appeal put it even more strongly: 'the special attention which the inspector is bound to give is of particular importance where the site concerned is of such universal value that protecting [it] is the concern of all mankind'. By coincidence this clarification of the law occurred between the end of our hearing and Mr MacDonald writing his conclusions. Having looked carefully at the reasons given for approval in our own case, neither we, nor more importantly Crombie, could find any specific mention of the word preserve. It was to be that omission which gave heart to the battle-cry of my opponents. But to our surprise and pleasure the Judicial Review failed to recommend the overturning of the original appeal and Mr Justice Hutchinson proceeded to confirm the safety of our Planning Consent.

We rather hoped that this set-back would bring an end to our battles, but the decision only served to strengthen the resolve of our opponents. The fight was now driven forward under the spirited leadership of a new Chief of Staff, Lord Raglan[17] himself, the chairman of The Bath Society. By his side, as ever, was the now battle-hardened Crombie who had lately been awarded an MBE for protecting Bath against marauding architects. This ratcheting up of the stakes was a dismal prospect for all concerned. Our costs were covered, to some extent, by having the Secretary of State as our ally. However, Peter North could ill-afford the time and uncertainty that this fresh attack brought with it. Our two opponents, with no formal legal support or training, successfully argued in the Court of Appeal against John Laws,[18] representing the Secretary of State, that the

17 Lord Raglan's great-great-great-grandfather, Fitzroy James Henry Somerset, lost an arm in 1815 fighting alongside the Duke of Wellington at Waterloo. If I was up against the big guns, then so now was he, just like his celebrated forebear.

18 Now Lord Justice Laws.

'first hearing' (the appeal) should be set aside and that a new inspector should be appointed to hear the whole case afresh.

I sat in the Royal Courts of Justice in the Strand throughout the case to test the strength of the arguments levelled against us. I had to admit Tony Crombie put up a particularly stout performance. If he and Raglan had been a couple of hickory-shafted golf clubs (a rather apt analogy) they might well have been described as 'rustless and polished'. Lord Glidewell agreed with Major Crombie's submission that the appeal inspector, Mr MacDonald, 'fell into error' (I *do* so enjoy those legal pleasantries!) in making a false comparison between the effect of my proposed building constructed on the field and that of a similar one constructed in the garden. The fact that any self-respecting architect would never have designed a similar building if it was to be sited in the garden had played no part in their Lordships' deliberations. Buildings are specifically designed for the place they are to be built, particularly so in this of all cases; other alternatives, I suggest, have little relevance.

Sadly the whole matter was referred back to Nicholas Ridley's successor Michael Heseltine for yet another round of argument and confrontation. This marathon was becoming not so much a planning application as a crippling test of stamina and patience.

Casualties

MY PHONE RANG. IT WAS PETER NORTH. 'HELLO,' I SAID WEARILY, 'SAD ABOUT the Court of Appeal; really dreadful news.'

'That, William, my dear friend, is but one of my sadnesses.' His voice sounded flat and dispirited. 'I'm afraid I simply can't go on. The rest of my business has taken a hit and I have no option but to throw in the towel.'

'I hope to God that all this Cavendish nonsense hasn't been the prime cause?' I knew only too well that it probably had. But Peter was a proud man and even if it was so, he would never have admitted it.

'I'm afraid I'm going to have to sell the site,' he murmured. 'I'll be asking about four hundred grand for the three acres, but of course I may not get it in this depressed market, particularly with the uncertainty of the new appeal – if it even happens.' He sounded terribly depressed. I wanted to pick him up and give him a hug. Instead we arranged to have lunch together in London where we could drown our sorrows over a glass of good claret, and forget the whole sorry business.

Matters were not improved when I heard of the untimely resignation of my champion, Tim Mowl. In February 1991 he announced that he had decided to leave his post as architectural correspondent on the *Bath Chronicle*: 'Sometimes, resignation is the only course.' (See *Appendix*).

He had been a fierce advocate of my scheme throughout the campaign, and had remained steadfast. Unfortunately his views were not the views that some of the good folk of Bath wished to read. And that wasn't the end of it. Unable to reconcile his obligations to both architecture and the City of Bath and unable to accommodate the defiant stance being asked of him by The Georgian Group, Tim resigned his role as spokesman on behalf of that august body too.

The Second Front

RELAXED IN THE KNOWLEDGE OF MY DEFEAT AT THE HANDS OF THEIR LORDS' Justice, Major Anthony Crombie was sitting happily in his tent with Lord Raglan and Peter Woodward of Bath Preservation Trust toasting their recent victory and carousing with local well-wishers. Unbeknown to them, however, I was busily gathering my troops to fight on. My cause was much strengthened by two matters: interest from the Prince of Wales; and my successful approach to Andrew Brownsword, a wealthy entrepreneur then living in the Royal Crescent, who I knew was prepared to take a risk. I suggested he might like to buy the site and mount a second appeal; a tall order and one which I had no right to expect him to seriously consider, but one I sincerely hoped he might entertain for it seemed to be the only hope.

He approached the proposition with a degree of caution, but encour-

---

19 Ken Biggs was and is a well known West of England contractor and by then specialised in conservation work.

aged by his wise friend, Ken Biggs,[19] Brownsword not only purchased the site in partnership with Bath solicitor Jonathan Wyld, but also took on my designs. The new owners embraced with enthusiasm the job of administering the *coups de grace*. Andrew Warner was re-engaged as the planning guru who, in turn, recommended Adrian Trevelyan Thomas, a charming and able barrister, to argue our case anew.

And so in the middle week of May 1992 the second hearing began. This time an enlarged scale model took centre stage. This brought in both the rising ground of High Common, opposite the site to the west, and the end of Lansdown Crescent which is well above and behind the site to the east. It was a question of *déja vu* for most of us. We had been through the whole performance twice before and knew all the arguments by heart. While I listened to the ebb and flow of evidence it gave me time to reflect on sketches for the treehouse which Prince Charles had asked me to design at Highgrove as a birthday present for his two young sons, Prince William and Prince Harry, which I had done at the first enquiry (See *Win Some, Lose Some*). At least I felt I was being productive, while the same tedious arguments were dusted off.

In his masterful summing up Trevelyan Thomas pointed out that it seemed perverse that Bath City Council had chosen formally to adopt a Local Town Plan in the June of 1990 which cast the Cavendish Lodge field as 'open space' when there had been a full-blown Planning Consent in existence for my scheme, for at least 18 months, since November 1988. As Adrian delivered those words I was watching Tony Crombie and saw the blood drain from his face. At that moment I realised the balance of argument had at last shifted decisively away from my opponents. But would the scales tip far enough in our direction to *win* this battle? The long wait for that final decision would be the ultimate test of my patience.

When the planning inspector closed his file at the end of the hearing and asked to see the site I knew, or thought I knew, victory was in sight. Amongst the long grass and cow parsley which enveloped the site four of my staff (Clare Bertram, my elder daughter, Mark Watson, Ted Brewster and John Daniels) had been busy cutting a clearing and carefully staking out in red and white plastic tape the line of the perimeter walls of the house. It is true that the footprint alone of a building tends to look smaller than you imagine it will. But this one looked big! I realised it would need a man of considerable vision to accept the loss of what was seen by some as an Elysian field, with a glorious southern aspect, butterflies and wild flowers. In that evening's paper there appeared a photograph of Major Crombie, Cherrill Copperwheat, Bath City's tree expert, and the inspector lost in the deep undergrowth while inspecting the ground.

Final Victory

WE HAD TO WAIT UNTIL 28 DECEMBER 1993, A FULL YEAR AFTER THE SECOND appeal was heard, for the decision to be handed down. I was delighted and relieved when it was finally acknowledged that my Grand House, with all its outbuildings, would indeed 'preserve' this sensitive part of Bath. I fancied I could hear the trumpet calls of victory echoing round the hills of Bath. Thus our case was entered into legal history with my old rival Anthony Crombie up there in lights but unable to enjoy the moment for which he had campaigned so hard and so long.

I was inundated with messages of goodwill particularly from those who lived in Cavendish Crescent. Well, I thought, if those were indeed their sentiments, if John Heath and his friends Douglas and Mary Home really did want my building, then it was high time to start digging the foundations and ordering in the stone before some little varmint decided to redraw the battle lines.

For the time being, however, all was quiet. I knew my opponents would have dearly liked to counter-attack through to the House of Lords but their guns had been spiked by the Law Lords, who had refused leave to appeal on the first hearing and would most likely still have resisted any such move. With relief I learned that Crombie had reluctantly decided to make a strategic withdrawal and retire 'hurt'. He would not, however, go quietly.

Small print in legal documents often throws up surprises and the conditions which were attached to this second approval had a sting in the tail. A fresh obstacle, which would all but bring me down, had been placed in my path. The city council had been given the power to approve or reject the detailed drawings of my design, and particularly my use of different types of stone, a fundamental part of the design. In general this would work against me, but on one crucial occasion, I am relieved to say, it came to my rescue.

Nothing in the short term mattered if Andrew Brownsword decided to sit on the approval and do nothing. But he was soon approached by Berkeley Homes who had gained a fine reputation for taking on such projects and doing them well. Negotiations were successful and on 9 June 1995 ownership passed from Andrew and his co-owner Jonathan Wyld to Beaufort Homes[20] with one important proviso:

> 'no buildings will be erected on the ... property ... other than those which have external elevations and site layout which are substantially the same as the buildings and site layout on the plans prepared by William Bertram and Fell which resulted in the consent (but excluding details of external materials contained in such plans ... to be agreed with Local Planning Authority in accordance with the consent).

It was that exclusion which would come to haunt me.

Allies

SHORTLY AFTER BEAUFORT TOOK POSSESSION I WAS ASKED BY THE NEW OWNERS if my firm would bid for preparing the drawings from which they could build. Knowing only too well the substantial amount of work involved in doing the job properly we put up what we thought was a realistic figure. Unfortunately this turned out to be about twice the sum of the Bristol firm of architects, Britten Hadley. So to my great concern that firm was duly appointed and soon set about converting my precious plans into their working drawings.

20 A subsidiary of Berkeley Homes.

Had I now lost control of my design? Well, not quite. A couple of months later a bundle of drawings from Hadley's dropped onto Angus Astley's desk at the planning office. Gus, the city's conservation officer, had been asked by Les Sparks to look after the Cavendish Lodge file and do what he could to curb my 'excesses'. In a covering letter Britten Hadley had asked Gus to approve *their* details of stonework, against those of my original designs. Gus took one look at them and rang me.

'William, have you seen what they've done to Cavendish?' he asked somewhat melodramatically, 'if not, then please do come down and take a look.' So I dropped everything and within ten minutes I was standing in his office poring over the drawings. What I saw disturbed me. I rolled up one set and tucking it firmly under my arm, looked Gus straight in the eye, 'I think I know what I have to do.' With hands thrust deep into my pockets and head down I walked slowly back to 5 Gay Street cursing beneath my breath. I was frustrated that the system tolerated another architect picking up my scheme, particularly *this* one with its long and bitter history, to work up his own details without sufficient under-standing of the thought and knowledge that had gone into the original design. It didn't seem right then, it still doesn't feel right now, and it's no way to achieve worthwhile pieces of architecture.

I began the task of bringing the design back from oblivion by enlarging to full size, Hadley's 1/5th-scale stone details which had just been sent to Astley. Cornices, which had been drawn to this smaller scale, suddenly took on their full weight and bulk. Projections in some cases had been drawn at three feet, nearly three times what I had shown. I then set about designing in freehand the much daintier sizes that they should have been. On 10 September 1995 I rang Ian Thomas, my contact at Beaufort Homes and told him that I'd seen the Britten Hadley draw-ings and had a few ideas on how he and his co-directors could save about a quarter of a million pounds in construction cost. I thought that would make him sit up and by Jiminy it did! I showed Thomas and his colleagues how important it was that all the stone sizes should exactly match the much smaller ones on my original drawings. We agreed a fee for the work and I immediately set about preparing full-size sections for all the cut stone. I soon realised that to get this right wasn't quite as easy as I'd first thought. The tendency when designing at full size is to under-scale the stone when you sketch it on the drawing board. It always looks too big. Sir Christopher Wren had a similar problem at St Paul's Cathedral. Anxious to get the grapes in the garland frieze in proportion he sent one of the men up the timber scaffolding to the appropriate level. He was instructed by the great man to blow into a pig's bladder until it was considered the right size. Only then was Wren, who remained at ground level, content to let the masons carve the fruit. So I decided the only way was to take my original 1/16th scale drawings (1:200) and with the help of a pair of old-fashioned dividers systematically transpose the size of every moulding, every column, every cornice and every window and doorcase into full-size drawings. Demanding though this was I resisted the temptation to modify any of the stones in the process. This way I knew that the finished building must look exactly like my original design drawing. (And it did!)

There were other important lessons to be learnt. The Britten Hadley drawings showed half-columns (in plan) to the porticos. If they had been built to that design there would have been no shadow-line and the columns would have appeared two-dimensional. What the great *capo-maestri* knew was that in such a situation a three-quarter engaged column allowed the curvature of the shaft to be fully appreciated and gave the façade vivid three-dimensional impact. To their credit Beaufort were most understanding. Their only concern was that the final design should be right, especially as they hoped to persuade me to get His Royal Highness to open the place! This however was something that I was continually being asked, and one which I was never prepared to pursue.

I introduced another little quirk into the design: a gentle sweep to the bottom corners of the pediments on both the main house and the lodges. I had always been unhappy with the traditional mitred end to the 's'-shaped moulding on the top of a cornice. To my eye it invariably looked out of proportion and a bit clipped. So on this occasion I gave it a gentle upward tilt, a bit like the ends of a handle-bar moustache. It certainly brings a sprightliness to the detail even though the purist might take issue and the general public neither notice nor care!

Advance

THE FIRST SOD OF THE NEW CAVENDISH LODGE WAS TURNED IN THE AUTUMN of 1996, ten years to the month from that first meeting with my old friend, Peter North. He rang me when he knew things were on the move. I could hear in his voice how excited he was, for it was still his baby. After all that had happened we were now at last on the home run. When next he visited Bath we had a leisurely lunch together at Woods, a restaurant opposite the Assembly Rooms, and afterwards wandered up to the site via the Circus, Margaret's Buildings and St James's Square. Just as we were approaching I noticed one of the workmen painting a little white mark on the top of the metal railings opposite the entrance to the site. He was being very careful about it and when he saw me watching him he waved.

'Thought you might like to see this Mr Bertram. I'm just about to put a little pencil line on this white paint and that will be used to centre up for the whole shooting match.' He looked up and winked. He knew the significance to both of us.

Wallis Western, the main contractors, under the inspirational leadership of Chris, pushed the job along very quickly. The natural springs which issued from the high banks in the garden were harnessed, and a major sewer which ran diagonally across the site was successfully rerouted allowing the foundations of the big house to be laid on time. Nothing, it seemed, would be allowed to hold up the builders or delay the work and before you could say 'Majorgrumble' the two little lodges next to Cavendish Road were nearing completion. The developers had sensibly decided to use them as exemplars in miniature for the more formidable work to come. Trevor Dring, a genius with limestone and a fine carver in his own right, was commissioned to provide and fix all the freestone. He employed most of his extended family, including his father, all of whom have stone craftsmanship in their blood. Each little nuance of my full-scale drawings was painstakingly created and the drystone walling was perfectly laid by Bob Powel and his troops. The enormity of their task didn't seem to worry them at all. It would certainly have fazed me! As it unfolded, the overall effect was magical. At least I thought so, but some folk had other ideas!

Rearguard Action

WRITING IN THE *CHRONICLE* UNDER THE HEADLINE 'FOR BETTER, OR WORSE' just after Christmas 1996 my old sparring Peter Woodward of The Bath Preservation Trust wrote: 'Finally perhaps neither for better nor worse, but certainly for richer, is the startling growth into reality of the new Cavendish Lodge, the culmination of decades of bickering. I would not dare to comment.'

How wise!

In December of that year Peter and Barbara Arnould took the bold step of buying the southern lodge. They were the first to move in, possibly because theirs was the only building that was finished! They didn't seem to mind that for the next year they would be acting as un-official custodians of the site while the contractors and landscapers finished their work. In fact they counted it a privilege to be living in this particular spot and watching the Big House, as they liked to call it, take shape. So you can understand their indignation when out of the blue a photographer and a certain Major Crombie, accompanied by Kenneth Powell, a greatly respected architectural critic, arrived unannounced on their doorstep. A photograph was taken of the Major posing with arms akimbo and looking smug right beside their much loved little home. An article appeared in the *Daily Telegraph* on 11 January 1997 (see *Appendix*) which carried in its headline Crombie's description of my lodges as 'a bizarre pair of semi-bungalows'.

'We are hopping mad about it. The setting has been wrecked and it's opened the door for more developers to invade Bath.'
I idly wondered who Crombie thought would be building in Bath if it

wasn't to be developers. After all they were the ones who, for 250 years, had created the very buildings he cherished.

Before going to press Ken Powell did allow me the opportunity to comment on the views he was about to express publicly. I confirmed that my scheme was not 'progressive' as the modernists would have it. I agreed with him that it could indeed be described as 'regressive' and, no, I wasn't in the least bit ashamed of that. I suggested that in a few years time, when it was finished, this great house would fade into the landscape and nobody would remember what all the fuss was about. He thought I was being optimistic! He finished his piece: 'For some, the development will always be a blot on the landscape. For others its 'regressive' style may suggest that Bath has simply lost its nerve.'

These sorts of comment didn't bother me but Peter Arnould was having none of it. He was furious, and fired back under the banner head-line 'Lodge is not an architectural monster' (see *Appendix*).

The gloves were being unlaced even before my building was finished. Then it was a free-for-all for anyone who wanted to join in the fun.

I was genuinely delighted by this attention. To have one's work crit-icised is a little hurtful but paradoxically it is also rather invigorating. To have one's work ignored, however, is *death*. My feelings could be summed up by Winston Churchill who once commented, 'I do not at all resent criticism, even when, for the sake of emphasis, it for a time parts company with reality!' But I fear Peter and Barbara Arnould were not so relaxed and not much amused.

Looking back I believe I was lucky that Beaufort Homes gave me the opportunity *and* authority to influence at least the *outside* of my building. No matter that what appeared to be my noble front door giving onto the balustraded belvedere was in reality only a side entrance. I am sure Palladio would have understood the artifice. In his Villa Barbaro the front door was not on the central axis but tucked away to one side behind the arcade. My dear friend Theo Williams[21] was not impressed. However I was not so fortunate with the inside. My original plan was to

---

21 Theo Williams (quantity surveyor extraordinaire) had in November 1995 sent me a charming hand-written letter warning me of the dangers of adopting some of the design shortcomings of John Wood the Elder!

create apartments with large drawing rooms, open fires and two good-sized bedrooms. This created a sense of space and some degree of sophistication. To my great sadness the selling agents, who shall remain nameless, advised the developers that three bedrooms would sell better than two. Unfortunately the Beaufort Homes people accepted that advice and the extra bedrooms were squeezed into the unchanged footprint of the building to the detriment of my fine spaces. Moreover during those ten long years of conflict the whole economy of the UK had changed. People were becoming better-off under the New Labour Government. Had I been asked to design the house in '97 rather then '86 when I first put pencil to paper I might have suggested combining two flats into one and giving each the benefit of two garages. By that time there were many who could easily have afforded three-quarters of a million pounds for a luxurious flat in a fine building in one of the world's most beautiful cities.

I have to confess that the damage to the interiors was not my only sadness. Gus Astley,[22] who hitherto had been so supportive, decided it was time to start curbing what he mistakenly saw as my wilfulness. At a moment when the main house had barely risen out of the ground he asked if he could come and see me. He opened up the plans of my original 1987 scheme, the ones that had not changed one jot in all those turbulent years. 'I rather thought,' he said diffidently, 'that the way you have shown those fine recessed ashlar panels on the north elevation might be introduced to advantage on the south side.'

My heart sank.

'Gus, my dear fellow, those stone panels are huge. They are thirteen feet wide and twenty feet high. I created them as a powerful element in the design of the north side where the elevation doesn't have much going for it. All the drystone walling which I show on the south elevation must be kept, except of course for the portico which I show in cut Bath stone. If you introduce these panels on either side of the pediment the eye will be drawn away from the focal point and will destroy the simplicity of the whole façade.'

22 Gus Astley died in 2003. I greatly miss his enthusiasm, knowledge, skills and friendship.

'Well William, let me put it this way – I hope you'll agree that I've given you all the help I could reasonably be expected to give. I really don't think this modest request should be allowed to spoil our relationship.'

'No, nor do I, but I also feel very strongly, Gus, that my original design should be allowed to stand. As you well know I've fought for over a decade to keep it intact. It's simply unreasonable for you to ask me to change it now.'

'I don't think you have quite grasped the significance of what I'm saying, William. I cannot, and will not approve the use of drystone walling in the positions you've shown on the southern elevation. I insist on the incorporation of those ashlar panels. I'm prepared, I'm afraid, to refuse your present application for the 'approval of details'. If you don't agree to this then the refusal will extend to all those full-size details you've already done; even though I would regret that.'

'What can I do to convince you?' I pleaded, recalling only too clearly the conditions of the planning approval which gave him the final say. 'You've been got at, Gus – I know you have. Please do not ask me to do this.'

'No, William, I've not been influenced by anything or anyone. This is my own opinion. I've thought long and hard and my decision is in the best interest of the building. And besides you have no options. You either agree or we're back to square one and another appeal!'

'You're joking?' But he wasn't. 'You say, Gus, you have the best interests of the building at heart. This piece was conceived by me – surely I should be allowed to determine such things?'

Any observer will see if they care to look that I capitulated.[23] To my mind the two panels do diminish the impact of the portico, just as I said they would. 'I told you so' isn't much comfort especially when it could so easily have been done right in the first place. But Gus was a charming man and he held his views just as forcefully as I held mine. The only difference this time was that he held the whip hand. Perhaps the thought of another couple of years of argument inside a courtroom didn't bother

23 The view of the south façade has been much compromised by the planting of a fir tree in the centre of the circular lawn. It should be removed and the grass restored to its former simplicity.

him, but for my part I had seen quite enough of them and he knew it. Maybe for posterity I should have insisted on another morse-coded message, this time being carved into those very same panels: 'Just look at the original designs!'

Parting Shots

Twelve years on in 2008, as I tell this story, the Big House is maturing. Those in Cavendish Crescent have not lost their views nor has the value of their homes declined – quite the contrary. Forty years of uncertainty for them is at an end; Cavendish is here to stay. Coachloads of English, Japanese and French tourists stop opposite the gates and take photographs. The Arnoulds live in their little lodgehouse and still love it. As you might expect, some are for the scheme, others passionately against it (see *Appendix*).

I had perhaps underestimated just how long the memories would last and how entrenched my opponents would become. At lunch in November 2006, a decade after I'd completed the scheme, I met for the first time Jacques and Frances Beney who had lived for two and a half years in the top lodge. Sometime ago they invited a friend and his wife to visit them. He had been employed in the planning department of the city council during the time of my troubles. Over a good-natured meal Jacques happened to mention how much they both enjoyed living there and how well they thought Cavendish Lodge as a whole fitted in. So incensed by this remark was their guest that he nearly choked. 'Absolutely wrong,' he said vehemently, 'Ghastly pastiche, we did everything we could to stop it. Should never have been allowed.'

Frances was taken aback. 'But people are astonished when we tell them it's only ten years old. Tell me, what would you have done instead?' But on that matter he chose, like so many of my critics, to remain silent!

For those of you who feel fit enough and are so inclined, try walking up the long, slow hill to Cavendish, preferably at midday when the sun shines obliquely across the tweedy texture of the fine Cotswold stone walls, or perhaps in the evening when the buildings blush a shade of pink as they reflect the setting sun. Ponder this tale of bloody intrigue, and whether this battle was worth the fight. Who knows, on still autumn days you might even catch the whiff of cordite:

> A damned nice thing – the nearest run thing you ever saw
> in your life ... By God, I don't think it would have done if I
> had not been [there].[24]

24 The Duke of Wellington after the Battle of Waterloo, 18 June 1815.

Win Some – Lose Some

THERE ON MY DESK WAS AN UNOPENED LETTER. THE ENVELOPE BORE THE marks of royalty, white with EIIR in a round stamp and crossed with blue pencil from side to side and from top to bottom. It wasn't the first letter I had received from Buckingham Palace and it certainly wouldn't be the last.

I sat down on my studio sofa and slit it open. I pressed the ends together and with two fingers drew out the little square envelope enclosing two small white sheets. It was hand-written and signed by Prince Charles and dated 4 April 1988. Would I very kindly design for the two princes a treehouse at Highgrove as combined birthday presents? He mentioned that he had identified an old holly tree amongst a number of others in his new arboretum; it was large enough and would, he thought be suitable for any structure I might think of. Two days later I wrote back to His Royal Highness and suggested, perhaps rather cheekily, that as this was for the boys then he might allow me to inter-view Prince William to find out what it was he had in mind. I knew his elder son was a formidable young man from an encounter a year earlier when he was but five years old.

It was in 1987, after I had completed my work on the Highgrove 'beehives', the little pavilions either side of the drawing room terrace, that Prince Charles very kindly invited me to his Christmas drinks party to celebrate the completion of all the works he had undertaken in and around the house. In those days, before Charles Morris had designed the Orchard Room (some distance from the house), entertaining was a much more informal and intimate affair. Fires were burning in both the study and drawing room. A large and beautifully decorated Christmas

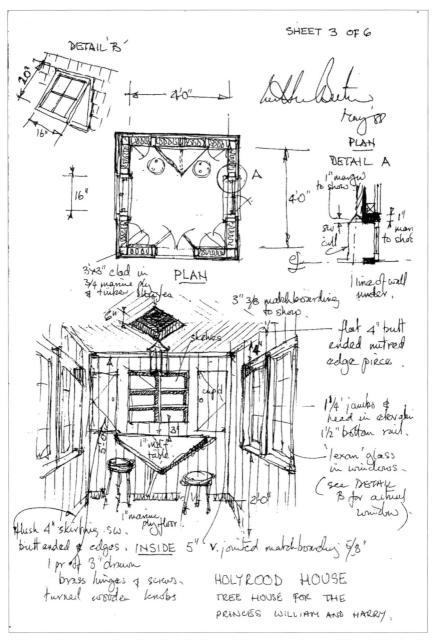

'I want it to be as high as possible so I can get away from everyone.'
One of my sketches for Hollyrood House

tree stood proudly in the hall and antique tables groaned with familiar family photographs. Both Prince Charles and the Princess of Wales were our hosts. She was dressed all in black with pearl earrings and pearl necklace. She looked as pretty and as statuesque as I had imagined although a good deal taller than I expected. There were some 50 people at the party including Felix Kelly, the artist responsible for the oil painting that had persuaded the Prince to embellish the façades of the house. This work had been put in hand for His Royal Highness by the architect Peter Falconer. There too were the young princes, well past their bedtime, wearing pyjamas and dressing gowns. They were earning their spurs by handing round plates of nibbles to the guests with varying success. As the elder of the two approached me I suggested he might like a breather so we sat down on a nearby sofa to have a chat. He got himself comfortable with his little legs sticking out in front of him, then, looking down into his half-full plate of sausages he asked. 'Who are you, Sir?'

'I'm the architect,' I told him, 'who designed those two little buildings just outside on the terrace.' I explained that there was one for him and one for his brother Harry, and if he looked inside he'd find that I had carved a little buzzy bee into the stone of the window cills.

'What was that for?' he asked.

'Well, that is how I sometimes sign my buildings. You see my name too, is William, just like yours, and the bee stands for the first letter of my surname, Bertram.'

Looking straight at me and fixing me with a knowing eye he announced in a very small high-pitched voice, 'And my name, Mr Bertram, is Prince William,' and proceeded to draw his little frame up to its full sitting height.

'And I am delighted to have met you, sir,' I said thinking to myself that reading fairy stories about kings and princes, frogs and princesses to this young man must indeed be an extraordinary experience.

At 9.30 on 18 April 1988, a year after that meeting, I arrived at the back door of Highgrove. His Royal Highness was already dressed in his shooting jacket and was encouraging those in his house party to put on their gumboots for the trek over to the wood. There stood his son and heir, and two of (Sir) David Frost's children who happened to be staying the night. Together we all tramped over the lawn to the arboretum. As we reached it Prince Charles stopped and pointed out a majestic, 35 foot-high holly tree. 'That's the one I thought we would use, Willie.' He then turned to his son. 'Now, Wills, Mr Bertram has come all the way from Bath to see you to find out what you would like. He's the person I've asked to help us with the design of your treehouse.'

Prince William thought for a moment, his fair head cocked to one side 'I want it to be as high as possible so I can get away from everyone and I want a rope ladder which I can pull up so no one can get at me,' he said all in one breath. There followed a long silence which I broke only to ask if that was it. Prince Charles looked at me and back at William, who, feeling that something more was required said, 'Can I go now and see the ponies Papa?' And with that the interview appeared to be at an end. Then off he went with his chums to the stables.

The Prince turned back to me, 'I'm afraid it's all down to you now, Willie. I'll be interested to see what you make of it. I think we should have a proper ladder as well as his rope, don't you, just to be on the safe side?'

Such commissions are a joy. Not so much because of who the client was in this case although that was a lot of fun, but because the scale of the problem is one that you can easily hold in your mind's eye. It was some days later that I happened on the idea of calling the little structure 'Hollyrood House'. That immediately gave me the key for all the many decisions I needed to make to bring this little folly to life.

I made my first sketches while I was reclining under the feathery canopy of an acer tree in the charming and peaceful garden created by my good friends Anton and Sue Young at Ridleys Cheer. I completed the sketches some time later while I was waiting to take the witness-stand at the public inquiry into my controversial scheme for Cavendish Lodge in Bath. This may seem odd to the uninitiated but any designer will tell you that there is no occasion so important as to inhibit a sketch. I've even used the back of a funeral service sheet to develop an idea! As I sat on those hard benches in the Guildhall debating chamber, I finessed my

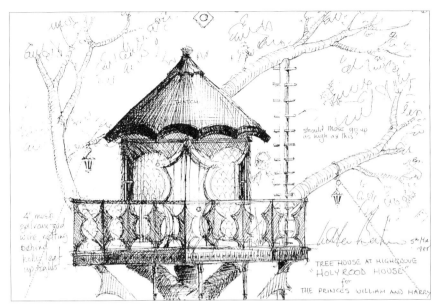

The treehouse, I explained, would be a long way up in the branches and there would be a pole with sticks in it so Prince Harry could climb up to it

design for the shape of the holly leaf which I would then use for the railings around the platform on which the little building sat, the scalloped eaves-line of the thatched roof and for the front door. By the time it came to give my evidence in front of the Inspector those drawings were more or less finished and quite detailed enough to be sent to Kensington Palace for royal approval, which I received by letter in August 1987. Unaltered, they were subsequently published in *The Garden at Highgrove*.[1]

Some time later, after we had carefully priced the work involved, His Royal Highness 'pressed the button', giving me and the team just enough time to complete the treehouse by 21 June 1989, Prince William's seventh birthday.

Shortly after we started it was reported that Prince Harry, the poor fellow, had to go into hospital for an operation, so to cheer him up I sent him the drawings I had done. The treehouse, I explained, would be a long way up in the branches and there would be a pole with sticks in it so he could climb up to it. He would be able to see through the other

1 *The Garden at Highgrove* by the HRH Prince of Wales and Candida Lycett Green (Weidenfeld & Nicolson 2000).

trees back to the house. I thought it would be difficult for people in the house to see him, which made it even better. I finished the letter by hoping that he liked what I'd drawn and that he would get better soon so he could enjoy the little place.

I entrusted the job of measuring the holly tree to my daughter Clare, a redhead. After she and a colleague, Nick Mathews, had finished recording accurately the girth of the trunk and position of all the branches, which was no easy task, she left Highgrove in her little black Renault by the back drive and joined the main road. The paparazzi were as usual camped opposite the entrance on the off chance of catching a glimpse of someone newsworthy. Immediately they saw Clare they mistook her for Prince Andrew's wife, Sarah Ferguson, the Duchess of York. The reporters snatched up their binoculars, stubbed out their cigarettes, leapt into their cars and gave chase. It was some five miles down the road before they realised their mistake. Clare realised what was happening and could hardly see the road through tears of laughter.

David Palmer, the local builder, who has helped me with most of the 30 or so projects for which I have been responsible at Highgrove, was now well on with the treehouse. The solid platform was in position supported by stout wooden brackets which I had arranged in a fan shape around the main trunk, a bit like the spokes of an umbrella. At one of our regular meetings Prince Charles and I had climbed the long and bouncy ladder to the top and were standing on the deck inspecting the works. We were perched some fourteen feet above the ground amongst branches, twigs and prickly leaves. At that moment Princess Diana walked beneath us with a gaggle of her friends. Initially, I have to admit, I didn't recognise her. The young woman I was looking down on was fair-haired, practically white. Her face was angular and thin. She was wearing long beige Bermuda shorts and a green stripy top and white canvas shoes. I looked at her pretty upturned face as she called up to her husband. 'I do hope you two know what you're doing. It all looks jolly dangerous to me!'

Prince Charles leaned over the temporary rail and shouted back 'Willie's got it all in hand, darling. Don't you worry.' I was touched by his confidence in me which I wasn't at all sure I shared! It dawned on me that on this occasion it really was me who was ultimately responsible for the safety of the future king.

The sadness was that after Hollyrood House had been made and the formal birthday tape-cutting ceremony performed by Prince Charles, the two princes very soon outgrew their small home. The holly tree itself eventually developed honey fungus, and the little thatched house was lifted off its platform and the tree was cut down. I was not present on this sad occasion nor, for some reason, was I consulted in its resiting. Those who visit Highgrove now see only what remains of my treehouse perched on a large deck raised a mere six feet off the ground. I really do think it has lost a bit of romance in translation! But on the positive side it certainly made it easier for Mario Testino to pose his photograph of His Royal Highness and the two princes looking out through my holly-leaf-shaped front door for his official 2003 Christmas card.

THE TELEPHONE IS A STRANGE INSTRUMENT. WHEN IT RINGS IT CAN BRING triumph or disaster, a mundane request or a call-to-arms. This time it was the soft voice of Patricia Kluge[2] speaking from Albemarle County, Virginia, in the United States.

'Is that Mr William Bertram I'm speaking to?' said a slow, sexy voice with just a drift of American lilt to it. 'I don't know if Prince Charles has mentioned me to you but I was over at Highgrove with him recently and saw your play house up in the top of the holly tree. He very sweetly gave me your telephone number. William, may I call you William? [She correctly assumed she could]. John and I would be so happy if you could find time to come over to Charlottesville and do something for our young son, John Junior. We think it would be just so special if you could.'

As it turned out His Royal Highness had explained the position to me. John Kluge was, he told me, the second richest man in America. That was in 1988, before Bill Gates had made his billions. Rupert Murdoch had paid John Kluge two billion dollars for Metromedia Corp, a series of local radio stations spreading from the Atlantic to the Pacific

2 Pronounced Kloogy.

'Welcome to Albemarle.' Home to Patricia and John Kluge

coasts. John had also sold, amongst other assets, the Harlem Globetrotters, for another $30 million.

The Prince thought the Kluges could afford just about anything even I might be able to think of! 'She, Pat, is an old friend,' he continued, 'I've given you a great build-up so go and have some fun. Anyway I'm sure you'll find them both very kind and charming.'

The arrangements were made and after an eight-hour economy flight (the mean old things!) to Washington I was driven by Liester,[3] their chauffeur, through the flat lands of the Eastern Seaboard, across the Mason-Dixon Line of Civil War fame, and on to Albemarle House.[4] It was tucked into the foothills below the legendary Blue Ridge Mountains, not far from Monticello where Thomas Jefferson had built himself an elegant Georgian mansion (begun in 1769). We drove past a pretty security post, and through some imposing automatic gates. From there the drive meandered picturesquely through the estate's own nine-hole golf course designed by Arnold Palmer. We skirted a spinney of mature ilex

3 With his accomplice, a Russian Countess, Liester was subsequently gaoled for murdering a local jeweller.

4 Well known now for its fine vineyard.

and, after a mile or so, rolled up to the pillared front door of a very grand all-American Georgian Revivalist home. The entire house party, all eleven of them, were assembled to greet me at the front door above an elegant flight of pretty curving stone steps. I eased myself out of the car feeling tired and crumpled, and not looking in the least like the suave British emissary of the Prince of Wales they might have expected. I felt more like a scruffy second-rate celebrity at a film premier who ought to have glammed up! I got the distinct impression they were a little disappointed.

'Welcome to Albemarle,' said my attractive 39-year-old hostess as she drifted down towards me. She took my arm firmly in hers. 'William Bertram, all the way from England. Let me introduce you'. It would be some time before I managed to remember all the names of my fellow guests but at first flush they sounded very influential and important. My suitcase was taken upstairs to the principal guest bedroom by the under-butler. When I had freshened up I went downstairs and followed Pat through a fine oak-panelled library[5] into a tiny side alcove. The room was fitted out as a very cosy and intimate little bar with a plush-covered banquette and burgundy-coloured walls. 'Now what can I get you, William?' She held up a crystal tumbler.

We sat close together and she proceeded to tell me about herself. Her large brown eyes transfixed me; a half smile played around the corners of full lips. I knew a little of her background but it was a bit of a surprise when she admitted that this was her second marriage. 'I grew up in Baghdad, came to the UK and married an Englishman who published glamour magazines. You've probably seen my pictures already [I hadn't]. Unfortunately they're all bosoms and beads. I'm not very proud of that. My husband at the time told me it would help my career as a dancer but I found out too late that he was much more interested in his own bank balance! It didn't last long.'

I looked down and squeezed the rim of my gin and tonic. 'If I may say so, Patricia, your circumstances do seem to have taken a turn for the better. How come?' I surreptitiously glanced down at my watch and

5 Beautifully crafted by Symms of Oxford.

realised it was, for me, three o'clock in the morning. I could hardly keep my eyes open. She got up and filled her glass with iced water. 'I met John while I was still married. We were both unsettled, and one day he said he thought we would make a very powerful combination. 'Why not come with me and I'll put you on Broadway?' And true to his word that is just about what he's done.' The door opened and the butler brought in a plate of smoked salmon. Pat explained that the rest of the party had already had dinner and hoped the sandwiches would fill the bill. She smiled and I rather enjoyed the pun! When eventually I got upstairs I lay on the eiderdown looking up at the ceiling conscious only that this had been one of the longest and most exhausting afternoons of my life. I fell asleep fully clothed.

Although I had gone to bed late I woke up early. One simply can't adjust to the difference of five hours in a single evening. It was four o'clock in the morning when I got up. The sun had not yet risen but the birds in the surrounding woodland were beginning to stir. I tried to remember a bit about the house. It had been built four years before in beautiful handmade pink brick with a slated roof above modillioned eaves, with over one hundred feet of façade on two storeys. It was attractively detailed with elegant Georgian sash windows, each keyed with Mexican shellstone. A triangular pediment formed a three-bay centrepiece. This was flanked by symmetrical links to a library wing at one end and a kitchen wing at the other. A wide and light-filled enfilade passage ran the whole length of the house, off which projected first the tall dining room and then an equally big drawing room. They were separated by a charming courtyard garden. In 1982 John Kluge had commissioned David Easton, the well-known New York interior designer to help them. David had sketched his first thoughts for the house on the back of a paper napkin while he and Pat were having tea at the Carlyle Hotel. Before they'd finished their buttered scones the bones of the design had been fixed. Not such an unusual way of working, in my experience! The backs of envelopes and other scraps of paper have always proved to be quite the best place to develop ideas!

That first morning I tip-toed quietly downstairs so as not to wake the household and stepped out onto the gravel drive. I needed some fresh air so I decided to walk all the way up to the main gate and back; a good two-mile round trip. Mist still hung over the two-acre lake and the rolling contours of the golf course sparkled with frost. Having worked up a healthy appetite I got back just as the sun was rising. I ran a bath and a little later settled down to bacon and eggs at a large table in the bay window of the kitchen.

I cannot now remember why, but it was Pat who cooked my breakfast, and while she was standing by the Aga with her back to me she told me that John would like to see me in his study when I'd finished. 'He wants to talk about John Junior's new playhouse.' I put my knife and fork neatly on my plate, as Nanny had taught me, pushed back my Windsor chair and followed her through the back door, out into the garden and up through the woods behind the house. She'd dressed casually for that crisp autumn morning in a green open-necked blouse and cardigan, faded blue jeans and open-toed sandals and blue nail varnish. We went about 100 yards along a path until we came to a traditional American log cabin nestling among the trees. Pat popped her head round the door and ushered me inside. 'I'll leave you two together,' she said, and pulled shut the old planked door with a satisfying clunk.

John Kluge was sitting at a large scrubbed wooden table covered with a few papers and one or two books. On the log wall behind him hung a large timber panel decorated with old rusty nails. He told me that these 'hand-cuts' were much prized by the early frontiersmen. (When they moved house they would burn down the old cabin and collect up the nails to reuse in the next.) The floor was waxed pine boards over which a couple of rough Apache Indian rugs had been casually thrown. A cotton-covered bashed-up sofa sat across one corner. 'Have a look around William. Come on, I'll show you my porch.' John got up from his delicate New England spindle-back chair clearly feeling it was time to shake my hand. He was five foot four inches tall, in his mid-seventies, grey and balding. He was wearing a pair of baggy trousers and worn-down slip-ons. He turned away and waved a hand for me to follow. He made his way to the corner of the cabin where he showed me a little open porch facing the sunshine edged with fancy wooden railings and low overhanging eaves. In the centre of the floor was an ancient rocking chair. Outside the birchwood descended into a deep valley shrouded in a blue haze. The sunshine beamed down through the leaves and made patterns on the porch floor. From the ravine below rose the muffled gurgle of a stream.

'I thought your study would be in the main house, Mr Kluge?' I said, more by way of a question than a statement. I wasn't really surprised by his reply.

'I spend a whole lot of my time out here, William. I just find it the best place to think and I like to do a whole lot o' that. I've got all the things I value round me. That desk is the first piece of furniture I ever bought in America after my parents emigrated from Germany back in the twenties; the little blue Dresden figure of a Lipizzaner and rider is just about my most treasured possession. I bought it when I made my first bit of money over here in the US. The house is all very well, but I like simple things. Pat's got a good eye and I let her enjoy herself putting the whole place together with David [Easton]. No, I like simplicity, just like this little place here. Not too many people know how the old pioneers built these cabins but I managed to get the one man in America who can still do it properly. I think he's done a great job, don't you?' I nodded. He sat down in the rocker and I pulled up a battered deckchair and lay back in anticipation of good natter.

'Would you mind, John, if I ask how you got started? Not everyone in life makes your sort of money.'

'Well, I got into billboards. Lots of 'em, all up and down the highways. I was advertising, in a big way, at a young age. Do you know what the basis of a good advertisement is William?' He knew I didn't know. 'Eight words. That's the key. If you can't get your message over in eight words or less then you've lost the guy. Think of it: 'Beans means Heinz'. Just three words. Tells you everything you want to know about beans. Even if you add 'Heinz 57 varieties' you've only got six or seven words. People just loved me for that and paid me a whole lot to think for 'em. Then there were the radio stations, but that's another story.'

'Now young man,' he said straightening up. 'Patricia tells me that you've done a great job for Charles and that you're going to do a great design for our John Junior. What I want is a really fun place for him to play in, built up here in the woods. Do you think you could do that for me? Don't worry about the cost, just let that imagination of yours off the hook. Our visitors are all going on an expedition today so it'll give you a chance to put some ideas together while we're gone. See you this evening for dinner, and I guess we can have a chat about it all tomorrow morning.'

As they were leaving, in a convoy of gleaming cars, I collected a sketchbook from my bedroom and wandered through the garden down to the swimming pool with its panoramic view over the golf course. No one seemed to be playing, but then I couldn't see all the greens. Thrushes were singing in the top branches of the tall pine trees, sunshine was sparkling off the ripples in the pool. It was all very peaceful and an ideal setting to get me going. I flopped down onto a pile of calico cushions in a large wicker chair, made sure that the sun was shining over my left shoulder so my hand didn't cast a shadow across the page, crossed my legs to support my pad and began to draw.

This was a completely different problem to the one I'd faced at High-grove. Here there appeared to be no limitations! I could do anything I wanted, or so I thought. In a spirit of unrestrained freedom I let my imagination rip. I started by asking myself what a five-year-old boy, going on six, would think was really good fun? Secret passages? Special ways of getting into and out of the play house? What about a moat around a castle built to half scale; perhaps a drawbridge powered by a water wheel with a lever and cogs to make it work; a waterfall that you walked under to get to a secret door into a dungeon? I plumped for all these, and a great hall to boot, with a big fireplace for having real log fires and cook-ups and a turreted spiral staircase going from dungeon right up to a battlemented rooftop. And what could be more fun than getting back down into the big hall than by a slide which shot you out of the same fireplace? (Assuming your buddy hadn't just started cooking!) That would be the sort of place I'd like to have had if I'd been

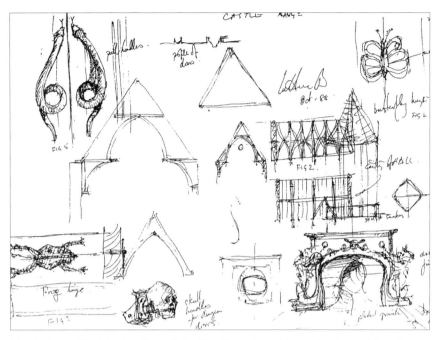

I busied myself with sketches of the fireplace, door hinges, knobs and handles

the five-year-old son of a billionaire step-father. If John Kluge wouldn't entertain such an expensive flight of fancy then no one would. I busied myself with my sketches until I had refined the ideas and had made a reasonable fist of putting them down on paper.

When I'd finished I put on my swimming trunks and plunged into the warm water of the pool. As I surfaced who should come pottering along but old man Kluge himself. 'Hey John,' I called out, blowing the spots of water off my face, 'I thought you were going out with the rest of them?'

He raised his arm and flicked an imaginary wisp from the air. 'Jeeze,' he said looking down at my drawing 'you really let yourself go there. I guess you must have known that mad King Ludwig who built that damned fairy castle, Neuschwanstein in Bavaria!' I pulled myself out of the water and flung a towel across my shoulders and sploshed over to where he was standing.

'Unlike Ludwig, I'm not mad, and this looks like a whole lot o' dollars

'I guess you must have known that mad King Ludwig!'

to me, William.' My heart sank. 'Better get my construction boys to throw a rule at it and see if it's do-able.' He put his arm round my shoulder and patted me silently then moved off, head down, deep in thought.

That evening the rest of the party arrived back from their outing and came and settled down to drinks beside the pool. They wanted to know how the castle worked and be shown all the details. As I spoke I sketched for them what I had in mind for the fireplace, the door hinges and handles.

Being with these people I got to realise pretty quickly that social hierarchy in the United States is determined not by birth, as in the United Kingdom, but by a combination of financial muscle and which of the Ivy League universities you attended. This settled your influence in the world. These two don't always coincide, but when they do you tend to be at the very top of the heap. Here I was rubbing shoulders with the great, the good, the powerful and the super-wealthy. I reckoned, quite rightly, that it didn't get much glitzier than this in the whole of the Union.

That evening we sat down twelve to dinner, in a dining room over-arched by a high-vaulted, richly decorated plaster ceiling, with walls hung with Brussels tapestries and gilded antique French mirrors. Among the guests were Mr and Mrs Callico – she was young and very beautiful; Gina Sopwith (Hawthorn), the Olympic downhill skier who often accompanied the Prince of Wales on his winter breaks in Kloesters; the Count and Countess Arnoud de Villagas, who looked after Kluge's collection of a hundred or so vintage horse-drawn carriages, which included a coach built by Ettore Bugatti for himself and his family. They also owned the Imperial Russian sleigh, a majestic piece of work in hand-painted wood and gold braided upholstery. I sat next to one of the head tutors of the architectural school at the University of Virginia,[6] a post for which he was well qualified. In 1550 his family commissioned Andrea Palladio to build them a house, La Rotunda, just outside Vicenza, and they have owned it ever since! For an architect this is like sitting down to sup with the Good Lord himself! Then there were Mr and Mrs Stein – he was running for Mayor of New York when Koch retired and clearly was angling for John Kluge to provide funds for his campaign.

After dinner the ladies left. Kluge pushed back his chair, lit a large Havana cigar, started the port and waited for conversation to flow. It turned out that he was about to sell his yacht, *The Virginian*, and was building a very much larger one, *The Virginian II*.

'What sort of engines have you gone for?' asked Stein, mentioning, rather foolishly I thought, that his new motor yacht had the very latest and most powerful pair of Volvos. From the far end of the long mahogany table, Max Frankel, the editor of the *New York Times*, who up until then had remained relatively quiet, entered the conversation. 'Hey Jarn, I was mighty surprised you didn't get in first and snap up that telephone business which my friend George got hold of the other day. I guess he's going to make a killing. If you'd wanted, it could have been yours.'

6 That delightful 'Academical Village' in Charlottesville, Virginia which was designed and laid out between 1810 and 1812 by Thomas Jefferson (3rd President) when he was 70.

There was a pause while old man Kluge screwed up his eyes against the smoke, took a long drag on his cigar and picked a bit of tobacco leaf from the end of his tongue. 'Why didn't I buy it? I'll tell you why I didn't. To be fair I did have a look at the finances and I came to the conclusion pretty quickly that to knock it into some sort of commercial shape it would have meant sacking a good 25 per cent of the workforce – over 350 people. Then I'd needed to have gotten the marketing right. And after all that effort and heartache what was in it for me? Just a hundred million bucks. Well who in the hell needs a hundred million bucks?' I felt like raising my hand but as it seemed no one else round the table needed a hundred million bucks I thought it rather bad form to let on that it wouldn't do my own finances any harm at all!

I went to bed with my head spinning. Again I woke early. It was a bright Sunday morning. Each morning in Virginia, even in October, seemed to be full of blue skies, sunshine and warmth. After breakfast we drove the mile across the estate to their private chapel, recently built on a slight rise and surrounded by trees. This charming little place had also been created for them by David Easton and was based closely on the Gothic designs of Batty Langley, the eccentric nineteenth-century English architect. We took our places in the soft cream and grey painted pews along with 50 of the 125 estate staff.

Father Laushway, wearing heavy vestments which had been designed for him by Pat and David Easton, took the Mass. I noticed that he didn't look too comfortable. Halfway through the service the reason became clear. The 'east' window was actually facing south. The combination of the sun shining through the large Gothic window behind the altar, and the weight of his robes, was gently cooking him. We said our prayers and sang our hymns then walked out into the fresh clean air of Virginia. Outside the church door the minister was relaxed and relieved to be cooling off. He bade us farewell.

It was such a beautiful day we decided it would do us all good to walk back to the house. John took the opportunity to come with me. 'William, I've just had my people look at your little castle for John Junior. Now don't get me wrong, I think it's a great little place you've come up with, but the figures just don't stack up. I guess it's gonna cost about a quarter of a million bucks. How does that sound to you? Seems one hellava lot to me.'

I was thinking back to the previous evening's hundred-million-dollar conversation. 'Sounds about right, John,' I said, wondering rather naively just how committed he was to the venture.

'Well,' he drawled, 'let's put it this way. When I saw David's sketches for the big house I just said, "let's build". But I guess with this one, Will, I'm afraid it's gotta be 'let's just take a rain check'.'

I have known people with little cash who are so inspired by a design that they are overwhelmed by the romance and excitement of it all. Somehow they find the money and build in spite of the cost. But the moral of this story is that however much money a client has, if he doesn't like what he sees he won't want to stump up. An architect has but one chance to get it right and if he misjudges the situation it is more than likely that he will not be given another.

As LUCK WOULD HAVE IT I WAS GIVEN A SECOND CHANCE. SOME YEARS LATER Patricia asked me to help her embellish the gardens at Albemarle. This time I took with me my trusted friend Mary Home. She would concentrate on planting schemes while I dealt with the structures.

The allée, planted by the Kluge's gifted landscape architect Francois Goffinet, was situated half way up the steep bank behind the house. I suggested to Pat that it might benefit from an eye-catcher at each end, where the avenue widened out into circular groves. I decided upon a pair of not-quite-matching classical pavilions, each with a little domed roof; one to be square and the other octagonal. I named one 'Monti' because the ground fell away sharply behind it. The other, with tongue in cheek, I called 'Cello' and adorned with internal decorations inspired by musical instruments.

It was important that these two buildings were diminutive if they were not to overpower the garden. So I decided to base my schemes on half the scale of the dome on Monticello, the nearby house designed for himself by Thomas Jefferson. This seemed entirely appropriate as the ex-President had taken a similar approach when drawing up his plans for the Rotunda at his famous University of Virginia at Charlottesville, where he determined his dome would be exactly half the dimensions of Emperor Hadrian's Pantheon in Rome.

Needless to say, all the fun was had by me in the process of design. Monti and Cello, my heavenly twins, were never built. In a long career I've learnt to celebrate the journey; just as well, for you may not always make it to your destination!

The End of the Beginning

THIS STORY DOES NOT HAVE, IN THE CONVENTIONAL SENSE, A BEGINNING, A middle and an end. It does have, however, an end which is its beginning and a beginning which is its end: and of course a middle, which I suppose has been there all the time. All new commissions usually start with a telephone call. This one was no exception but it was unusual and was, and still is, the one which makes me feel both the proudest and humblest.

I was rung by Peregrine Churchill, nephew to the great Sir Winston and son of Jack, Sir Winston's brother. Would I care to come over for lunch one day soon to his house at Vernham Dean in Hampshire to discuss the possibility of redesigning Sir Winston's grave in the church-yard at Bladon, just across the park from Blenheim Palace? My reaction to this request was one of speechlessness – not a characteristic for which I'm known. 'Of course I would,' I said and asked him where on earth he'd got my name. Peregrine dismissed my question in favour of making a date for our meeting and promised to make everything much clearer when we met.

And so it was that under a pale blue sky on a warm November day in 1992 I found myself skirting the gentle undulations of Tidcombe Downs and negotiating the narrow hedge-lined lanes which linked the small villages of flint and thatched cottages. As I drove on, my mind was not entirely focused on the road ahead but on Winston Churchill, the great war leader, the man with whom I would so closely be involved over the coming year or two!

I HAD BEEN A VERY SMALL BOY DURING THE SECOND WORLD WAR BUT I HELD vivid memories of it. The clearest of these concerned the aerodrome at

Shenington, just the other side of the valley from my home at Alkerton near Banbury. Each night I would lie in bed listening to the Wellingtons roaring over the house one after the other on their way to bomb some distant German city. Early each morning I was woken by the steady beat of their engines as they crept back home. Night after night this happened and became as natural to me as picking wild flowers in springtime. Shenlow Hill, at the western end of the runway, was a hazard to both taking-off and landing, proving the nemesis of many planes. The dull thud of a violent explosion would interrupt the regular order of things and I would, next day, inspect the pitiful remains of the grey, burnt fuselage and the flying paraphernalia scattered across the scorched hillside.

Shenington[1] was manned by regular RAF ground crew and girls who had joined the WAAFs. We didn't see much of them, but on one treacherous night I was brought full-face into their world. It had been raining hard the whole day and by dark there was a heavy thunderstorm. It was winter and the days were drawing in. The steep hill outside the gardener's cottage, the old School House, where I was staying for a few days, was wet and slippery. I lay in the darkness listening to the relentless rain and watching the lightning flickering behind my bedroom curtains. Suddenly the front door of the cottage burst open. I could hear shouting. I quickly got out of bed and crept along the landing to the top of the stairs where I sat, clutching my knees, looking down upon the terrible scene below. George, a local farmhand, and one of the Home Guard stood in the doorway holding, as best they could, a woman whose face had been smashed to pieces. A mixture of blood and rain dripped from her lolling cheek which fell away from her face exposing a long line of white teeth. She was whimpering and screaming in equal measure. Horace and Ethel High, our gardener and his wife, laid her down gently on the kitchen floor and tried to stem the blood with towels. From where I was sitting I could just see what was happening through a chink in the

1 Completed in October 1941 the aerodrome was officially known as RAF Edge Hill. From this airfield the prototype of the Gloster Meteor undertook its maiden flight on 4 February 1942. On 17April the first jet-powered fighter plane was flown from Edge Hill to de Havilland's airfield at Hatfield where it was demonstrated to the Prime Minister Winston Churchill in the company of the designer of the turbojet Mr Frank Whittle.

door. Suddenly I heard convulsions and deafening screams. I put my hands over my ears and ran back to the warmth of my bed shaking with fear. I pulled the covers over my head and tried to sleep.

Over breakfast the next morning Mr High said to me, 'Poor girl, she really was in a bad way. Did you hear anything, Bill?' He said that the brakes had failed on her bike at the top of the hill and she'd hit the stone wall by Tanner's Pool's gates full tilt. 'Didn't have a chance,' he said quietly.

'Is she going to be all right, Highboy?' I asked. He told me that the ambulance had taken her away to Horton General in Banbury. 'I'm sure she'll be looked after nicely,' he said, trying to reassure me. 'They're very clever in there and you see if they don't put her back together again, just like old Humpty Dumpty.' He spread some dripping on a burnt piece of toast and tried to reassure me. 'Mark my words, she'll be as right as rain in no time.' But I wasn't having any of it. I thought she was going to die. To a small boy at that particular moment the war and all its bloody ways seemed very close indeed.

I WAS SO WRAPPED UP IN MY THOUGHTS THAT I GOT HOPELESSLY LOST. I DID eventually find Fairdown, an unpretentious house of two storeys with white rendered walls, a slate roof, overgrown drive and rather more than its fair share of creepers. As I got out of the car Yvonne, Peregrine's charming French wife, opened the front door. She extended a long graceful hand which I was tempted to kiss in the gallic manner. 'You must be Villiam,' she said in the soft lilt of a Parisienne, 'Peregrine is inside, he will be so pleased to see you.' She led me into a bright hall with a long south-facing window, through a pale green dining room and into a dark study. 'Villiam is here, my dear,' she said as she gestured towards an old man of some eighty years who bore a striking resemblance to Sir Winston himself. Peregrine eased out of a deep leather armchair and shook my hand.

'Grand of you to come, Mr Bertram; sit down and have a drink.'

He already had glasses and the necessary bottles on a silver tray beside him. He waved a vague hand towards a chair opposite him and we sat down together.

'Most extraordinary thing you being here,' he said, by way of introduction. 'I'm an engineer by profession and my young director knows John Lewis, the solicitor, who knows you?' His voice rose slightly as if in question. 'I asked him the other day if he could put me in touch with someone who might be able to help; and the first person he thought of was you.' Peregrine then went on to ask if I had any experience in designing graves which, in all truth, I had to admit I hadn't.

'Well, no matter,' he went on, 'designers are designers. I'm sure you'll manage, but it isn't going to be easy.' I felt reassured by his confidence in me but I had to ask him why it was thought necessary to redesign the grave at all.

'You haven't seen it then?' he replied. 'Perhaps we'd better go in to lunch and then, if you wouldn't mind, William, I'd like you to drive us both over to Bladon. It will be easier to explain when we're there.'

During a simple lunch I got a little of the flavour of what I might be letting myself in for. Sir Winston's grave, not surprisingly, had become a place of pilgrimage. Folk from all over the world came to see it, to remember lost relatives in war and to experience the peacefulness of the simple country churchyard where their hero was buried. The state of the grave, or more accurately graves, for there are 20 or so other family graves surrounding Winston's, was a profound disappointment to those thousands of visitors. Peregrine himself was the chairman of the trustees of Sir Winston's estate and it was through his letter box, and that of his co-trustee young Winston Churchill MP, that an endless flow of damning comments fell. 'The family simply has to do something about it,' sighed Peregrine easing himself up from the table. 'That I hope is where you come in, William.'

We went back into his study for coffee. It was a cosy room. The walls were lined with books, mostly albums with little white labels chronicling WSC's letters in date order. 'Are those the originals?' I asked. Peregrine got up and pulled out one volume and opened it. The letter itself was held with corner tabs, like an old photo album. He picked one off the page and handed it to me, 'That's one of the letters to my father written whilst Winston was in the trenches during the First War. There are lots of them in here.' I read it and carefully handed it back to him, suddenly overcome by the thought that the Great Man's hand had held that very piece of paper too.

'That, I take it, is also one of his,' I said, pointing to a picture over the fireplace. It was a painting of a river overhung with trees. I fancied Winston had captured the reflections off the water very well. 'I'm lucky to have that,' said Peregrine looking at it affectionately. 'You have no idea how possessive the Old Man was about his pictures. In my youth I used to go down to Chartwell for the odd weekend. On one such occasion I went off to find my uncle, whom I discovered working in his studio, which he had made for himself in the cottage at the bottom of the garden. Amongst the canvases propped up against a plan-chest I found a good likeness which he had done of my mother.[2] Winston was sitting at his easel, in his smock, painting. As I stood in the doorway he turned to me, took his cigar out of his mouth, saw me looking at the picture and asked if I would like it. Naturally I was delighted.'

'So, young Peregrine, my boy,' exclaimed Winston with gusto, 'you shall have it.' And with that he got to his feet and proceeded to wrap it up in tissue paper. 'You run along now, you can take it with you when you leave; I'll have it ready for you in the hall.'

When it was time to go, Winston presented him with the portrait but kept a very firm grip of it. 'You'd like it framed, I'm sure,' he said still hanging on. 'No,' replied Peregrine, 'don't worry, I'll take care of that,' and he tugged on his end of the canvas hoping to pull it from his grasp. Winston wasn't giving in without a fight. 'I really do think that it would be most unfair of me to ask you to spend your hard-earned cash on an expensive frame. I know just the sort which would suit it best,' and with that Winston gave a final, sharp tug. Having thus retrieved it, he tucked the picture under his arm and promised to let him know when it would be ready, properly framed. Peregrine looked out through the window and continued with a deep sigh, 'and do you know, William, I didn't see that picture again for over twenty years!'

2 Lady Gwendoline Churchill (see *Sir Winston Churchill: His Life and his Paintings*, David Coombs and Minnie S Churchill, 1995).

'So, what do you reckon was his best painting?' I asked. 'Oh,' said Peregrine, 'without doubt a still-life he did of half-empty brandy and whisky bottles. He'd arranged them on a sunlit window sill which gave lots of interesting light and shade in the liquid. It turned out very well. He was pleased with it anyway, but when he showed it to Clemmie she insisted that he destroy it; which rather reluctantly he did.[3] You see, it was at a time when he was drinking far more than she thought was good for him and she didn't want to encourage it. Winston told me about it afterwards. With a roguish twinkle in his eye he confessed to me, 'You know, Peregrine, I couldn't have done half as well if I'd been sober!'

Peregrine got up unsteadily and went over to his desk where he picked up a sheet of paper. 'Here,' he said as he passed my chair, 'I thought you ought to know who you're going to be dealing with in this enterprise. I haven't as yet got round to forming the Churchill Graves Trust but it'll come and these will be the Trustees.' I ran my eye down the list. It was headed by young Winston, the MP for Davyhulme. He is my age and I'd first come across him, aged 15, in the south of France at the Hotel du Cap in Antibes. To my eternal jealousy he'd been presented with a speedboat by an admirer of his grandfather.[4] Now he was to be chairman of the Trustees. Then there was his aunt Lady Soames, youngest daughter of Sir Winston. From what he said I gathered that Peregrine and Mary were not on the best of terms, although it seemed to me to be mostly Peregrine's problem. The Duke of Marlborough, or Sunny, as he is known to the family, was the third trustee, followed by the Reverend Roger Humphreys, the Rector of Bladon and Woodstock. 'You'll find them all simple enough to deal with, William, as long as you make clear what you want to do. Once you've established their confidence even Mary will pipe down! And Humphreys will do what Marlborough tells him.' Well, I thought, that all sounds pretty straight-forward, but I had to pinch myself to make sure I wasn't dreaming.

Just then Yvonne popped her head round the door. 'I think it's time we got going; by the time we get back here it will be dark,' and to rein-

---

3 Later he painted another such still life which now hangs in the dining room at Chartwell.

4 He well remembered being given the boat and confessed to me that it was as much of a surprise to him as it was to the other guests at the Club Nautique.

force her point she stood holding out an overcoat for her husband. It took about an hour to get to the churchyard. Whilst we drove through the Oxfordshire countryside I was regaled with stories of the chilly Christmases that Peregrine had enjoyed at Blenheim. 'Funny really,' he said, 'As a child I thought everyone had a hat and coat-rack in their drawing rooms. We used to get toasty warm by the huge log fire then, when the gong went for lunch, we all got up, put on our outdoor gear, marched along miles of freezing passages to the dining room, took off our coats and hats and settled down at the table.' He looked out of the car window as I drove along and said wistfully, 'But the best bit of all was tobogganing. In those days every winter, it seemed, the lake froze. We chose the steepest of its banks to sledge down and would slide across the ice for hundreds of yards. We used to have competitions to see who could go the furthest.' He turned and looked at me. 'That reminds me, I want you to design a memorial for Winston in the Great Park on the site of the Old Woodstock Manor.[5] It would be a good spot because it's where Winston proposed to young Clementine Hozier. Mind you, we may fall foul of the Marlboroughs – I haven't spoken seriously of it yet; but all in good time.' On my return to his house I did a 30-second sketch to show him what might be possible.

We turned left off the road to Witney, drove up a steep lane between stone cottages and down Church Lane, and parked by the lych gate. Yvonne was quickly round to help her husband out of the car and all three of us entered the churchyard. An old crumbly concrete path ahead of us split into two, one branch leading to the south porch of the church, the other straight on past the tower. As we broached the slight ridge by the west door there, beyond and below us, sloped an even wider concrete apron running along the left-hand side of a group of grave stones. Rising from the middle of these was a fine stone cross with a green copper wreath at its base. I looked down at the black and white label which rather surprisingly indicated that here lay, not Sir Winston as I had anticipated, but Lord Randolph Churchill, Winston's father. Then my eye fell on the flat slab of stone covered in lettering right next to the path. It

5 Sadly pulled down in 1709 by Sarah, the first Duchess of Marlborough, much against the advice of Sir John Vanbrugh, her architect.

took a moment to realise that I was actually standing right beside Sir Winston's grave. It was laid more or less flush with the ground and surrounded by gravel embedded in mud. His daughter Mary Soames had, as always, made sure that there was a fresh posy of flowers in a little basket with a fond note beside it.

We stood back and leaned on a single galvanised pipe rail which ran along the back edge of the widened path. Softly Yvonne asked me what I thought. My mind raced; first impressions are often the most instinctive and invariably prove to be right but you don't always want to share them in case you have second thoughts.

'Well I don't think it's right that everyone can walk between the graves,' I whispered. And as if to prove my point at that very moment a coachload of visitors arrived. The driver took up an authoritative position standing right on top of Sir Winston and Clementine's stone. After he had made his little speech he invited his fellow passengers to have their photographs taken with him. This lack of respect made me feel quite angry.

As they trundled off, Peregrine raised one eyebrow and bending forward invited me to listen to what he had to say. 'The stone was designed by Mary, so when you come to present your plans, William, you may encounter some resistance to its redesign. I don't know what you think but it isn't what people who come here expect; they feel let down.' I rather agreed with him and said, 'It would also be nice if there was somewhere for people to sit and contemplate rather than having to lean on this ghastly rail.' I walked round to the east side of the group of graves, followed by Peregrine who leaned heavily on his stick. He drew from his pocketbook a small, dog-eared photograph and handed it to me. It was of Winston standing under the yew tree which still overhung the graves. He was wearing a Homburg hat and he too was leaning on a walking stick. 'That's the position the Old Man said he wanted to be buried,' said Peregrine, 'It was Mary who chose the present plot. Typically she turned his grave round to face west, unlike every other grave in this churchyard or most others.' I had to disagree with him. 'I think on this occasion Mary did the right thing,' I said, 'apart from the fact that

Winston would probably have appreciated being different, it does mean that we can keep visitors to the path because they can read the inscription the right way round.' I reflected further. Clearly it had been his wish to be laid to rest in a peaceful country churchyard and, like a salmon returning to its own river, he wanted to be as close to his birthplace at Blenheim as possible. What he hadn't wanted was the pomp of St Paul's or of Westminster Abbey. He probably realised that on his long journey from London to Bladon he would be carried into the hearts of a grateful nation. I thought my job was to preserve that simple feeling of peace and dignity. 'I'll do my best to produce a design which does justice to his memory,' I said quietly and Peregrine seemed happy with that.

When I came to think more deeply about the design the first thing to resolve was the relationship of the graves to one another. Of course they had to remain where they were, but the site sloped in two directions and when it rained the mud between the stones ran in rivulets taking the gravel with it. I immediately struck upon the idea of forming a series of two-directional stepped plinths, each one edged in granite and each dedicated to a single grave. This took care of the slopes and was as robust a concept as Winston's powerful character demanded. I then turned my attention to the design of the stone itself. My first ideas were rather flamboyant: a large lump of white marble on which would be carved a book, a sword and the Garter cape, which I intended to be draped over one corner. To get some reaction to this design I sent the sketch to, amongst others, Lord Wraxall,[6] a friend whose opinion I respected and whom I knew had been at the War Office on Winston's staff during the Second World War. He wrote back a kind letter suggesting that lesser men might require such embellishments, but for Winston, he thought the very simplest of stones would do.

So I returned to my sketchbook and designed a stone which I thought might simply evoke Sir Winston the man. It was about a foot high, three feet three and half inches wide[7] and exactly his height in length. To find out what that dimension was I rang Blenheim and a helpful girl meas-

6 Of Tyntesfield, that outstanding confection of Victorian Gothic Revival.
7 One metre, in celebration of WSC's vision of a United Europe.

ured one of Winston's boilersuits, consulted their records and confirmed that he was, in his heyday, precisely five feet seven and a half inches tall. The gleaming white Portland stone would be placed upon a three-inch raised step, on which wreaths could be laid. I gave each surface a slight camber to throw off the rainwater and improve the proportions, just as Sir Edwin Lutyens had done when designing, on a slightly larger scale, the Cenotaph in Whitehall. Then I decided to infill with Cotswold pitched stone the space between it and the kerb-stone steps of Portuguese granite.[8] On top of the stone itself, and in relief carving, I set out the lettering and dates of the Great Man himself and of his wife, both of whom occupy that singular tomb: Winston Leonard Spencer Churchill 1874-1965; Clementine Ogilvy Spencer Churchill 1885-1977.

Then I turned my attention to the broader design issues which involved the site as a whole. Gone would be the grey concrete path through the churchyard. Proper honey-coloured stone flags with pitched stone edging to match the graves would take its place. Gone, too, the gas-pipe railing, in favour of stone seats. These were inspired by the war memorial at Mells in Somerset, another of Lutyens's little masterpieces. And in would come a protective chain to deter the coach drivers! The final touch was the rainwater gulleys. I thought these should reflect the age of Empire, so I copied the ones that I had seen in the pavements of the Piazza del Campidoglio, the very seat of power of Imperial Rome. Winston, I thought, would have been amused that the original had been designed by Michelangelo.

Armed with all this material I was ready to face the Trustees. 'Are you coming to the meeting?' I asked Peregrine when I knew that there was to be lunch at Charlbury given by the Duke of Marlborough. 'No, no dear boy, you don't need me. I'm now out of it, other than to find a way to pay the bills. I'm working behind the scenes. If all goes well I may just be able to sell Winston's papers. That would more than cover the cost.' He wished me luck.

Although the Duke of Marlborough has his own private apartments hung with the Blenheim tapestries at the Palace, he lives some way off in

---

8 Chosen to mark Portugal's 700-year alliance with England.

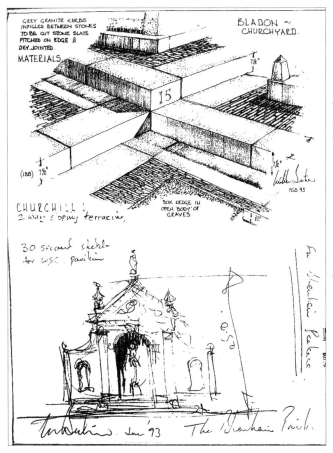

I immediately thought of stepped plinths edged in granite

My 30-second design for Sir Winston's memorial in the Great Park at Blenheim

a house which is the very antithesis of the splendour of Blenheim. It has been transformed into the most perfect small English country chateau. There is a gentleness to its setting, surrounded as it is by trees and trim hedging, striped lawns and neatly cut edges. The interior is a glorious example of architectural symmetry. The dining room is elegantly tall and full of light with, on this occasion, the burnished mahogany table perfectly set with old glass and silver, polished and sparkling. All that was missing were the guests.

Young Winston arrived after me and parked his Jaguar beneath the clock tower of the stable block. He had with him the Garter pennant which marked the Queen's investiture of Sir Winston with the Honour of Knight Companion of the Most Noble Order of the Garter on 24

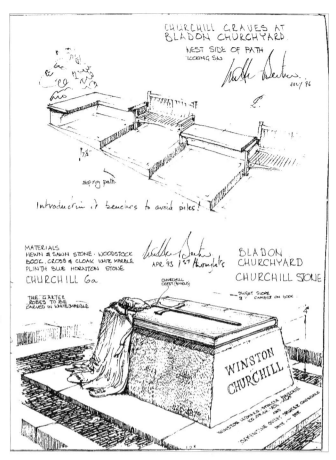

'William, couldn't you interrupt the continuous stone seat with a wooden one to avoid piles!'

My flamboyant ideas for Sir Winston, with book, sword and garter cape, were swiftly replaced by something much simpler and more powerful

April 1953.[9] The unfaded colours shone through the clear plastic bag in which it was folded. With it draped across both outstretched arms he offered it to the Duke of Marlborough, who was standing at the front door to greet him. 'I think that my grandfather would have liked this to be kept at Blenheim,' Winston said. 'Perhaps, Sunny, you might display it with all his other things?' His Grace was clearly taken aback by this generosity. For me the gesture opened a window into young Winston's character that, perhaps, he had allowed to remain closed for too long.

We went in to lunch and I found myself sitting between Mary Soames and Rosita, the pretty American wife of my host. The conversation flowed easily, as did fine wines. Everyone except me seemed to be writing

9 A Garter Knight's banner hangs in St George's Chapel at Windsor whilst the knight is alive. At death it is passed to the family. A replica of Winston's hangs in the study at Chartwell.

a book and much was made of the difficulties in dealing with publishers. I gathered that Mary was in the last throes of completing her latest, entitled *Speaking for Themselves*, which was a collection of the letters exchanged by her father and mother.[10] She told me that it had been really difficult editing them down to just one volume. 'There are fascinating insights in so many of their letters, you know; but I was told that a second volume simply wouldn't sell enough copies to make it worthwhile. Pity really! I suppose they know what's best,' she said. Then Roger apologised that his book was more of a pamphlet. It was called, appropriately enough, *The Church and Tourism*. If anyone was qualified to write on such a topic then we all agreed that he was the man to do it.

From the head of the table the Duke turned the conversation to matters in hand. 'I hear from Peregrine, William, that you have it in mind not only to sort out the rest of the graves but also to give Sir Winston's a new look. Before we go to the churchyard perhaps you'd like to tell us a bit about it.'

I turned to Mary. 'Lady Soames,' I said, 'I realise that I have to tread very carefully here. I know that you had the present gravestone carved and that you must be very fond of it, but do you really think it's up to snuff?'

She put her hand on my arm and said quietly, 'What you've got to remember, William, is that when my father died, his was the only name on the stone. I have to admit that it does look more cluttered now that his name is joined by my mother's. I had to do it like that, don't you see? After all she is there with him. But,' she graciously went on, 'I'm sure you have some good ideas for us, which is why you're here.'

I opened a large envelope and took from it half a dozen copies of my design for the new stone, one for each of us. I ran through my thinking and all went well until I got to the lettering on top of it. 'I think that Sir Winston's name and dates should be rather larger than Clementine's. You see, your mother's name, being nearer the path, will appear to be bigger than your father's if we don't adjust the scale.'

There was a long pause while Mary looked round the table to gather

10 Some of the very ones which I had so recently held.

My proposed layout for the churchyard at Bladon

support for what she was about to say to me. 'William, what you must understand is that we are a very ordinary family, really just like anyone else's, at least as far as all this is concerned. To us my mother was a very important influence on my father.' She looked over at her nephew. 'As far as we're concerned, both their names are of equal importance and therefore, I believe, should be the same size.'

'If you think for one moment that yours is an ordinary family I don't think you have any conception of the affection in which the nation holds you. This stone will become an object of great significance for the thousands, if not millions, who will visit your father's grave. I do think it is important to balance these things.' I explained that I had prepared six different settings for the lettering, all drawn full size, with Clementine's name progressively smaller on each one. The smallest was about three-quarters the size of Sir Winston's.

We got up from lunch and drove in convoy to Bladon, literally as the crow flew. The Duke led the way in his black Range Rover. He opened the private gate on the very western axis to Blenheim Park, drove down his new lime avenue, around the Victory Column, across Vanbrugh's half submerged stone bridge straddling Capability Brown's great lake and then swept us majestically into the cobbled forecourt of the Palace itself.

'I see the Duke has had his balls regilded,' twinkled Roger Humphreys looking up at the cupolas, reiterating one of Sir Winston's favourite jokes. We turned left to pass between the armoury, a symmetrical pair of low side-wings heavily adorned with Vanbrugh's whimsy to warfare; the decoration appropriately inspired by the cannonball. And eventually we arrived at the little village hall, a black clapboard structure with pretty white bargeboards next to the church. We entered the churchyard and walked to the graves. It was some time before the visitors to Winston's tomb realised that a discussion about the future shape of the graves was taking place right in their midst. Soon however they were nudging each other and glancing in our direction as first they recognised Mary Soames and then young Winston.

'Roger,' said the Duke, 'I believe there's a cup of tea waiting for us in the hall. Shall we go in and have a look at William's designs for the lettering?' My colleague, Ted Brewster, had already laid out on the floor the six large drawings in descending order of size. I suggested that the best way to get a proper feel for the problem would be for the trustees to stand on the trestle table which ran down the length of the room. They could then, I explained, look at each design in roughly the same way as they'd be seen in situ, and then let me know which one they liked best. So, with a certain unsteadiness, the Duke of Marlborough, Lady Soames, Winston Churchill MP and the Reverend Roger Humphreys climbed on to the table and shuffled up and down conferring urgently with each other. After a couple of minutes Mary called the discussion to order. 'William,' she said looking down at me, 'we have all chosen the one at this end,' and she pointed down at the drawing which had Clementine's name considerably smaller than her husband's. 'I quite see what you were getting at during lunch. Do you think, perhaps, it might be even smaller?'

'No,' I said reassuringly, 'I think you've got it absolutely right.'

Winston asked if there was anything planned for the end of the stone. 'If not,' he went on, 'I think we should just have the word CHURCHILL carved in bold letters, facing the path; simple, but perhaps the more effective for it. How do you all feel?'

'I think we all feel very happy with how the whole matter is progressing, don't you Sunny?' said Mary in her soft, authoritative voice. His Grace looked round at the assembled company and said, 'I suggest the first thing that might be changed is the amount of stone seating along the path. I like the design and I'm all for having places to sit, but as Winston came from a cavalry regiment I think a few more wooden benches might avoid … piles!' He turned to me and asked if I would like to look into it. I was rather attached to my line of stone seats. They provided the necessary enclosure from the rest of the churchyard on the west side of the path. The simplicity of that design would be compromised by this latest suggestion. However, having got the whole of my scheme all but accepted I thought it rather churlish to make a fuss. So I promised to see what could be done.

The Duke then pursued his second idea. 'I take it that we want the graves to be as labour-saving as possible? I'm looking at these box hedges everywhere. I've got miles of them at Blenheim and they take an awful lot of looking after. Has any thought been given to having something that wouldn't need any help at all, like plastic box hedges, instead? Lot to be said for it.' His voice trailed off into silence.

'Really, Sunny,' said Mary, 'how could you? That's as bad as Montagu's suggestion that Stonehenge should be copied in fibreglass to preserve the original.' She turned to me. 'Don't listen to him William, you just carry on as you are.'

'Just a thought,' said Sunny with a smile; and we all affectionately pulled his leg.

The cost of the work was established by Peter Gunning, our quantity surveyor, and a faculty to implement the design was granted by the diocese. Joslins of Oxford were contracted to carry out the work. They embarked upon this with craftsmanship and good humour under the amiable leadership of Roy Kelly. It had always been planned to lift every gravestone and carefully store them a mile or so down the road at their yard. Then the rains came and the site, behind its mesh safety barriers, began to look more and more like the Battle of the Somme. If that wasn't bad enough, a website carried a photograph of the site in this condition accompanied by a scurrilous article about the desecration of the grave, criticising the family for not looking after it properly. As a non-user of the world-wide-web I thought nothing of it, but it did upset the trustees. Then to brighten things they heard that Peregrine had secured the funds by selling the Churchill papers to the nation for £11 million. As Chairman of the Heritage Lottery Fund, Jacob Rothschild had proudly announced the purchase, but perhaps had not been prepared for the adverse reaction it provoked. For the second time in a week the family were castigated in the press with leading articles accusing them of greed. Some tabloids even suggested that Winston's papers already belonged to the nation, and if they didn't, they jolly well should. Poor old Peregrine wasn't happy either. He told me that a lot of Winston's papers were his personal property and the deal only went through when he agreed to put them up to complete the set. 'I would have had to accept all this stuff and nonsense if I'd benefited from the sale, but I haven't made a penny; never intended to.' He sounded very down.

The work at Bladon progressed steadily. The public watched as best they could, held back behind the wire screens and saddened that they had come so far only to be faced with a building site. But largely they were good-humoured and understood the situation. Then, when the work was all but complete and looking quite splendid, someone riding a horse decided to take a short-cut through the churchyard, right across the new graves leaving hoof marks behind it and knocking over some of the fledgling box hedging. 'Just another one of those things which one has to contend with,' said Roger philosophically, 'I don't think there's too much damage.' So we replaced the stones which had been marked and replanted the bushes.

The kerbstones were given their legends indicating what relationship the occupant had to Winston: his father; his mother;[11] his brother Jack

11 The famous Jennie Jerome, a Long Island beauty.

and his wife; Peregrine's mother,[12] Christopher Soames and his family and so on. And Consuelo. I wasn't going to be allowed to forget Consuelo Vanderbilt, who had married the 9th Duke. She had no direct relationship to the Churchill line but Sunny was adamant that she should be acknowledged. Perhaps he felt that the family ties to America would thereby maintain their strength.

On the morning of Monday 8 May 1998, the anniversary of VE Day, under a blue sky and with just the faintest of breezes, the Service of Rededication took place at the newly fashioned graveside of Sir Winston and Lady Churchill. Through each gate of the little churchyard at Bladon came family and friends, those involved in the building, the professional teams guiding them and many others.

Lady Soames, quiet and dignified in a pale blue coat and skirt, stooped down and placed a posy of flowers at the end of the stone beneath the crisply incised name of CHURCHILL. She straightened and paused for a moment looking down at the grave. She then turned and joined her nephew Winston and his new and sophisticated American wife, Luce (Engelen). She whispered something to them and then moved over to greet the American philanthropist, Damon Wells. He had been very generous in making money available to bridge the financial gap, allowing us to get on with the work before all the funding was in place. He especially wanted to be associated with the stone itself. His admiration for Sir Winston was profound and he felt that his personal contribution should be seen as a gesture from the whole of the American people. At an emotional meeting of the Trustees some two years later he would be invited to join the Trustees himself.

Striding down the path ahead of the Duchess and the Marquis of Blandford, the Duke of Marlborough acknowledged the assembled company and leaned down to place a family wreath on the tomb. A number of passers-by, not knowing of the occasion, stood back to watch whilst villagers, who were only too well aware, came in their Sunday bests to send the Old Man on his way once again. The television crews set up their camera positions away from the throng on the east side of

12 Peregrine died on 19 March 2002; his ashes are buried with her.

The Lady Soames DBE, his Grace the Duke of Marlborough and Winston Churcill – all of whom constituted the Churchill Graves Committee

the graves, with pink lilac in flower as their backcloth. Sue Saville the ITN reporter, wearing her trademark electric blue coat and skirt, would interview Winston after the service. He spoke movingly of his grandfather. He looked so much like him that he could for all the world have been Sir Winston himself. I too would be asked to say a few words as the designer (but they would come out all wrong and to my relief would be cut from that evening's television news).

Beside me stood my wife Victoria. She above all deserved to be there, if for no other reason than for having put up with my monosyllabic presence whilst designing the scheme. I was also accompanied by my trusted team: Anthony Fell, the son of my business partner Peter Fell, who saw to the day-to-day running of the contract; John Daniels who prepared detailed plans; Ted Brewster who filled in the gaps and Anton Young who helped to identify suitable box hedging called 'Memorial', and made sure that it was fed, watered and clipped tight. Joslins were represented in full, led by the indominitable Kelly, with his troops fell-in behind, notably Bill Brown who had done such a skillful job of carving the stone

Lance Cpl Mark Holt and Trumpet Major Barry Whitlock sound 'The Last Post'

with all its complicated lettering.

Opposite me stood a small contingent of representatives of both the French and Danish Resistance. They stood quietly to attention, heads bowed in the purple shadow of the church tower. The Danes particularly had shown their devotion and gratitude to Churchill's wartime achievements: for what he had done for them as a nation and for the world as a whole. Every year without fail they had, on the anniversary of the end of the Second World War, made a pilgrimage to Bladon as a mark of respect. To them therefore, and only to them, had been accorded the honour of having their memorial plaque near to the grave.

A hush fell upon the scene as the Reverend Roger Humphreys walked slowly down the path clutching his Order of Service, white surplice billowing in the breeze. He stopped, looked round and welcomed his informal congregation. He then nodded to the leader of St Martin's Church choir which broke the silence with a rendering of 'O sing joyfully', by Adrian Batten. Their voices held on the wind for a moment then drifted across the village and on towards Blenheim Palace.

Winston Churchill, in a firm, strong delivery, read from the Book of Wisdom. 'The righteous live for ever. And in the Lord is their Reward ...' I detected the slightest tremble in his voice as he ended the reading: 'And the faithful shall abide with Him in love; Because grace and mercy are to His chosen.' I believe he was relieved and thankful that the rector was responsible for the Act of Rededication itself.

There was a pause; no one spoke; no one moved; just the rustle of the wind through the leaves of the tall trees surrounding us and the silent drift of clouds overhead. Barry Whitlock and Mark Holt, the pair of trumpeters representing the band of the Queen's Royal Lancers, slowly raised their gleaming instruments and placed them carefully to their lips. With just a nod out rang the sombre call of 'The Last Post', followed immediately by the much more joyful trill of 'Reveille'. If Sir Winston had been listening, as I am sure he was, his mind would have cast back exactly one hundred years to the part he played as Lieutenant WS Churchill of the 21st Lancers in the charge at Omdurman on 2 September, 1898.

As the service continued I have to confess that my mind wandered back to those war years and that fateful night for the poor WAAF so horribly injured when she crashed her bicycle. She may have played only the smallest of parts in the Great Man's war machine, but each little cog was needed to keep that machine running. I was sure, looking round at the scene in front of me, that the ghost of her spirit was there, amongst us, as close to her war-time leader as it was possible to get. Through my daydream I was only just conscious of Roger's presence and only faintly aware of him saying 'And now I would invite all those present to join with me in the hymn, 'O God our help in ages past, our hope for years to come.' I was then swept up in a joyful chorus of a hundred voices until that final crescendo of the words 'and our eternal home.' Amen. Silence. We stood there, heads bowed, and were again left alone with our thoughts.

It was the end of a wonderful day; the end of an inspiring piece of work; and I suppose for the grave of Sir Winston and Clementine Churchill it was indeed the end of a new beginning.

'Twas Easier Said

For which of you, intending to build a tower,
sitteth not down first, and counteth the cost,
whether he have sufficient to finish it?
Luke C.14, V.28

THERE IS TOLD IN THE BIBLE AN ACCOUNT OF THE MAN WHO PLANS A GREAT banquet and invites all his friends, relations and acquaintances to join him for the feast. Without exception they make lame excuses for declining his invitation. When he throws open the doors no one turns up. So he decides to go out into the streets and alleyways and invite the poor and disadvantaged to come and eat his food and drink his wine. The story which I am about to tell has much of the sadness, joy, lack of consideration, triumph of the human spirit and despair of that ancient parable.

I first met the Reverend Beverley Tasker at a committee meeting chaired by Colonel Bill Roberts, who not only ran the affairs of the Duchy of Cornwall around Bath and beyond as if it were his own personal fiefdom, free in his own mind from the irksome constraints of the Treasury, but also those of the feoffees of the Compton Dando Church Estate Trust. We were a mixed bunch, we trustees; experienced, well-to-do, the only qualification being that we lived within a nine-mile radius of the village. My long-standing friend, Peter Harrison, had some years before become steward, a professional appointment which entailed running the committee's affairs and entering the minutes into a large and ancient leather-bound book. Into the flyleaf had been pasted a yellowing parchment which listed the rules by which the Trust had been governed in an unbroken line since the reign of Queen Elizabeth I. I'm not sure why I was there; probably to act as a sounding-board for the Church architect, Julian Hannam, or, more likely, as it turned out, to become chairman myself when Bill Roberts's time came.

On 25 November 1976 I attended my first meeting. We gathered in the rectory around the dining room table. Much earlier that morning Barbara Tasker had lit the fire, but the winter cold had penetrated so deeply into the thick stone walls that it took some time to warm up. Even with the benefit of an internal glow from a glass of Harvey's Bristol Cream sherry some of us kept our coats on.

'Well, Tasker,' opened Bill in his booming voice, 'we the feoffees welcome you to the parish. Tell me, have you had a chance to look at the finances?' Beverley, who had not long been the incumbent, carefully tidied his notes with the tips of his fingers. 'Well, mister chairman, we were indeed most fortunate to have the BBC down last week to make a recording in the church.'

'What, of you singing, Rector?' chuckled the Colonel with evident pleasure.

'Actually no. They came to record the silence. Apparently the church possesses the very best quality of absolute nothingness that can be found anywhere, at least around Bristol.'

Bill leaned forward grinning broadly. 'Sounds pretty far-fetched to me. Well I hope they've paid up and the coffers are now well and truly filled. I take it then Rector, you won't now be needing any extra cash from us this year to bail out the PCC?'

The Reverend Tasker wasn't at all sure whether this was a joke or not. He knew that the funds we had available for distribution were limited, but didn't quite know on what they could be spent. 'Well, I was rather hoping that this bill for cleaning the choir's white linen vestments might fall within the scope of the trust,' he said tentatively pushing a bedraggled-looking invoice towards the chairman. The colonel asked the steward to read out from the great leather book the conditions under which payment might be made. It proved inconclusive.

'I fear, Vicar,' said the chairman with the merest twinkle in his eye, 'that this is, how shall I put it, a rather grey area?!' The feoffees to a man fell about laughing, as did Tasker. Amid the hubbub, however, Bill Roberts could be seen signing off the laundry account. He pushed the cheque over to Beverley, 'but on this occasion I think we are all of the opinion that as you are a new boy, Rector, we should be generous.' The gesture was calculated to give Beverley the feeling that he was not only welcome in his new post but was amongst friends and accepted by all concerned.

Acceptance was not, however, something my friend the Reverend Tasker was to experience when, a year or two later, he took the living of All Saints, Long Ashton, a ribbon of a village as its name suggests, south west of Bristol. The congregation included wealthy families whose fore-bears had made their money as merchant venturers, and those quiet gentlefolk who go about their daily business without fuss; much like any other community.

Tasker was a man who liked to get on: on with his flock and on with the job of making the best of things. He is one of that rare breed who can inspire a person to achieve far more than they ever thought possible. He also had a forthrightness of opinion about religious matters which unfortunately did not always commend itself to his superiors.

He looked around his church. It was large by village standards with a wide nave overarched by a white barrel-vaulted ceiling running the full length of the building from the intricately carved rood screen to the tall pointed arch supporting the stone tower. The tower itself rose majestically to four storeys and was topped with impressive crenellation. The rest he decided was also in reasonably good shape. An army of dedicated parishioners took it in turns to clean the brasses, do the flowers, sweep the aisles, and polish the pews, as in so many lovingly tended parish churches up and down the country. And the place glowed with pride.

One morning the vicar of All Saints walked down to the end of the church, pulled back a blue velvet curtain by the west door and uncovered, to his surprise, a corner beneath the tower filled with mops, vases, ladders and a bucket with half a dozen dead mice in the bottom of it! A secondhand kitchen wall cabinet full of assorted china sat incongruously on a trestle table. This was not, he thought, the sort of thing one wanted to see along the processional route from altar to west door. So he determined to do something about it. The church architect was called in and asked to prepare plans to sort out the mess and give some consideration to how best encourage the congregation to linger in the church after the service so they might gossip and get to know one another before dashing home to save the Sunday joint.

The modest scheme which was presented to the church council only went as far as a little housekeeping, the introduction of a loo and not much else. With it came an estimate of the likely, relatively modest cost, and a fee account from the architect for his pains. About this time the Bishop of Bath and Wells, the Right Reverend George Carey, decided to ask all the parishes in the diocese for an increase in their quota, a payment to central funds which many already found intolerably high.

News leaked out of Beverley's new tower scheme. Those families who had supported the church over the years were naturally anxious about the bill which might be attached. The architect's plans were duly pinned up and comments were invited. No one wrote very much, but there descended upon the church and its hapless vicar a distancing of spirit and a whispering campaign. More particularly it was directed against the idea of any further embellishment of the church especially as it was anticipated that the old guard would most likely be called upon to pay for it. To make matters even more difficult the bishop was made aware that the new incumbent was not an entirely welcome addition to the community and exception had been taken to some of his more unconventional interpretations of the scriptures. Those in authority listened, took soundings and conceded that such criticism might be justified.

Meantime Beverley Tasker gave no one but his wife Barbara and his faithful secretary, Valerie Bond, any idea of how this feeling of rejection was affecting him. In the small hours he would lie awake and pray in silence that the force for good he wanted to promote in his flock would be accepted for what it was; a way to unite his congregation in common purpose, not to divide them.

Up the hill in an ancient cottage one David Evans looked on at the developing crisis and didn't like what he saw at all. He and Rosemary, his wife, were not native to Long Ashton, and understood little of the social undercurrents which so profoundly affected the life of the new vicar. All he did know was that sitting back and not getting involved was not an option.

So one morning he rang the vicar. 'Beverley, tell me, how are you? I've been anxiously watching your battle over the tower project. Do you think there is anything I can do to help?' Tasker could hardly believe his ears. Could this be, he wondered, the answer to his prayers? Was this the David who was going to take on and defeat the Goliaths?

When a soul is suffering from profound disillusionment, as by this time Beverley most certainly was, each turn of the screw deepens despondency. It sometimes needs only a kind word, unexpected generosity or the metaphorical arm around a shoulder to halt the slide and lighten the gloom. Once the merest flicker of hope has been ignited it just requires a gentle puff to make it glow. That telephone call proved to be the kindling that lit Tasker's fire.

Together he and David Evans decided to make a fresh start. So Beverley rang me. 'You do churches, William, don't you? I was just wondering if you might have time in your busy schedule to take on All Saints? It's a lovely church.'

I had made it a rule that I would not take on the responsibilities of church architect unless there was something to get my teeth into. There are those of my profession who delight in finding the brass foundry that cast the original window catches when a few more are required, but that, I fear, is not for me. 'Rather depends, Beverley, on what else there is to do. A bit of re-ordering perhaps? Anyway it would be fun to work alongside you again.'

'Would sorting out the back of the church under the tower be enough of a challenge, William? We've had a scheme prepared, but it simply doesn't go far enough, and our architect has gone with it. He quite understands and with all the infighting that's going on, is quite pleased to be out of it.'

'What infighting?'

'Look, why not come over and I'll tell you what's what.'

A week later I found myself driving down the long high street. I pulled over into the middle of the busy road and turned into Church Lane. The tower was immediately ahead of me as I dropped gently down between high rusty stone walls and turned left beside the well tended churchyard and on round to the vicarage drive beyond. I drew up beside a bright yellow MGB sports car. The front door of the house opened with a flourish and there stood Beverley – short, stocky, with a full head of curly black hair. He was grinning.

I nodded towards the car. 'This yours?'

'Had it for years, William,' he said proudly, 'might go for a spin after we've done some work. It's still a great pleasure. Takes my mind off things, sometimes.' He had been a chaplain in the Royal Air Force and clearly still had his pilot's wings on. He walked me round the rectory which was smothered in roses. 'Pretty isn't it?' he said pointing to the creamy white clusters. 'It's called "Rambling Rector".' His head dropped, 'and I reckon that just about sums it all up.'

A glass of sherry was waiting for me in his study and so too was David Evans. I sat down next to him on an old sofa. Tasker spun his swivel chair round to face me. 'Bit of challenge for you here, William. You'll need all your skills as an architect and all the persuasive powers of a diplomat.' He picked up a small leather-bound book and let it fall open to show an engraving. He passed it over to me. There on the side of a manor house was depicted an intricate oriel window supported, for good measure, by a stone buttress. I looked at both David and Beverley in turn. I took a sip of sherry and waited.

'I don't know how you are going to achieve it, William, but I want to put a floor into the tower to make an extra room where the choir can practise and we can hold our PCC meetings. That,' he said pointing at the picture, 'is the sort of way I'd like to maintain contact with the body of the church.'

'Not an oriel window inside the church, Beverley? I'm sure it's do-able, but it's going to be pretty expensive.'

'Well, William, I think you'll find there is just such a window in St

George's Chapel at Windsor, and as for cost, if that is your only misgiving then I must say I am encouraged. If you think you can develop my idea then that's wonderful. Perhaps we should go and take a look.' And with that he unlocked the front door and walked us out into the sunshine, across the lawn, through a small door in the churchyard wall and into the deep shade of the church.

Once inside I could see that in one corner, by the font, stood an easel displaying some sketches of the previous proposal. I didn't look in case I was influenced. Then I spotted a three-sided heavily carved oak screen which was clamped around the inside face of the draughty west door. Propped against walls and all around the floor were the bits and pieces of cleaning stuff which, I was quietly informed, were the reason I had been summoned.

It is odd, being an architect. One minute you are no more than a disengaged onlooker, the next an enthusiastic participant. It was the presence of this carved lobby screen, designed by the well known early-twentieth-century Bristol architect Sir George Oatley[1] that caught my imagination. Here was a beautifully crafted piece of work which to my mind was entirely wasted where it was and deserved to be found a new home in the church.

'If it is your intention, Beverley, to fill in,' and I waved an arm above my head to encompass the void beneath the ceiling of the ringing chamber 'to contain this space with a new floor, two important things will have to happen. The first is that we must raise these three fine marble memorial tablets to the Smythe family, because if we don't it will be impossible to put in the floor where it needs to go. The second,' and here I could no longer disguise my growing enthusiasm, 'is, that with a bit of luck, Sir George's little memorial lobby can be opened out like a triptych to form a full width screen below the oriel. We can use it to shield all the gubbins the church helpers need, the loos, the stairs, the store, the galley and so on.'

Fumbling for my measuring tape I walked over to the screen. 'Here David, take this would you, and hold it onto the wall next to the door?'

1 Oatley was also responsible for the Wills Building, that high Gothic confection at the top of Park Street in Bristol.

I then marched purposefully round the lobby until I reached the other side and pulled tight the linen tape. I made a mental note of the measurement. 'Now for the clincher,' I said. 'Let's measure across the archway.' We pulled it taut and I turned my thumb over to read the dimension. 'Well, well,' I mused, 'that screen might have been made for it.' By this time my imagination was in over-drive. A clear image was forming in my mind. Before it faded I sat down in one of the pews and made a quick sketch of what I thought the window and the screen below might look like. It took no more than five minutes. 'That sort of thing, Vicar?' I suggested, handing up the drawing.

He studied it carefully. 'This is quite splendid. Can I keep it, William? It's just what's needed for the newsletter. Gives enough to whet the appetite, but not enough to show the detail. It may just do the trick.'

I left Beverley, Valerie his secretary and David in the church with the promise that after sending my people to do some measuring I'd work up the scheme in rather more detail. My staff on this occasion consisted of my long-suffering wife, Victoria, who was expected to help manhandle the church ladders, with Clare, my daughter, then employed by my firm. All went well until the two of them needed to manoeuvre the extended aluminium ladder to another spot and proceeded to lose control of it; not only of the ladder, but of themselves too. As they fought to balance it stifled giggles filtered towards an aged couple who were deep in prayer seated in a pew half way down the nave and blissfully unaware of impending calamity. Eventually, however, and thankfully without mishap, my two crept from the church like naughty schoolchildren having got all the precious dimensions I needed to start my designs.

It was decided that it would be much better to unveil the scheme to the congregation when, and only when, I had got everything in reasonable detail. The impact of a presentation can sometimes be strengthened if the drawings themselves are so beautiful that even the most jaundiced critic has to acknowledge there is some merit to them. So I set about designing the big window. As this was going to be the element that would either make or break the day I drew it up as carefully as I could. I decided to introduce oak rods to give extra definition to the angles of the oriel,

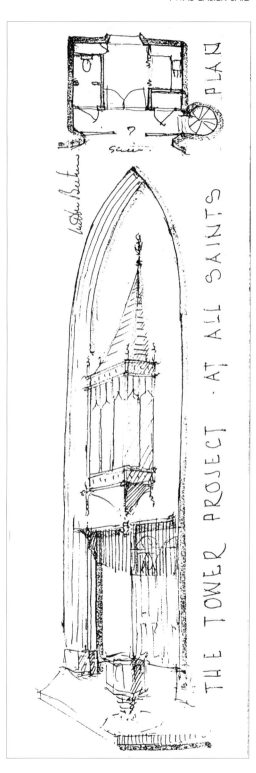

PLAN

THE TOWER PROJECT · AT ALL SAINTS

I sat down in one of the pews and made a quick, five-minute sketch of what I thought the window and the screen might look like which I thought needed a visual boost. I merely flicked four squiggles on the top of each of the 'churchwarden staves' which I would develop in more detail later.

Then one evening when I felt in the mood I took out my sketchpad and set to with a soft-nosed pencil to work up those squiggles into something with a bit more relevance. I chose the shepherd's crook and the bishop's mitre to represent the Church, and the orb and crown to represent the State. My elbow was working freely and the drawing came easily to me. It was all beginning to look rather fine.

Eventually the day in September 1991 arrived when the scheme was to be presented. The whole of Long Ashton it seemed had turned out to hear what their new church architect had to say for himself. Beverley opened the meeting with a few encouraging words and then gave me the floor. I introduced myself, but I'd hardly got into my stride when a commanding voice from the back of the church demanded to know what my scheme was likely to cost. 'Oh God!' I saw the vicar mouth, 'you deal with it, William.'

I turned back towards the congregation, 'Since you ask, sir, my best estimate, as I stand here this evening ...'

'Get on with it then!' came a second voice.

I continued as if nothing had happened, ...'is about one hundred and twenty thousand pounds – give or take.'

'Does that include your hefty fees, Mr Bertram?'

'Those, I fear, will be in addition to that figure.'

My inquisitor turned for moral support to a cabal of like-minded friends sitting next to him. 'Thought as much. What gives you the idea that this sort of money is ...' But at that moment David Evans, who was sitting three rows back from the pulpit and close to where I was standing rose very slowly from his pew, looked squarely in the direction of my adversary, then addressed me.

'William, I have had the privilege to study your most excellent designs for the back of the church,' and he again turned towards the west door to face the overflowing pews behind him. 'The Parochial Church Council has for years grappled with the changing demands of our congregation

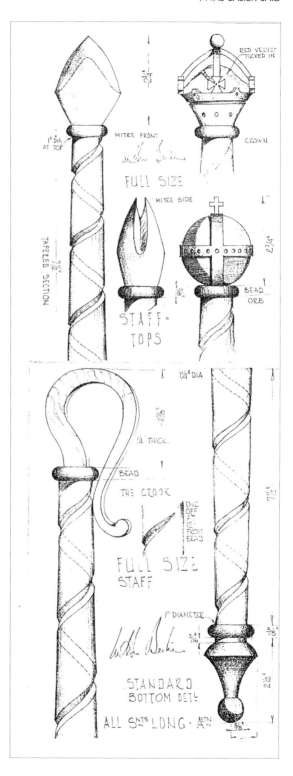

I chose the shepherd's crook and the bishop's mitre to represent the Church, and the orb and crown to represent the State and I think the scheme you have brought to us will enhance the way we all use this church. But more importantly, perhaps, it will leave a fine architectural legacy. I have nothing,' and he repeated the word more powerfully, 'nothing but praise. As for the money, I have no doubt whatsoever that it will come. I am quite sure there will be many who will wish to be associated with such a beautiful addition to this fine and much-loved parish church.' David then sat down to murmured appreciation.

My own cautious reaction was that he might have rather overstepped the mark; but not a bit of it.

Shortly after this exchange the meeting broke up, with the non-believers the first to leave. Nevertheless I was soon surrounded by the less vociferous elements of that congregation who wanted to know how they might help. Would 20 pounds be any good – would 100? Then a rather wonderful thing happened. Beverley, who had been deep in conversation with an elderly gentleman, came over to me. 'I think, William, my prayers may not have fallen on stony ground,' he whispered. 'I've just been told that he is going to have a word with his family and hopes to convince them that he should make a gift of the oriel window.'[2]

From that moment on, like one of Hans Christian Andersen's fairy tales, money for the tower project began, slowly at first, but then in substantial sums, to arrive in the church coffers. Spurred on by this initial success, a Faculty for the work was obtained from the Diocese of Bath and Wells and contracts drawn up with Stansells, the builder, and with Ken Biggs, whose craftsmen would make the window itself.

Under the gentle leadership of Philip Le Sueur, a Jerseyman, the work proceeded in fine order until we had successfully re-established the processional route through to the west door which had to pass the store cupboard, new loo, stairs and galley kitchen. This was elegantly achieved by the introduction of secret doors in oak-panelled walls. And eventually all was finished. It had been paid for by the generosity of not only those in the village but by those who no longer lived in Long Ashton and who had heard what was happening to their beloved church. The service of dedication was taken by the Rt Rev Donald Arden to a packed

2 The secret of Roy Ware's generosity has been kept until this book.

church, on November 5 1995, four years after I presented my scheme. All those involved were proud of the result.[3]

I thought that might be the end of my association with the Reverend Beverley Tasker. In the process of our adventure I was delighted to see that he had regained his sense of humour, had been lifted out of despair by the support of his friends and was once again a fully functioning advocate for the Church of England.

About a year later I got a telephone call from him. 'I've been meaning to ring you for some time, William. I'd like to give you some lunch as a 'thank-you' for all you did.' A week later we found ourselves sitting comfortably across a round table covered in a white starched tablecloth at Hunstrete House, an expensive hotel near Bath.

'You remember that I told you I was looking into what logic can bring to the church? Well I've been working on the concept of God; really teasing out all the anomalies and inconsistencies and applying pure logic to what I've found.'

'And, Beverley, what have you discovered?'

'Rather surprisingly for a man of the cloth, perhaps, I've found that pure logic indicates that our dear Lord does not, in fact, exist. Never has done! I've looked at it from all sides and I still come up with the same answer.'

'Oh dear what a pity,' I heard myself say. 'Doesn't that rather worry you, Beverley, when you remember what happened at the church, all the bad blood and eventually winning through? I do think you might have come up with something a little more favourable towards the Good Lord.' He smiled and looked thoughtful. 'Yes, I think I may have missed something don't you? It may need a little more work!'

But as things turned out for Beverley even the most far-sighted church member might have felt that indeed there really was no God, no loving Father on whom, ultimately, one could rely.

The Reverend Tasker was in the last year of his ministry. The lady

3 Amongst whom were: Mike Addicott and Roland Fear the master joiners who made the window under the supervision of Tim Church; Roy Bishop who did the carving; John Owen who gilded; and Colin Stokes who designed the stained glass. Paul Wyatt, Ken Biggs' son-in-law, and Daryl Bridges, oversaw the installation and Adam Cloote looked after the scheme on site for me.

cleaners who cared for the church had been augmented by a pensioner who offered to help clean the brasses and dust the pews. One day the old man strolled over to the rectory and Beverely asked him if he would clean the glass in my oriel window. He tried to use the long-handled mop with which Beverley had supplied him with but it hadn't worked. The vicar told him not to bother and to do something less demanding and left him to it. But later that day the pensioner's wife rang the vicarage. She was clearly upset and told Beverley that her husband had fallen off a ladder while cleaning the window and had broken his collar bone. He was lying in a pew looking like death when Beverley found him. An ambulance was called and the poor fellow was carted off to hospital.

In due course it was suggested that a claim for the accident should be put to the insurers and Beverley offered to help prepare the papers for his old friend. There was a long pause. 'I don't think we can do that,' said his wife quietly. 'We've already approached a firm who say that they will fight his case against the church and if they can't win compensation for us then they won't charge anything.' The vicar suggested to her, with as much tact as he could muster, that that was probably not the best way to have gone about things.

Within days of the accident a thick envelope dropped onto the vicarage doormat. Beverley slit it open and, with mounting concern, read the contents. There were about 50 legal questions he was required to answer. He quickly scanned through them. 'What risk analysis had he carried out before allowing his 'employee' to embark upon the work in question?' Beverley rang me to share his bewilderment and frustration. 'What do you say to some of these absurdities, William? Am I really expected to do a risk assessment before a sixty-year-old gentleman is allowed to clean the brasses? He had no right to be up that ladder in the first place. The world seems to have turned upside down, and me with it!'

'Have you sent this stuff to HQ?' I asked. 'Surely they can sort it out for you. After all it's their church and presumably their insurance policy that will suffer.'

'They don't seem to want to know, William. Say it's my problem and any claims may have to be settled outside their jurisdiction. Quite honestly the worry of it all is really beginning to get me and Barbara down.' His voice tailed off into a black silence.

'But you're retiring soon.'

'I know, and I shall tell the church solicitors that when I go I want to hear no more of it. No more letters, no questions – nothing.' He sounded distraught and angry and clearly found it increasingly difficult to accept what had happened.

But the trauma didn't end there. For a year into retirement the vicar had to deal with the situation until eventually the church decided that in the interest of good order the matter should be settled. At last Beverley and Barbara felt sufficiently relaxed to drift quietly into retirement. Both retreated into the bosom of their family, with their memories, their books and writings and started a new life in a small cottage in the heart of Warwickshire.

The Reverend Tasker was never a retiring character, but after a full life of service to his community and his country he might have been forgiven for hoping that when retirement came, the Good Lord, if indeed he was watching over his staff, might have offered him a rather softer landing.

Yet the window now stands as a proud testament to the single-mindedness of a man who still managed to inspire those around him whilst he himself was deeply down-hearted. Beverley had been under no illusion as to the antagonism he was likely to encounter nor the difficulties he faced, but he persevered. 'Mark my words, William,' he had said prophetically, when we first met to discuss it, 'this project will, I fear, be a good deal easier to discuss than ever it will be ... to achieve!'

A Sting in the Tale

I FLOPPED DOWN INTO A DEEP ARMCHAIR AND TOOK UP THE *ARCHITECTS'*
Journal of August 1989 and casually flipped through the advertisements.
My eye caught the details of a residential course at Manchester Business
School under the intriguing headline 'How to Influence Clients and win
Commissions', or something along those lines. I never thought of myself
as particularly bad at attracting clients, but did feel that it might well be
a good idea to know what my fellow architects were up to. So I enrolled.

We students were a diverse lot. We came from all corners of the
profession. Some were about to throw their architectural hats in the ring
and start practices on their own or with friends. Others were still
employed in both private practice and local government and were trying
to pluck up enough courage to do so. Then there were the old hands,
like me, who simply wanted to know how we'd get on when put up
against younger colleagues with a competitive streak.

The central task we were given was to respond in an interview with
an unknown client who wanted to build a factory to process, of all
things, fatty acids, and who was going to choose one of us as his architect. I wasn't at all sure that I would have been very keen if he had chosen
me anyway, but that I was told wasn't the point! We were split into teams
of three and were encouraged to organise ourselves to cover each aspect
of our presentation.

After we had made our play, and in true American management style,
our videoed performances were carefully analysed and everyone was
congratulated on their competence. Except, that was, for me! I was
singled out to be hauled over the coals. What, you may ask, was my crime?
Why, asking the client if he could assure my team that he actually owned,

or at the very least had an option, on the site on which he proposed to build his new factory. I received a warning from my tutor.

'You simply cannot ask such a direct question, Bertram; not if you want to retain the respect of your client and any commission that may come your way. Frankly, it's no business of yours whether he owns the site or not!'

My fellow students all nodded in agreement. I, on the other hand, was nonplussed. 'But surely there isn't much point in spending valuable time getting close to a client if he cannot confirm something as fundamental as that,' I argued. However, my protestations were considered to be wholly without merit. From then on I was consigned to the back of the classroom to learn what I might from the rest of the proceedings.

When it came to the psychometric test, which it was claimed helped analyse character traits, mine were judged to be about as far removed from potential success in attracting clients as it was possible to get. In fact my little star-shaped emblem was practically off the graph!

'The unusual aspect of William's character, which cannot be said for some of you,' opined the course director at the end-of-week dinner, 'is that, although coming bottom of the class, he does at least acknowledge his shortcomings!' Great, I thought! That was all very well and was probably aimed at giving my fellow students a warm glow. I was not about to change my character nor, for that matter, my own method of assessing the trustworthiness or good faith of any potential client, a testing process at the best of times. If misjudged it could and indeed would prove very expensive. It was far too complex a matter simply to follow what were, for me, untried methods.

It was with some relief, therefore, that I responded with characteristic enthusiasm to yet another call-to-arms from my old friend Mr Tham. He wanted me to join him on a visit to Prague to look at the possibility of converting the old Swiss Embassy into a luxurious hotel for Blakeney Hotels.[1] John is nothing if not a romantic. He had named his company after the Scarlet Pimpernel, with whom, I may say, he has something in common.

---

1 By this time Blakeney Hotels was known as The Cliveden Group.

The Velvet Revolution, which unshackled Czechoslovakia from its Soviet master, had occurred a year before on 17 September, 1989. The nation was beginning, once again, to find its voice through Vaclav Havel, the poet-philosopher turned reluctant political leader. Moves were afoot to restore to the population their belongings which, together with their houses, had been systematically recorded by the Russians and all their chattels carefully warehoused. The Salm Palace, in which we were interested, was the property of the new government and therefore free from the lengthy negotiations which bedevilled those involved in Restitution.

Blakeney Hotels had been approached by Lord (Jacob) Rothschild through his colleague Tony Bromovsky, to create an establishment to rival Cliveden and the Royal Crescent Hotel in Bath. Our team, led by John Tham, had been responsible for both these ventures and it was thought that the city of Prague, with its new-found freedom, could now begin to offer an element of luxury. This new partnership was to work well. Lord Rothschild had recently raised the funds for the refurbishment of Spencer House, the London home of the family of Her Royal Highness Diana the Princess of Wales. He was already involved in a number of projects in the Czech Republic which were designed to help the fledgling state get back onto a sound financial footing. I felt confident that I was in good hands.

Tony Bromovsky was to be our minder. He knew the city well and had made it his business to understand who were the powerbrokers in Prague, who could get things done and who would be able to unlock otherwise closed doors. There were essentially two elements to the project which concerned him. The first was to attract sufficient financial backing to cover the large sums needed to convert the Salm Palace. The building had been empty for some years and was in a sorry state. The second was to convince the government that our group was capable of taking over the palace and running it as a fine hotel. We soon found that we were not the only contenders. It had already been decided that there should be a competition open to all comers.

The first thing to do, then, was to have a good look at what was on offer. So we flew to Prague. The airport was a ponderous building of

1970s vintage. The place was very much like the busy arrivals hall of a large railway station. It reminded me of so many other mid-European gatherings where everyone, including officials, seemed to be wearing either black, beige or brown. The only smiles, it seemed, were on our own faces. Tony Bromovsky was waiting to greet us. We bundled our cases into the back of a Mercedes taxi and set off at breakneck speed along a concrete dual-carriageway lined with high-rise suburban tenements. If town planners were a little more imaginative and alive to first impressions they would make processional routes from airport to city centre a rather more uplifting experience.

Prague is a beautiful city of spires and domes, of pinnacles and palaces, of statues and bridges and quaint medieval streets. Unlike Warsaw, which from necessity in part had to be rebuilt in replica, Prague did not suffer the outrage of the Luftwaffe's blitzkrieg. The buildings here are just as the architects and craftsmen who built them with such gloriously unfettered freedom of expression had left them.

The city is made up of five historic towns merged by their proximity. Like any well-fortified town the castle, one of the first manifestations of this golden city, was built on a ridge overlooking the crossing-point of the wide and steady-flowing river Vltava. Fortification gave way to ecclesiastical and political power and Hradčany Castle was transformed when Empress Maria Theresa commissioned the Viennese court architect Pacassi to give the buildings a unifying Neo-Classical façade.

The great princely families, who owned much of the Czech Republic in their own right, made it their business to be near the seat of power. The Czernins and the Lobkowitzs built their grand palaces in the heart of the old city. The Schwarzenbergs however perched theirs alongside the castle itself and in time the Salm Palace was built beside it.

We decided that we would walk to Hradčany Square, the site of the Salm, from our hotel, the Intercontinental – a building of such monstrous brutalism that I felt ashamed to be staying there when all around us were charming examples from every historical period and every architectural fashion. Perhaps its address, on a street named 'Revolucioni', should have forewarned me!

We made our way to Staromestske Namesti, the Old Town Square, an open cobbled arena dominated by the twin towers of the fourteenth-century Teyn church. It rose in stone and slate magnificence above the Baroque façades which elbowed their neighbours for position around the edge. Little did we know of the architectural treasures that lay beneath our feet – all but abandoned due to flooding, leaving many of the houses with Romanesque rooms hidden in their basements.

Down Celetna Street I watched a horse-drawn cart full of brown coal being unloaded into the bunker of one of the town houses. There was a faint smell of sulphur in the air which hung beneath an overcast sky and even found its noxious way along the tree-lined banks of the river.

The three of us, John Tham, John Mann our structural engineer from Bath[2] and I, set off down a cobbled side street to avoid the trams, on our way to the Charles Bridge. Nothing could have prepared us for the glorious view we were about to see. At either end of the bridge gate towers protect the carriageway, whose seventeen arches sit confidently astride the river at its widest point. Other than for ceremonial occasions it is now restricted to pedestrians who can enjoy an open-air picture gallery stretching from one end to the other. Artists show their own work, much of it inspired by the many sandstone sculptures which decorate the bridge's parapets. In the distance above the tumble of clay-tiled roofs, copper domes and stone spires we could make out the cliff-like façade of the Salm Palace. It was not, it has to be said, the most inspiring building in the city, but it fitted in quite well. As the evening closed in and the milk-green floodlights came on we walked slowly up the hill towards Hradčany Square. We stopped for a breather at the top of the slope and looked back at the twinkling lights of the city beneath us. Overhead the velvet black of the sky was smudged by the drift of sulphur clouds fed from a thousand chimneypots.

I cleared my throat as the acrid fumes assailed my lungs. I began wheezing and coughing uncontrollably. That cough stayed with me for the four days we were there and for a fortnight afterwards. This was not,

2 In the final event Robert Bowles of Alan Baxter & Associates undertook the structural engineering.

I thought, a good sign if one was setting out to create a very special rendezvous for the most discerning visitors to the city.

As we approached the Palace itself there was much activity. A crew with arc lights and actors dressed in French costumes were in the process of filming. My concern for the suitability of the Salm Palace as a luxury hotel was further deepened when I found that it had been chosen as the setting for the prison in a television series. Richard E Grant was playing Sir Percy Blakeney, the Scarlet Pimpernel, no less! John Tham was greatly amused by the coincidence, but we both felt that perhaps on this occasion the omen was not particularly significant. To paraphrase Charles Dickens in *The Tale of Two Cities,* 'we didn't know whether we were about to enjoy the best of times or the worst of times'.

We left the bustle of movie-making and walked out of the square at the far end towards the Little Quarter leaving the brooding presence of St Vitus Cathedral and the Castle behind us. Smog hung in the narrow cobbled alleyways with tree-sized street lamps doing their best to penetrate the gloom. We came across a well patronised and noisy restaurant behind an arcaded pavement and took our places round a large table dressed in a smart red and white checked cloth. A strong smell of sauerkraut and boiled meat drifted out from the kitchens. The menu was not exactly *haute cuisine*, but then we never expected it to be. On offer was boiled ham and a generous portion of steamed vegetables, all garnished with the ubiquitous dumplings. And the cost? About one tenth of what we would have paid at home, had we been able to find such a feast.

John Tham was in great form. 'Tomorrow,' he announced enthusiastically, 'I've set up a meeting with the manager of our hotel to try to tease out the economics of the place.' Apparently he had also arranged an appointment with the city's building department, followed by lunch with Mia and Micki Flick, the heirs to the Mercedes-Benz fortune. This had been instigated by Tony Bromovsky in the hope of persuading them to invest in the project.

The next morning we were ushered into our hotel manager's office where he gave us a cordial welcome. Earlier that day over breakfast the three of us had been discussing the general level of pay for the hotel staff.

Some of them spoke passable English which, to our never-ending surprise, had been learned at school. From brief conversations with them it was clear that they were still being employed on scales which had been current during the Communist era. We, on the other hand, were paying for our rooms at New York rates. Their revolution had been rather more 'nylon' than 'velvet'. Taxi drivers were particularly aware of what Westerners were prepared to pay and would programme their meters accordingly by simply shifting the decimal point!

In our discussion that morning the question of return on capital arose. 'I suppose,' queried Tham, 'this hotel of yours must be one of the most profitable Intercontintentals in the world?'

The manager looked as if he had been mortally offended. 'No, no Mr Tham, you have got it all wrong. This hotel is not *one* of the most profitable in the world, it is *the* most profitable of all Intercontinentals.'

As we walked from his office we had the same thought. If such a powerfully ugly hotel could make such returns then even the Salm Palace, with its prison-like gates, overlooking the charming panorama of this magnificent city, might well hold its own. There was indeed money to be made in running such an establishment. All that was needed was investment.

But before we saw potential partners we met the state officials who were responsible for monitoring the reconstruction and restoration of the city's historic buildings. We could just see the old Town Hall with its twin astronomical clocks peeping through the twentieth-century windows of our meeting room. The building we were in was on the site of one that had been destroyed in the last days of the Second World War. The replacement, like all stylish architectural infills, had called for a designer with imagination. The planning policy appeared to be that new work should reflect the very best of its period and the old should be lovingly restored and should, under no circumstances, be modified or tinkered with. At least they had a recognisable philosophy.

We enjoyed a spirited talk by the head of the department who clearly loved and lived restoration. It was impressed upon us how carefully conservation work should be carried out especially where works of art,

Prague.
Salm Palace
is at the left
side of the T
junction

such as frescoes and antique plasterwork, were concerned. So that we could experience this delicate process at first hand we were placed in the tender care of a powerfully-built foreman, who looked quite capable of representing the Czech Republic in the shot put. We dutifully followed him down a narrow street and were ushered into a medieval structure shrouded in timber scaffolding. As the door opened the noise of Kango hammers was deafening. Through the dust we could just make out large chunks of plaster being punched off the walls. Immediately above all this activity were beautiful wall paintings protected only by a thin film of clear plastic hanging from a batten nailed to the plastered wall just above them. The contrast from what we'd just been told should be happening and what was actually going on could not have been more striking. We thought, perhaps, the authorities would be prepared to turn a blind eye to their own rules. Subsequent events were to prove us wrong!

We arrived at the restaurant ten minutes late. It was full of people, but there was no mistaking the Flicks. He was tall, blue-eyed, well-built and fair-headed: the epitome of the German aristocrat. She was small, dark, pretty and knew it. Herr Flick rose slowly from his chair as we entered and waved a hand across the empty chairs inviting us to join them. He was relaxed and attentive as John Tham explained how he would market the Salm Palace Hotel and the likely patronage he was expecting. Flick asked me how easy it would be to convert the building. I should not perhaps have been quite so bullish because I foresaw many problems. It seemed churlish to put obstacles in his way when we were there to secure funds. Our pitch, however, left him in little doubt that we were out cap in hand. Micki took on the look of a U-boat commander who had just received orders to carry out a particularly risky operation. He was non-committal and, as it turned out, remained so.

We were now ready to meet the architects who held copies of the measured plans of the Salm Palace. We left the restaurant making our way via the river walk to their offices. It was a pleasant enough stroll and gave us a chance to understand the city a little better. Prague had for too many years been under the heel of the Soviets; only in the late 60s, under the charismatic leadership of Alexander Dubček, had it briefly enjoyed a taste of freedom in what became known as the Prague Spring. What was instantly apparent was the legacy of the Communist era. Very few buildings had been built during their time and the ones that had been were not up to much. Fortunately few historic buildings had been demolished. On the contrary, they had been left more or less intact. Nor had they been restored, which allowed them to deteriorate in their own way and at their own pace. An interesting example of preservation through neglect. But the restoration of this historic fabric by the new order was now becoming urgent. In contrast getting about on foot was a joy. All the pavements had been renewed with patterned setts in contrasting shades. Kerbstones were true and level and the roads had recently been drained and cobbled. The infinite number of flights of steps had been squared up and rebuilt using old stone. What the Soviets had chosen to spend their limited budgets on had worked well; it had been an expedient solution to an age-old problem.

The plans we collected had been prepared under the Communist administration. My fear that they would not come up to the high standard of those exquisite hand-drawn measured surveys produced for me by my friend Simeon Zell[3] proved to be unfounded. Here we had equally good, if not better, drawings with which to explore the Salm Palace and

3 For the past quarter of a century, all my measured surveys of historic buildings have been prepared by Simeon Zell – a vital first step in the preparation of any design.

prepare our scheme for its conversion.

The menacing iron gates were unlocked and we entered a cobbled yard surrounded on three sides by a four-storey stuccoed building. Some might have described it as being typical of Austro-Hungarian Empire style. It surely had none of the charm of a Bohemian palace; no frills, no ornate cornicework, no uplifting decoration around row upon row of rectangular metal windows. The principal entrance was not where one expected it to be, in the middle, but off to one side and rather crudely cut through a pumice-like stone dado. Inside the hallway the cobbling continued in an uninterrupted sweep and out through another arch into a second courtyard which was dominated by the forbidding black and white scraffiti walls of the Schwarzenberg Palace next door.

The ground floor rooms were typical of many others we had seen in Prague with high vaulted ceilings which were distempered white to enhance their sculptural shape. Windows overlooked the magical spirescape of the city below, but the cills were just a little too high to be able to enjoy the view when seated. The two staircases, on the other hand, were very beautiful, wide and easy-going; one drifted effortlessly up to the very top of the building.

If this palace were to yield sufficient rooms to make it a worthwhile proposition it quickly became clear that the attics held the clue. At the top of the principal staircase a vast roof space disappeared into gloom in both directions. The floor was firm and entirely paved in large clay floor tiles. This was most encouraging, but it was the roof structure itself which presented the biggest challenge. Cedarwood beams, some 50 feet long and a foot and half square, spanned between a forest of beautifully carpentered trusses of the most complex and intriguing design. These supported a massive tiled roof. If we could rely on a run of good fortune I thought we might be able to keep all the rooms downstairs and make up bedroom numbers in this gloriously under-used space. Little did I know that I was in for a stern lesson indeed.

Over the following six months I visited the city twice. On the first occasion I took with me a scale model of part of the roof structure, made for me by my colleague Ted Brewster. We'd also prepared a companion model to show how we might modify the timbers to achieve rooms in the roof. I had both of them with me when I met the building people in Prague who extended to us the welcome luxury of conducting the meeting in English! Following an hour of intense discussion we all agreed that my suggestion of opening up the roof with dormers (pretty ones, I hasten to add!) was not the way forward. We settled for using the narrow horizontal slots which ran just below the eaves and above the tiled frieze as the only acceptable way to bring light and air into this new accommodation.

Rather foolishly, as it turned out, I left the meeting thinking I'd got somewhere and relayed the good news to my clients. It was only when I returned on my second visit, having carefully worked up my plans, that I realised that all was not quite as straightforward as I had thought. This meeting was held in Prague Castle itself, not a stone's throw from the Salm Palace. Guards enforced tight security over all visitors and it took us half an hour to be accepted into the inner sanctum.

The chairman was flanked by representatives from all the interested civic departments. There were men from the tourist office, officials from the historic fabric lobby, engineers from the drainage executive, traffic controllers and the agency responsible for pedestrians. Three rather frightening-looking men from the Ministry of Culture occupied the end of the table. I got the impression they saw me as the enemy. It was, by any measure, a daunting bureaucratic array, but for me not nearly as worrying as the chairman's opening remarks. After welcoming us to the meeting and introducing his colleagues (all with unpronounceable names) he stood up to make his point. 'Mr Bertram, I would like you to understand that this will be positively the last meeting we shall have that will be held in English. The next ones will be conducted entirely in Czech!' He then turned to his structural engineer and offered him the opening salvo. I knew the fellow well, just as well as the representative on his left from the historic fabric department; after all, I comforted myself, it was with them that I had so recently discussed my scheme for the attics. They both pored over my latest plans for the top floor. It was their spokesman's next remark that floored me. 'What, Mr Bertram, are all these rooms doing up here?' he asked pointing aggressively at the drawing and fixing me with a quizzical eye from beneath bushy brows.

Naturally I was taken aback although I felt that it might not be a good idea to show it. 'Well, we did agree, the last time we met, how best to modify the roof timbers, to make space for the bedrooms. All I've done in the meantime is to draw it up.' I looked at him with raised eyebrows in an effort to make my point and frame a question without appearing to do either. I really wasn't prepared for his reply.

'We agreed, sir, how to modify the roof for the one bedroom you showed me. I do not remember agreeing to your changing any of the other timbers.'

Clearly this negotiation was not going to be straightforward. I quite understood that they wanted us to respect the importance of the existing fabric even when considering the most modest of alterations. But this was ridiculous. I realised that I had to forget the comparatively easy-going relationship I enjoyed when dealing with our own English Heritage people on similar matters and be prepared to change my attitude entirely. Indeed it was only sensible to show courtesy if I wanted to be taken seriously. I realised I had a lot to do if our consortium was to have any chance of winning. A 'beauty parade', to whittle down the list to a manageable number, had been scheduled for our next, and most crucial, visit to Prague.

Back in London we held a council-of-war. It took place on the top floor of Spencer House under the chairmanship of Jacob Rothschild.[4] I learned a great deal about running such meetings from his lordship. He let us know that he would be late and we should start without him. After about half an hour he arrived, took his place at the head of the table and asked to be brought up to speed. He listened attentively, then looking round the table asked us to agree with him what the conclusions of our discussion should be. With that accomplished he gathered up his files, apologised for leaving early and wished us luck. Our meeting lasted an hour and a half; his very valuable contribution a mere ten minutes!

The pressure was now on. Not only was it my responsibility to

4 Edward Bulmer had joined our team and gave his ideas for the decor at this meeting.

prepare all the drawings, but also to arrange for them to be bound and the text translated into Czech. Quite by chance this turned out to be a little simpler than I had anticipated. Working in the offices of Bath City planning department was one of my *bêtes noires* in the shape of Ludek Majer.[5] He and I shared a healthy disregard for one another which had, over the years, developed into a kind of friendship. I thought he might be able to help me.

'You are a very lucky fellow,' he said in his broken English after hearing how important it was for me to get Czech grammar and spelling absolutely right. 'I've just been home to Prague and while there I bought the latest Czech typewriter which of course incorporates all the proper hieroglyphics.' When Ludek heard of the powerful team that had been assembled he was only too delighted to be counted as one of us. He offered to type the text, and, more importantly, prepare the translation. It was a stroke of good fortune and I'm glad to say went some way to further strengthening our relationship.

When I had assembled all the photographs, prepared my design drawings and written the story I took them down to my friend Hylton Bayntun-Coward who ran George Bayntun the famous bookbinders, down by the railway station in Bath. He marshalled his staff over one weekend and made up a dozen beautifully-finished imperial-sized leather-bound portfolios. It nearly killed them!

We were now all set to take Prague by storm. We found out early on, and with some relief, that the interview was to be held in English. We were to be the last of the four international teams to present our scheme. There had been two groups before lunch and one after, before our turn. The same panel of influential judges had been sitting throughout the day, cocooned in a soaring, gilded Baroque reception room on the first floor of Prague Castle. They had listened to an avalanche of facts and figures and had studied piles of drawings whilst trying their best to take in the complexities of the different schemes. When it came to our turn, at five o'clock in the evening, they looked all in.

Lord Rothschild led our presentation followed by John Tham. They

5 Ludek Majer is now Development Controller at Canterbury City Council.

had rehearsed their slide show of befores and afters, but even so the speed of Jacob's delivery was impressive. All eyes were on the screen as he dashed through seventy slides of Spencer House in a matter of two minutes. It was a highly effective way of giving a snapshot of what might also be done to a building such as the Salm Palace.

This was followed by Tham at a slightly more leisurely pace using Cliveden as his subject. Then it was my turn. Each pair of judges was given one of the large portfolios. I propped up my copy on an easel and used a long pointer. On these occasions I like to wield a big stick – makes for feeling in command! I then explained the salient points of my design. I spoke quickly and with genuine enthusiasm. I looked around through the near-impenetrable cigarette smoke and felt that my audience needed gingering up. It was quite clear that the rigours of the day were taking their toll. I paused in mid-flow. Karl Schwarzenberg,[6] head of one of the great Hapsburg houses, was slumped in his seat with his chin firmly resting on his chest and lightly snoring. It was important that not only he, the landlord of the next-door palace to the Salm, was taking note of proceedings, but that everyone else in the room was too.

'Don't you think that is right, Herr Schwarzenberg?' I asked politely, just to see how much he had taken in. Not a move. But he did stop snoring and then opened one eye and looked in my direction. He pulled himself up, half turned towards me and waved his hand. 'Ja, Ja,' he muttered, and proceeded to focus intently on the drawings in front of him. But from then on he and his colleagues sat up and paid attention just in case they too might be questioned!

After the meeting, Jacob handed me a scruffy bit of paper. It was a note that had been passed to him by Schwarzenberg during my presentation. It ran, 'I like your architect, Mr Bertram, very much, but I do wish he would address me by my proper title of 'Prince' and not 'Herr'. It does make such a difference.' I could only hope that it wouldn't be the gaffe which scuppered our chances. I should not have worried.

Within the month we heard the welcome news that ours was the bid that had won the day. We held a celebration party in London and geared

6 As I write Karl Schwarzenberg is Foreign Minister of the Czech Republic and I hear is enjoying every minute of it!

ourselves to brush up our Czech and begin the exciting process of settling down to the detailed design. However, we were in for a rude shock. Work was suddenly halted. There was a problem. The Prague authorities had been thrown into confusion. The Pezold family was claiming that they, not the state, were the rightful owner. The Salm Palace along with any family heirlooms still in store, should, they maintained, be restored to them.

The lawyers in Prague could do nothing but assemble all the information they held to prove them wrong. What we hoped would be settled in weeks ran into months, then into years. And still there was no definitive resolution to the impasse. In the meantime the brown coal burners had been banned and the air pollution cleaned up. Others in the great capital city had developed luxury hotels elsewhere and the Salm Palace fell deeper and deeper into the pit of neglect.[7]

The question of ownership has still not been settled. The battle still rages. Meanwhile Blakeney sold their lease on Cliveden to a consortium involving the internet billionaire Bill Gates. John Tham swopped the high-profile, high-pressure life of dealing with the demanding rich for the more tranquil waters of the West Indies and the far south west of England, and the Salm Palace deal proved to have been stillborn.

But I wouldn't have missed the Prague adventure for the world. I would probably never have visited nor fallen in love with that beautiful city nor bent my mind to the possibilities of working in such a demanding place. I believe we could have achieved marvellous things there. But I simply couldn't rid my mind of that week at the Manchester Business School and the outspokenness of my tutor. No, it may not be any of my business whether or not my clients own their buildings, but I can tell you it sure as hell makes the wheels go round!

7 The Salm Palace remains in limbo. The Hon Victoria Spicka wrote to her cousin, Charlotte Bayntun-Coward, in January 2008: 'Finally what you wrote about your friend William Bertram's winning scheme for the Salm Palace here in Prague makes perfect sense ... The Pezold family from old Austria are great friends of Lucie's and Lucie has done a lot of the translating of legal documents for the family in their ... bid to get the Palace returned to them! It isn't just the land on which the Palace stands that should belong to them but the whole Palace as well – plus many other wonderful Castles thoughout Bohemia and Moravia ... but I doubt they'll be successful ... in the meantime, the poor old Salm Palace is deteriorating badly which is sad and bad!'

The Last Word

'The best is only just good enough'

THERE ARE MANY MORE STORIES WHICH SPRING TO MIND AS I WRITE. ONCE the door is opened and the leaves of recollection ruffled, it is surprising what can be found beneath them and in long-forgotten corners. Writing is companionable and I don't want to close the book.

You may remember the story of my 'Brief Encounter' with the man on the train and the advice he gave which turned out to be so useful. There have been a number of occasions when I've been introduced to the *mot juste*; phrases which once heard are never forgotten. I remember my earliest lesson on the adverse effect of criticism. It was Mr Beard, the art master at Rottingdean, my prep school,[1] in Sussex, who told me that under no circumstances should you criticise an artist. At the time he was marking a pencil drawing I'd done of two pieces of wood jointed together. I knew it wasn't a very good sketch and was quite expecting some harsh words from him. 'Only ever offer encouragement,' he said, 'they will know, only too well, if their work isn't up to scratch; they'll resent you telling 'em what they already know. Now run along and get on with it!' He had made his point with me, at least! Later as a student of architecture and as a full blown practitioner I too can testify to the corrosiveness of criticism on the one hand and the profound effects of encouragement on the other.

'Never ignore your gut instinct,' suggested Forsyth Lawson, the first architect I ever worked for. He ran a successful practice in Banbury building arts-and-crafts stone houses for the gentry. At the age of just seventeen I joined him as office boy and was as raw as they come. This

---

1 Pulled down in the '60s to make way for SOGAT's headquarters.

was my way of finding out whether I really did want to spend the rest of my life being an architect. That first day told me all I needed to know.

I was delighted when I realised that the whole day consisted of doing art. As art was a particularly pleasant subject and one for which I was reasonably well equipped this came as a welcome surprise. School had presumed to teach me a lot of things that I didn't really want to know and for which no master ever gave good reason for making me learn. However after that first day in the office I was in no doubt that this was the way of life I wanted. Architecture, it seemed, was firmly fixed in reality, a refreshing change from what I deemed the vagueness of academia. Then I was thrown in at the deep end.

It concerned an old lady who needed a porch designed for the front of her bungalow; not a particularly challenging brief, but what, in my eyes, made it most interesting was that she wanted to hang her parrot cage from the ceiling. 'Now, Bill,' said Mr Lawson unfolding a scrap of paper onto which he had pencilled some figures, 'the cage is two foot six inches high and the old girl is five foot three inches tall. What I want you to do is to prepare a nice little sketch which shows just how pretty her porch can be and with some reassurance that she isn't going to bang her head on the bottom of the cage.' I was in seventh heaven.

But not for long. Not only was I the unpaid apprentice, but also the tea boy. At four o'clock that first afternoon I climbed to the attics and found the kettle. I then realised that I hadn't the first idea how to go about it. To make matters worse I didn't feel I could parade my ignorance in front of any member of staff. I did know that hot water and tea leaves were the principal ingredients, so I set about preparing what I hoped would produce a decent brew. I filled the kettle with cold water and then sprinkled a couple of spoonfuls of loose tea onto the surface. I lit the gas, moved the kettle onto the ring and waited expectantly. The water boiled and with great satisfaction I began filling the rows of mugs. Out came what appeared to be clean hot water, but with bits! I cautiously lifted the lid to see what had gone wrong. To my dismay I found that most of my precious tea leaves had stuck to the inside of the kettle. Feeling rather stupid I spent a quarter of an hour trying unsuccessfully to wash them out when the door burst open and in strode the bearded figure of the senior partner.

'What on earth do you think you're doing?' he boomed. 'We're all getting parched down stairs. Perhaps I can give you a hand?' I felt awful, especially when he told me that he wanted to see me before I went home. Was this going to be one of the shortest apprenticeships ever? That evening I gingerly knocked at his door. 'Got anywhere with that porch?' he asked as soon as I'd gone in. I pushed a tentative sketch across his desk and waited. He picked it up and turned his chair towards the light. 'I'm glad to say this looks rather more successful than your efforts at making tea! Now, Bertram,' he said still facing the window, 'I hope you've enjoyed your day?' I responded to him with great enthusiasm. He turned back to face me. 'Although there is nothing I can put my finger on, I get the feeling that you may well be cut out for this sort of work ... could be wrong, seldom am. Mind you, seven years of studying should sort you out, but I fancy you'll do pretty well.' Those few words of encouragement have been my talisman ever since.

I have had, on occasions, to interview potential new members of staff. Some came with qualifications which exactly mirrored the job on offer, others with very few qualifications but with useful experience. Invariably I chose the latter, for it was they who were least likely to threaten my intuitive way of working. It was they I felt who would get on with the rest of us. To those who had missed out I could never provide a logical justification for my decision. Sadly, of course, nowadays the excuse 'it's just my gut feeling' will no longer do.

I was fortunate to have got to know my father quite well. That may seem a strange thing to admit, but for the first three years of my life I was unaware that he played any part in my upbringing. I can recall in the early years of the Second World War standing expectantly at the front door of our beautiful Cotswold home waiting for my first glimpse of the stranger who I had been told was my father. He was on his way home from fighting the war in north Africa. I had, of course seen a photograph of him, but in that confused childish way I had mistaken the combination of his white buttonhole and the white flash of his dress shirt for a daffodil! It was hardly surprising that I was mystified at what, or rather who, I was about to meet. Then around the corner of the house came this man who, when he saw me, stopped in his tracks, flung open his arms and called out my name. In my excitement I dropped my teddy and ran as fast as my little legs could carry me, not into the embrace of a stranger, but to someone who in the twinkling of an eye epitomised everything in the world that a daddy should be.

In the years that followed my father would become my mentor, one of my first clients and one of my fiercest critics. It so happened that when I decided to strike out on my own he generously asked me to convert a barn in Shenington, the next village, which he had just bought from Mr Tew, the local butcher. The deal he proposed was that, apart from my fee, we would split the profit when it was sold. Well, he never did sell it. As the contract drew to its close my mother took me aside and told me that they had fallen in love with the place that I had created and had decided to move into it themselves. And it was there, at High Barn, just along the lane from the aerodrome (see *The End of the Beginning*), that they enjoyed their final years together.

Towards the end of his life, when he had been left on his own following the death of my mother, we became even closer. Whenever possible I would drive up from Bath so that we could be together, break the monotony of his loneliness and catch up on things. The dining room had been turned into his bedroom and I would set up my drawing board next to his bed so I could continue designing whilst we chatted. He was deeply interested in all aspects of my life and was especially proud of my work for Prince Charles. 'Tell me, how do you get on with the Prince's stuff, Willie?'

'Like you, Papa, I sometimes think it's rather like that old adage "when all's been said and done, rather more's been said"! But having said that we seem to get on famously.' There was a pause. 'You know dear boy, Sir John Harding, who became a field marshal, was my boss at the War Office. He had a marvellous way of putting it, "Never confuse the word 'discussion' with the word 'decision'." He was quite one of the cleverest men I ever came across; grasped the essentials, never had a wasteful thought and his directions to his staff were very precise. "Order, Counter-order, Disorder," was his maxim and one which you'd do well to heed yourself.'

I walked over to him. 'Come on you old bugger, let's get these pillows plumped up.' He looked up at me tenderly. 'Thank you, my dear fellow. Now do tell me, how are things going generally. Making any money?' He smoothed down the sheet, folded his hands and waited patiently for my reply.

'Of course I am, but you know, Papa I really do think I'm getting better and better at designing the older I get. My imagination is in rude working order and I feel as fit as a flea. I enjoy architecture so much that I reckon I'll go on to the bitter end. Frankly I can't see myself ever retiring.'

He looked up at me from beneath a cocked eyebrow. 'I'm delighted to hear what you say, my friend, but may this old buffer offer you a little piece of advice?' I looked down at him fondly and nodded. 'Whether or not you retire, Willie, is I fear, a decision that your clients will make, not you!'

Appendix to The Battle for Cavendish Lodge

As I WISH TO GIVE SPACE not only to those who kindly supported our plans for Cavendish Lodge, but also to those who decidedly did not, I am including here just a selection from the many column inches devoted to this hard-fought campaign.

Battle Joined
From Bath Evening Chronicle *February 1991*

A Fairy Tale: The Old Soldier and the Newspaper Chase

ONCE UPON A TIME, there was an old soldier who was sad that he had never been a knight in shining armour. He had never passed the exams on how to build beautiful castles and rescue maidens from dragons, and he didn't think much of the knights who had.

To get into the town where the old soldier lived, knights had to fight their way through a great tangled forest of committees, which had grown up around it. This meant that only the bravest and best knights could ever get into the town. The thorniest committee was called 'Planning', and the old soldier would love to have looked after it, but the townsfolk never asked him to do so because he was always grumbling and complaining.

He thought and he thought and he thought, and he decided that he would grow his own committees to make the forest even more impenetrable. He grew as many as he could, all over the town.

'You get power and influence,' he said to himself, 'by being a man of letters.' So he wrote letters all over the place, especially to the Planning Committee. He wrote so many grumbling letters that the townspeople called him 'Old Majorgrumble'. There was one person in the town who liked Old Majorgrumble, and he was the town crier called 'Chronicle'.

Chronicle loved to have complaints to cry all over the town, so he asked Old Majorgrumble what he was grumbling about every day.

Old Majorgrumble got so excited by Chronicle's attention, that he went out and bought a great big scrap book to keep all his grumbles from Chronicle's broadsheet in. He even invented a new way of grumbling called 'doublegrumble'. All he had to do was to read out some of his old grumbles from the scrap book to Chronicle, who would cry them all over the town all over again. This made Old Majorgrumble very happy, because it looked as if there were even more grumbles that there really were.

One day, a knight cut his way right through the impenetrable forest of committees around the town, and through all the committees that Old Majorgrumble had grown, and proposed to build a beautiful castle right in the middle of the town. Old Majorgrumble got his friend Chronicle to call on the townspeople to rise up against the knight, but they said that they rather liked the idea of a beautiful castle in the middle of their town. Old Majorgrumble wrote to the highest courts in the land, but they too said that they liked the design of the castle and anyway, it would be much nicer than Old Majorgrumble's overgrown tangle of committees.

Poor Old Majorgrumble.

By Filbert

OBJECTORS TO THE PLANNING APPLICATION included David Brain, a prominent local architect. He had designed, but then withdrawn, his own rather unimaginative and insipid scheme for the site; one of no fewer than eleven applications on the Cavendish Lodge site submitted in the previous ten years. Brain, a man who courted publicity quite as much as did Crombie, took it upon himself to weigh into the debate describing my scheme as 'monstrous' and 'Mickey Mouse Georgian, and very large Mickey Mouse Georgian at that. John Wood would have turned in his grave if he could have heard William Bertram describe his building as "pure Palladian".' [Which I hadn't!] (*Bath Evening Chronicle*, 7 February 1997)

That's as maybe, but what I did know was that both Wood and Palladio would have recognised the genesis of my design and, I like to think, would have done much the same given the characters and conditions that confronted me. And others agreed. My old friend Tim Mowl, the respected architectural historian, with a scholarly book on John Wood to his name, wrote:

In Bath eighteenth-century development was planned by architects and builders, not tree planters. The city's hillsides are a subtle fusion of architecture with landscape. Buildings came first, planting later. Now, at the end of the twentieth century the hills are apparently no-go areas, permanently to be pickled in aspic ... Although I am the area's Georgian Group representative I want nothing to do with it. Down in the city centre planners have allowed buildings which would not even grace Ceaucescu's Rumania – I speak of course of sheltered housing and doctors' surgeries. How can these enhance the conservation areas and Bertram's country house design actively detract from them?

However, his enthusiasm was questioned by the editor of the *Architects' Journal*:

In his piece Mowl informs the world that 'there is only one William Bertram, one architect with panache, ready to design a classical building that takes risks. This new Cavendish Lodge that he proposes for the wooded site below Cavendish Crescent is a prodigy ... the pediments promise vintage Bertram, noble yet self mocking ... As of old, Bath has produced an architect of originality and determination, able to create a design that compliments and enriches a splendid site but also proposes a viable solution ...

So far so good I thought, but the article proceeded on less happy lines:

I publish an elevation of the scheme designed by the wondrous

Bertram and leave it to my readers to decide whether an historian of 18th-century classicism can be relied upon to get it right when assessing a piece of 20th-century architecture. (*Bath Evening Chronicle*, 9 April 1990)

Tim took it all in good part. He'd taken on the establishment many times before and I rather fancy relished the intellectual challenge.

Hugh Crallen, an architect of the old school, a Bath City Councillor, and an active member of the Preservation Trust also felt strongly enough to write:

What a pleasure to read Dr Tim Mowl's uninhibited praise of the Bertram design ... he is absolutely right. This is no ignorant bit of neo-Georgian pastiche. On the contrary, Mr Bertram uses the well-tried classical repertoire with love and feeling, showing special respect for the qualities of the difficult site. How wise he was to ignore the puny and unimaginative brief which the Council provided to guide potential developers. It would indeed be a tragedy if this admirable scheme should be frustrated by the intensive lobbying of one or two people whose opinions are unrepresentative of informed local opinion – let alone Bath citizens at large.

Crombie and the Bath planners might with advantage have taken note of an article in the *Daily Telegraph* (February '04) by George Trefgarne on eighteenth-century development under the headline 'The economy could use another Bath':

The design covenants [for the terraces] applied only to the front [façades]… There were regulations, but they were drawn up [...] by freely contracting parties and not arbitrarily imposed by governments. The modern property developer […] is driven mad by endless footling rules […a]ll innovation is smothered, and the most abundant building material is not brick, but red tape.

In February '91: Douglas Home, a resident of Cavendish Crescent and from the beginning a staunch advocate of my scheme, wrote under the headline 'Bertram's plan most inspiring':

> I remember the time when we local residents were told to get used to the idea that something would inevitably be built to replace the former Cavendish Lodge; and most of us accepted this because some of this land was designated for building ... and the rest was a scruffy wilderness. Our only concern was the quality of the proposed building. We were relieved when the planners rejected a number of designs more suitable for Heathrow and I say 'relieved' because the most appalling buildings, reminiscent of the worst Soviet type, have been allowed in (other) parts of Bath. Then came William Bertram's plan, which was, frankly, the most inspiring and exciting building to be proposed for Bath ... [in 40 years] (*Bath Evening Chronicle*, 13 Feb 1991)

Mary Home's decisive intervention towards the end of the second Enquiry remains an inspiration and an abiding memory:

> Major Crombie officially represents The Bath Preservation Trust at this enquiry, but the Trust is about as democratic as the average Trades Union, and members are not at all happy with the block vote. He does not represent our views, or those of many other members we have spoken to. I don't know about The Bath Society but I think the same probably applies.

She continued:

> We are lucky enough to have a really inspired architect working in Bath in our lifetime. By the way, sir, I do urge you to go and have a look at the front of his Dower House [The Royal Crescent Hotel] if you have not already done so, for it is enchanting! Mr Bertram has given us this beautiful design for that grotty, rat-infested

wasteland next to us. We are so grateful to have THIS proposed building in place of the modern horrors that we were faced with earlier, and indeed might do so again if this appeal were [to be] rejected. So WHY THE QUIBBLING? WHY THE PETTY NIT-PICKING that goes on and on and on? Is it a bit too formal? Is it a bit too countrified? Incidentally, [even] the National Trust describe Dyrham Park as 'strongly reminiscent of a town house of its period' so what, may one ask, is wrong with Mr Bertram's interpretation here?

So please, Sir, LET MR BERTRAM BUILD HIS MAGNIFICENT HOUSE, politely set back as it is from Cavendish Crescent where he suggests, and it will enhance the area immeasurably and, indeed, benefit the whole of Bath too.

Casualties

On Tim Mowl's resignation David Turner wrote uncharitably:

> …nothing suited his tenure of the post so well as his departure from it. If he is offering his resignation the opportunity should be seized … (*Bath Evening Chronicle*, 11 Feb 1991)

A Mockler joined in:

> There is something petulant and ungenerous about it [Mowl's resignation]… almost as if he had taken the Court of Appeal's decision as a personal insult.

But Kathleen Williams expressed a more sympathetic view:

> I have been a member of The Georgian Group since the mid '50s and know what wonderful work they [including Tim Mowl] are doing for this country. It is a tragedy that … Cavendish Lodge is now lost to us …

And the Editor of the *Chronicle* added, in a note:

> 'in fact I declined to accept Tim Mowl's resignation and he
> continues as our architectural correspondent.'

(all in *Bath Evening Chronicle*, 19 Feb 1991)

Rearguard Action

Kenneth Powell finished his article with a pompous sideswipe at both
the Prince of Wales and me:

> The effect is not unpleasant though the architecture ... is pretty
> pedestrian with none of the drama of Wood's, father and son ...
> the building looks incongruous ... as with so much late 20th
> century classical architecture of the Highgrove School, the project
> lacks both the simplicity and the seriousness of its historic models
> and there is something two-dimensional about the New
> Cavendish Lodge. [...]
> For some, the development will always be a blot on the landscape.
> For others its 'regressive' style may suggest that Bath has simply
> lost its nerve. (*Weekend Telegraph*, 11 Jan 1997)

Peter Arnould responded with:

> 'Lodge is not an architectural monster'

> Nobody asked them [Crombie, Powell and Brain] to air their
> views on Cavendish Lodge, but having done so, they must expect
> an equally vigorous response and should not be too surprised if it
> gets a little rough. The achievement of Andreas [sic] Palladio was
> to incorporate in his designs for domestic architecture the classic
> orders previously found [only] in official Roman buildings. All
> over Italy there are original Palladio villas whose influence can

clearly be seen in Cavendish Lodge ... Its pedimented façade with pilaster columns is unmistakenly Palladio as is the raised base. [The use] of Cotswold stone relief ... is not only a permissible [but] a welcome visual effect ...' The attentions of David Brain's profession has left a rich legacy of appalling buildings of staggering insensitivity, but William Bertram's Cavendish Lodge is certainly not one of them. (*Bath Evening Chronicle*, 13 Aug 1997)

Judith Constantine (Couchman) could not have put more succinctly my own thoughts on the endless references I was subjected to about the 'perfect solution' for the site promoted by Brain.

[You] might be forgiven for not realizing that the so-called 'perfect plan' for Cavendish Lodge site, described by David Brain ... was of course David Brain's own work. What distinguished new building is there in Bath, or for that matter anywhere, which has been designed by this man. Need one say more? (*Bath Evening Chronicle*, 14 Feb 1997)

In a particularly amusing article with the headline 'Stone fit for pigsties' Steve Billett commented:

[This] is not a town house, though compared to its neighbours, it seems to me to have the inspiration of a sliced loaf ... My second anger [is that the lodges] are built not in Bath stone but faced with open jointed Cotswold stone which farmers use for their cowsheds and pigsties. Is there another house in Bath like it? If so I'd like to see it ...

Parting Shots

As 'Cavendish' was being topped out (the moment when the roof carcassing is completed) in the autumn of 1996, Tom Gorst wrote:

I confess I had my doubts ... but last Wednesday I laid my doubts to rest ... Was it worth going through 30 years of arguing to get it?.. Well I am convinced it was. This new [Cavendish Lodge] is, in my view, quite simply the most significant piece of post-war architecture in the city. (*Bath Evening Chronicle*, 17 Dec 1997)

No such unequivocal praise in Michael Forsyth's update of Pevsner's *Architectural Guide to Bath*:

The scheme is well detailed and the style and scale acceptable, but the ostentatious formal axial approach and Cotswold dry walling-effect stone are unsympathetic to the neighbourhood's quiet, picturesque Regency buildings.

John Curtis in his book entitled *Bath 2001* wrote:

New buildings in Bath have often been criticized for being out of scale and unsympathetic to their more elegant neighbours. These new apartments [Cavendish Lodge] built in the mid 1990s are a welcome exception.

Writing earlier this year Edward Goring, whose mantle as Evening Chronicler was eventually assumed by Tim Mowl, casts his mind back to 1987 when my proposed building caused such a stir in the Council Chamber. In that debate Marianna Clarke, who was ward councillor for Lansdown in which the Cavendish Lodge site rests, and who opposed my scheme from the outset, exhorted her fellow councillors to think 20, 50 or even 100 years ahead. Alderman William Shepherd weighed in with:

Bath is becoming not Bath but just another city. Future generations will be justified in condemning us.

Mary Rawlings, one time Mayor of Bath, reinforced that view:

Most of the recent blocks of flats [Ballance Street flats had just been completed, and presumably Cavendish Lodge] are a disgrace to the City. Bath should be a city for brilliantly designed buildings of international repute.

Kirsten Elliott and Neill Mennear reproduce in their beautifully presented book on Bath a delightful double-page spread of Cavendish Lodge from High Common. It shows the buildings surrounded by trees in full leaf with a caption that reads 'this pseudo-Georgian block of retirement houses sits unhappily among the crescents of Georgian Bath.' If they thought it was that bad then why give it such prominence?

In February 1997 after the official opening Alistair Bovey, an engineer practising in the city, penned me a supportive and very welcome note:

I feel that all of us involved in the building industry here in Bath owe you our appreciation for battling through ... against the odds. This city really must learn how to move forward and I am pleased that you have helped in securing another rung to the ladder.

And last but not least, in February 2007 I was astonished and delighted to receive a letter from Sonia Dickinson, who lives at number 16:

Two years ago I moved into Cavendish Lodge having spent more than twenty five years living on Sion Hill (just 300 yards from Cavendish Lodge) and much earlier having been a child here. I just wanted to write a line to let you know how delighted I am to be here ... and to thank you for all your work in creating the building and its setting.

Index

(illustrations in **bold**)

[signature] · JUNE 1994 · Clive House.